NIETZSCHE'S A

MW00845671

Friedrich Nietzsche's complex connection to Charles Darwin has been much explored, and both scholarly and popular opinions have tended to assume a convergence in their thinking. In this study, Dirk Johnson challenges that assumption and takes seriously Nietzsche's own explicitly stated "anti-Darwinism." He argues for the importance of Darwin for the development of Nietzsche's philosophy, but he places emphasis on the antagonistic character of their relationship and suggests that Nietzsche's mature critique against Darwin represents the key to understanding his broader (anti-)Darwinian position. He also offers an original reinterpretation of the *Genealogy of Morals*, a text long considered sympathetic to Darwinian naturalism, but which he argues should be taken as Nietzsche's most sophisticated critique of both Darwin and his followers. His book will appeal to all who are interested in the philosophy of Nietzsche and its cultural context.

DIRK R. JOHNSON is Associate Professor of Modern Languages at Hampden-Sydney College, USA.

NIETZSCHE'S
ANTI-DARWINISM

DIRK R. JOHNSON

CAMBRIDGE
UNIVERSITY PRESS

CAMBRIDGE UNIVERSITY PRESS
Cambridge, New York, Melbourne, Madrid, Cape Town,
Singapore, São Paulo, Delhi, Mexico City

Cambridge University Press
The Edinburgh Building, Cambridge CB2 8RU, UK

Published in the United States of America by Cambridge University Press, New York

www.cambridge.org
Information on this title: www.cambridge.org/9781107621527

First published 2010
First paperback edition 2013

A catalogue record for this publication is available from the British Library

Library of Congress Cataloguing in Publication Data
Johnson, Dirk Robert, 1963–
Nietzsche's anti-Darwinism / Dirk Johnson.
p.   cm.
Includes bibliographical references and index.
ISBN 978-0-521-19678-9 (hardback)
1. Nietzsche, Friedrich Wilhelm, 1844–1900.   2. Nietzsche, Friedrich Wilhelm,
1844–1900. Zur Genealogie der Moral.   3. Darwin, Charles, 1809–1882.   I. Title.
B3317.J64 2010
576.8′2–dc22
2010022335

ISBN 978-1-107-62152-7 Paperback

My mind seems to have become a kind of machine for grinding general laws out of large collections of facts, but why this should have caused the atrophy of that part of the brain alone, on which the higher tastes depend, I cannot conceive.

Darwin, Autobiography, 139

For most people the intellect is an awkward, gloomy, creaking machine that is hard to start: when they want to work with this machine and think well, they call it "taking the matter *seriously*" – oh, how taxing good thinking must be for them! The lovely human beast seems to lose its good mood when it thinks well; it becomes "serious!" And "where laughter and gaiety are found, thinking is good for nothing" – that is the prejudice of this serious beast against all "gay science."

Nietzsche, The Gay Science, 327

In spite of that philosopher who, being a true Englishman, tried to give laughter a bad reputation among all thoughtful people –, "laughter is a terrible infirmity of human nature, and one that every thinking mind will endeavour to overcome" (Hobbes) –, I would go so far as to allow myself a rank order of philosophers based on the rank of their laughter – right up to those who are capable of *golden* laughter.

Nietzsche, Beyond Good and Evil, 294

Contents

Acknowledgements

I would like to acknowledge a handful of people who have helped me with this project. First of all, I would like to thank Walther Zimmerli, whose positive response to a graduate-school seminar paper on Nietzsche and Darwin motivated me to pursue the topic in greater depth. Since then, a small group of Nietzsche scholars from around the world have encouraged me – in particular, Paul Loeb at the University of Puget Sound; Paul van Tongeren and the scholars of the Nietzsche Research Group at Radboud University, the Netherlands; and Robin Small at the University of Auckland, New Zealand. I also acknowledge my dissertation committee at Indiana University, who supported my decision to tackle this subject. I am grateful to James Janowski and Dieudonné Afatsawo, two incisive readers who commented on earlier drafts, and David Capper, a former student who helped compile an initial bibliography. My friend Jim Arieti patiently gave of his time and experience in helping to compile the index. Financial support from Hampden-Sydney College and its Summer Fellowships made research for this monograph possible, and conference stipends allowed me to present material at academic conferences. My colleagues and friends in the modern languages department at Hampden-Sydney have been a source of steady encouragement over the years. Gerry Randall at the Walter Bortz Library of Hampden-Sydney College helped to acquire titles quickly through interlibrary loan. My particular thanks go to Richard McClintock, who developed the elegant and striking cover design for this project. Finally, no words can express the thanks I owe to my lovely wife, Patrizia, and our two wonderful children, Lucas and Henrik. This book is for them.

Abbreviations

Translations of Nietzsche's works are abbreviated as follows:

A	*The Antichrist*, translated by Judith Norman (Cambridge: Cambridge University Press, 2005)
BGE	*Beyond Good and Evil*, translated by Judith Norman (Cambridge: Cambridge University Press, 2002)
CW	*Case of Wagner*, translated by Judith Norman (Cambridge: Cambridge University Press, 2005)
D	*Daybreak*, translated by R.J. Hollingdale (Cambridge: Cambridge University Press, 1997)
DS	*David Strauss*, translated by Richard T. Gray (in *Unfashionable Observations*, translated by Richard T. Gray [Stanford: Stanford University Press, 1995])
EH	*Ecce Homo*, translated by Judith Norman (Cambridge: Cambridge University Press, 2005)
GM	*On the Genealogy of Morality*, translated by Carol Diethe (Cambridge: Cambridge University Press, 1997)
GS	*The Gay Science*, translated by Josefine Nauckhoff (Cambridge: Cambridge University Press, 2001)
HC	*Homer's Contest* (*KSA* I, 783–92), translated by Dirk Johnson
HH	*Human, All Too Human*, translated by R.J. Hollingdale (Cambridge: Cambridge University Press, 1996)
TI	*Twilight of the Idols*, translated by Judith Norman (Cambridge: Cambridge University Press, 2005)
UM	*Untimely Meditations*, translated by Richard T. Gray (Stanford: Stanford University Press, 1995)
WP	*The Will to Power*, translated and edited by Walter Kaufmann (New York: Random House, 1967)
Z	*Thus Spoke Zarathustra*, translated by Adrian del Caro (Cambridge: Cambridge University Press, 2006)

Quotations from Nietzsche's notebooks are from *Kritische Studienausgabe in 15 Bänden*, edited by Giorgio Colli and Mazzino Montinari (Berlin: de Gruyter, 1980), abbreviated as *KSA*

Quotations from his letters are from *Sämtliche Briefe: Kritische Studienausgabe in 8 Bänden*, edited by Giorgio Colli and Mazzino Montinari (Berlin: de Gruyter, 1986), abbreviated as *KSB*

All quotations from the notebooks and the letters are my translations.

Introduction

Friedrich Nietzsche's complex relationship to Charles Darwin has been much explored, and readers have placed the two thinkers in conjunction from the very beginning. Nietzsche himself alluded to Darwinian interpretations of his ideas as early as 1888. In *Ecce Homo* (*EH*), he felt compelled to disparage the "scholarly cattle," who suggested that his *Übermensch* reflected Darwinian sympathies (*EH* "Why I Write Such Good Books" 1). In recent years, numerous studies have returned to the Nietzsche–Darwin axis, indicating that they recognize Nietzsche's connection to Darwin reflects a significant component of his thought.[1]

While the first objective of this study is to argue for the pre-eminence of Darwin for the development and articulation of Nietzsche's philosophy, its main thrust is to point to the *antagonistic* character of their relationship and to show how Nietzsche's final critique against Darwin and

---

[1] Studies in the first wave of critical reception often focused on the Darwinian resonances in Nietzsche, e.g. Alexander Tille, *Von Darwin bis Nietzsche: Ein Buch Entwicklungsethik* (Leipzig: Naumann, 1893); Oskar Ewald, "Darwin und Nietzsche," *Zeitschrift für Philosophie und philosophische Kritik* 136 (1909): 159–79; Claire Richter, *Nietzsche et les Théories biologiques contemporaines* (Paris: Mercure de France, 1911); Raoul Richter, *Essays* (Leipzig: Felix Meiner, 1913); and Ludwig Haas, "Der Darwinismus bei Nietzsche" (Ph.D. dissertation, Giessen, 1932). In recent years, scholarly interest in the Darwin angle has revived, and three full-length studies have tackled the question: Gregory Moore, *Nietzsche, Biology, and Metaphor* (Cambridge: Cambridge University Press, 2002); John Richardson, *Nietzsche's New Darwinism* (New York: Oxford University Press, 2004); and Edith Düsing, *Nietzsches Denkweg: Theologie, Darwinismus, Nihilismus* (Munich: W. Fink, 2006). This list does not include individual journal articles, such as Werner Stegmeier, "Darwin, Darwinismus, Nietzsche," *Nietzsche-Studien* 16 (1987): 246–87 and (more recently) Michael Skowron, "Nietzsches 'Anti-Darwinismus'," *Nietzsche-Studien* 37 (2008): 160–94, or the many studies where Darwin receives significant chapter treatments, such as in George J. Stack, *Lange and Nietzsche* (New York: de Gruyter, 1983); Irving Zeitlin, *Nietzsche: A Re-Examination* (Cambridge: Polity Press, 1994); Keith Ansell-Pearson, *Viroid Life: Perspectives on Nietzsche and the Transhuman Condition* (New York: Routledge, 1997); or Robin Small, *Nietzsche and Rée: A Star Friendship* (Oxford: Oxford University Press, 2005), to name but a few. Then there is Daniel Dennett, *Darwin's Dangerous Idea: Evolution and the Meanings of Life* (New York: Simon & Schuster, 1995), which has a separate section dedicated to Nietzsche ("Nietzsche's Just So Stories").

his followers might represent the key to understanding his broader (anti-) Darwinian position. In that sense, this second, much more significant objective will be to clarify the ambiguity behind Nietzsche's own unambiguously expressed final opposition to Darwin.

Of course, this approach entails taking his final opposition seriously. In some ways, my study will start from the end and proceed to the beginning. It will look for the subtle incongruities and the discrepancies between their thought-systems in order to unearth the fault lines between them. If Nietzsche was serious about his final antagonism, which I will argue he was, then this study will explain how a full-blown critique of Darwin could have emerged toward the end of his career after he had initially revealed close affinities with him and his ideas.

In a recent monograph, Ruth Abbey criticizes interpretations that concentrate on Nietzsche's radical late philosophy at the expense of his open-ended, multi-perspectival middle period. She detects scholarly prejudice against the middle period born from a spell that Nietzsche himself has successfully cast: "this image of Nietzsche as an autonomous and wholly individual thinker is accepted partly because we are held captive by the picture he draws of himself, for in his later works Nietzsche repeatedly invents himself as inventor rather than legatee."[2] While I share Abbey's high estimation of the middle period, both for its own sake and as the fertile seedbed of his later philosophy, I am skeptical of her negative assessment regarding the final period.

In the one case of Darwin, for example, the "anti-Darwinian" animus reflected in Nietzsche's late "Anti-Darwin" passages is neither sudden nor unprecedented. It arises from ten years of subtle questioning in the middle period that renders his opposition in the later works both explicable and credible. The best approach to the final period, then, is not to be seduced by Nietzsche's rhetorical hyperbole or Martin Heidegger's stylization of him as the "destroyer of the Western tradition" and "Platonism." It is to try to make sense of how and why he might have arrived at those antagonisms, including his final opposition to Darwin. At the same time, this study will argue for the pre-eminence of Darwin for understanding the transition to the late works, since Darwin, perhaps more than any other modern thinker, made his mature period possible, in effect allowing him "to become who he was."

Before proceeding, I will need to establish some of the guiding premises of my study and take issue with some common popular and

---

[2] Ruth Abbey, *Nietzsche's Middle Period* (New York: Oxford University Press, 2000), 141.

scholarly misperceptions. My first premise will be to argue that Nietzsche's exchange with Darwin was constant and ongoing and that it framed his philosophy from beginning to end. This perspective might be surprising; after all, Darwin does not appear often in his published work. References to Darwin, for example, are far eclipsed by those to Wagner or Schopenhauer.[3] Also, Daniel Dennett's observation that "Nietzsche probably never read Darwin"[4] is probably not far from the truth. He does not appear to have read *The Origin of Species* (1859) or even *The Descent of Man* (1871), the work with the greatest outward affinity to his project. These two facts alone have compelled commentators either to dismiss his position on Darwin altogether or to classify it as only a minor preoccupation.

The criticisms that Nietzsche did not refer to Darwin enough, or that he had insufficient firsthand knowledge of his theories, are misguided. For one, they fail to take into account that Darwin, whose science had broken with traditional metaphysics and had established a naturalist grounding for morality, quite simply represented the absolute starting point and unspoken framework for *all* of Nietzsche's subsequent investigations from the middle period on. For Nietzsche, *Darwin* represented much more than the theory of "natural selection" or the birth of evolutionary science. More than anything else, *Darwin* signified a radical break with conventional forms of morality. In that sense, Nietzsche's thinking always gravitated within a Darwinian orbit, and an analysis of his engagement with Darwin cannot and should not be reduced to explicit references. It must go below the surface and must examine the broader historical and cultural context of his experimentation with Darwin-inspired, i.e. "genealogical," perspectives in the wake of the "Darwinian revolution" (Himmelfarb).[5]

As far as his knowledge of Darwin is concerned, Nietzsche understood Darwin and the implications of his theories both early and well. If one considers that he and Darwin were roughly contemporaneous, that Darwin's ideas first had to be mediated through a foreign language and culture, and that the scientist's reputation was still in the process of being

---

[3] In a database search of Nietzsche's works, Wagner received 653 direct hits; Schopenhauer 415; and Darwin merely 21. (This of course does not include related terms such as *Darwinismus* or *darwinistisch*.)

[4] Dennett, *Darwin's Dangerous Idea*, 461.

[5] Düsing claims that Nietzsche's exposure to the Darwinian worldview overturned the comforting religious assumptions he held in his youth: "In all stages of his intellectual development, Nietzsche's explicit or implicit debate with both Strauss and Darwin had left volcanic crater-holes in his philosophical thought and pushed it into the direction of an anti-Christian biologism" (Düsing, *Nietzsches Denkweg*, 12).

solidified, Nietzsche early on grasped his significance.[6] Furthermore, Nietzsche wrestled with his insights at a far deeper level than many others who considered themselves "Darwinian." Of course, his interest in Darwin does not mean that he pursued his philosophy as a "Darwinian" or that he subjected his own philosophy and goals to Darwinian objectives. This he expressly did not. It means that he understood him *at least as well as* others who had subscribed themselves with far greater fervor and commitment to Darwin and his cause.

At the same time, Nietzsche's reservations concerning Darwin were *philosophical*; he did not approach his ideas as unimpeachable science. Thus, those commentators who seek to dismiss Nietzsche's position – for example, because he supposedly gets "natural selection" or "fitness" "wrong" – or those scholars, in turn, who attempt to place his biological notions on a one-to-one correlation with Darwin's misunderstand both his approach as well as the originality of his final perspective.[7] His antagonism emerges from his foundational critique of Darwin's cardinal assumptions, including his understanding of "nature"; his adoption of the altruism–egoism model; his assumptions about "man" and "human nature"; his prioritization and understanding of competition and struggle; his belief in self-preservation; even his belief in causality, to name but a few. His critique was not based on Darwinism qua biological science.

The second premise relates to the question of whether Nietzsche's polemical stance, particularly in the *Genealogy of Morals* (*GM*), truly incorporates Darwin or instead targets Social Darwinists, who had begun to apply his ideas to all aspects of humanity, including society and morality. This is a thorny question and, unfortunately, Nietzsche himself is not

---

[6] In *Nietzsche and "the English": The Influence of British and American Thinking on His Philosophy* (Amherst, NY: Humanity Books, 2008), Thomas Brobjer reassesses the importance of the Anglo-American tradition for Nietzsche's philosophy. One assumes that the "English" influence would be self-evident; yet it still goes underappreciated in most accounts. (On the other hand, there are numerous studies on "Nietzsche and the French.")

[7] The uncertainty and ambivalence which the Nietzsche–Darwin relationship evokes are reflected in the hedging comments that often qualify that relationship. Not able to accept Nietzsche's antagonism at face value, scholars try to make sense of it: "It is by no means clear that Nietzsche's critique of Darwin is either coherent or convincing" (Ansell-Pearson, *Viroid Life*, 105). "Although he says a great deal 'against Darwin,' there is no doubt that his thinking was stimulated by Darwinian conceptions and that he creatively adapted its principles to his own interpretation of life" (Stack, *Nietzsche and Lange*, 180). "Nietzsche accepted the validity of Darwin's theory and understood it well in most respects. He does appear, however, to have missed the significance of Darwin's work for his own philosophy" (Zeitlin, *Nietzsche: A Re-Examination*, 127). "[A]s we turn to his criticisms of Darwin, we find that many of those are ill informed: Nietzsche attacks him for positions Darwin doesn't hold. Often, Nietzsche's 'corrections' bring him to points Darwin already holds" (Richardson, *Nietzsche's New Darwinism*, 16–17).

entirely clear on the matter. Whereas his texts sometimes address specific sympathizers and their ideas (e.g. Rée, Spencer, as well as other so-called "English psychologists"), at other times they lump Darwin together with the Darwinists and in the final period, they challenge Darwin directly ("Anti-Darwin"). The question is crucial for the following reason. If one believes that Nietzsche's "polemic" targeted vulgar popularizations but exempted Darwin, one will tend to view the two men as compatible: both trying to establish a new basis for morality along naturalist lines. But if one agrees that Nietzsche also implicated Darwin, and not only his followers, one must clarify as far as possible the procedural basis for this claim.

First, Nietzsche himself chooses not to distinguish between Darwin, his followers, and compatible thinkers. In several passages throughout his works, Nietzsche refers to Darwin in the same critical breath as other British natural-law theorists such as the "English psychologists" of *GM*. The reason for this, to repeat, is that his interest in Darwin was a broader philosophical one. On that basis, Nietzsche clearly saw Darwin operating within the same tradition, school of thought, and perspectives as his British predecessors and contemporaries; many of the latter may not even have considered themselves "Darwinists" in an explicit sense. Nietzsche's critique of Spencer or Mill, for example – who in their own way both strove to remain independent from Darwin – equally implicated the latter, because his perspective took into account, and sought to challenge, an entire philosophical tradition: a so-called "English" school of thought. Therefore, Darwin could not escape his broader critique of the "English psychologists," for Nietzsche treated him as an equal partner within a larger philosophical enterprise that attempted to establish morality on a new non-metaphysical, naturalist platform.[8]

---

[8] My position here is essentially no different from Robert Young's, who criticizes Darwinian "exceptionalism" within scholarship: "There has been a tendency on the part of historians of science to isolate Darwin in two related ways. The first is to single him out from the mainstream of nineteenth-century naturalism in Britain and allow 'Darwinism' to stand duty for the wider movement of which it was in fact but a part. The second is the tendency to single out his evolutionary theory and to demarcate it sharply from those of his predecessors and contemporaries ... Charles Darwin is thus made to stand out as a figure of comparatively unalloyed scientific status and is treated in relative isolation from the social and intellectual context in which he worked and into which his theory was received" (Robert Young, "Darwin's Metaphor: Does Nature Select?" *Monist* 55 [1971], 442–43). Edward Manier's *The Young Darwin and his Cultural Circle: A Study of the Influences Which Helped Shape the Language and Logic of the First Drafts of the Theory of Natural Selection* (Dordrecht, Holland: D. Reidel Publishing, 1978) discusses Darwin's debt to a wide range of literary personalities who decisively influenced his thinking in advance of the *Origin's* publication.

Nietzsche's method here should not surprise us. After all, the *Descent* quotes with approval both current and earlier scientists and thinkers who approached the "moral sense" along compatible lines.[9] Moreover, Darwin places himself squarely within the reputable tradition of English empiricists and naturalists; and he further admires the moral examples of Aurelius and Kant,[10] all of whom offered him a congenial conceptual basis for a morality, whose existence he sought to naturalize.[11] One can articulate the correlation between Darwin and his sympathizers in the following way: whereas Darwin had introduced the theory of "natural selection" in the *Origin*, turning it into the "Bible" for evolutionary thought ever since, he wrote as just another "Darwinist" in the *Descent*, where he applied evolutionary insights to human nature. That is not to argue that Darwin did not approach the "moral question" and apply his insights to the matter of man with greater depth, clarity, and sophistication than his supporters; he often did; but his analysis was only one out of the many possible explanations for the emergence and development of the moral sense based on his model of natural selection.

At the same time, Nietzsche *did* estimate Darwin higher than his followers and accord him greater respect. One can detect here an inherent tension between these two poles: that is, seeing Darwin as just one member of a larger "English school" and, simultaneously, granting him *primus inter pares* status. Part of that tension results from Nietzsche's tacit admiration for the "Darwin" of the *Origin*, i.e. the major historical and philosophical innovator who had placed the thinking about man and his relationship to nature on a new footing – and therefore impelled Nietzsche to place his own philosophy on a new footing. But at another level, Nietzsche's final critique of Darwin reflected a highly stylized form of personal opposition which separated and elevated founders of historical "movements" from their "lesser" followers. Both positions emerged from a common insight: Nietzsche understood that the new evolutionary theories were decisive and were beginning to form the basis for a challenging, original, though competitive explanatory model in the realm of morality and beyond.

---

[9] "Mr. Bain gives a list of twenty-six British authors who have written on this subject [the 'moral sense'], and whose names are familiar to every reader; to these, Mr. Bain's own name, and those of Mr. Lecky, Mr. Shadworth Hodgson, and Sir J. Lubbock, as well as of others, may be added" (Charles Darwin, *The Descent of Man, and Selection in Relation to Sex* [Princeton: Princeton University Press, 1981], 71fn).
[10] Ibid.   [11] Darwin, *Descent*, 71.

The third major premise suggests that *GM* is Nietzsche's first sustained and systematic critique of Darwin. *GM* represents a problematic case study; after all, Darwin does not loom prominently within the text, and Nietzsche seems to polemicize against a broader collective of "English psychologists." But according to my previous argument, Nietzsche *does* recognize him as a member of this latter school of thought; it is only that he challenges the larger issue of Darwinian perspectives on morality in *GM*, whereas he begins to single out Darwin, the individual, in the post-*GM Twilight of the Idols* (1889) and in his notebooks.

What motivated Nietzsche's shift to a more personal style of critique? The issue is complicated, and I will explore it in greater detail in my analysis of his late thought in Chapter 3. However, I will show there that *GM* subverts Darwin's arguments themselves; it does not treat them as separate or superior. In fact, I will challenge the impression that his late "Anti-Darwin" passages are somehow sudden, unprecedented, or out of character with the rest of his philosophy. Indeed, if one treats *GM* as the first major installment of his larger emerging critique of Darwin(ism); and one understands, further, how these arguments compromise Darwin himself, not only his many late-century followers and imitators, then the "Anti-Darwin" passages merely become a logical, natural consequence, a stylistic variant, of his earlier preoccupations.

The fourth and final premise is that *GM* should not only be viewed as a direct challenge to Darwin as well as Nietzsche's first major theoretical assault on him; I will also contend that its arguments only truly make sense and reveal their hidden meanings in their function *as* polemic. By this, I do not mean to suggest that one can read *GM* in only one way. I also do not wish to deny that it is a fruitful, rewarding, and engaging work on many different levels and for many different audiences and disciplines. I merely suggest that one should recognize how its arguments have a provisional character and serve a subversive function. In such a reading, the text does not offer an alternative naturalist platform or build further on naturalist premises. Nietzsche's only means to challenge the historical supremacy of naturalism, I will argue, is to enter into its discursive parameters and engage it from within, to offer credible alternatives and hypotheses, to point out weak spots and inconsistencies, and to assume the guise of a naturalist in order to discredit naturalism.[12]

---

[12] In the Preface to *GM*, he writes that it befits "a positive mind" "to replace the improbable with the more probable and in some circumstances to replace one error with another" (*GM* "Preface," 4).

But how can *GM* – a text so informed about and so infused with "naturalist" rhetoric – seriously be considered "*anti*-naturalist"?[13] Does not Nietzsche's style of argumentation, his use of biological tropes and metaphors, and many of his central positions in the text prove that he was a naturalist through and through? These are serious objections, to which I will need to respond. Once again, Nietzsche adopted the discourse of both the naturalists and the Darwinists, because it was the only means to subvert their framework and to challenge their mounting success. According to Nietzsche's understanding of the ascetic ideal, which he formulates most fully in *GM* III, the naturalization of morality proved morality's great adaptability and flexibility as well as its ability to enter into new guises according to the "historical" circumstances. It was entirely consistent, then, for Nietzsche to tackle the issue of morality in the most recent contemporary arena, where it offered the most credible, powerful, and persuasive explanatory paradigm: nineteenth-century biological naturalism as exemplified by the success of Darwin and his paradigm.

Do I mean to suggest, then, that Nietzsche did not subscribe to the biological and physiological rhetoric in *GM*? No; I will argue that one part of that terminology was conditioned by the discursive requirements of nineteenth-century "naturalism," by its implicit rules and assumptions; the other part *did* form the basis of his philosophical repertoire. But one must learn to distinguish between using biological and physiological insights as a means to realize non-naturalist, anti-metaphysical objectives and using them as building blocks for a broader naturalist agenda. With "naturalism,"[14] I mean a self-contained philosophical program and school of thought, a paradigm of nature, in which the naturalization of morality assumes a prominent position; or, as D.H. Monro has stated, "to give an account of morality without invoking any moral facts or entities."[15] Whereas Nietzsche viewed the clear-eyed naturalization of discourse in his times as a great victory over philosophical idealism, he remained skeptical of how remnants of that idealism still informed the terminology and

---

[13] Brian Leiter proposes an alternative assessment: "The *Genealogy*, and Nietzsche's mature philosophy generally, proposes a *naturalistic* explanation, i.e., an explanation that is continuous with both the results and methods of the sciences" (Brian Leiter, *Nietzsche on Morality* [New York: Routledge, 2002], 11).

[14] For Leiter, "[n]aturalism in philosophy is, typically, in the first instance, a *methodological* view about how one should do philosophy: philosophical inquiry, on this view, should be continuous with empirical inquiry in the sciences" (Leiter, *Nietzsche on Morality*, 3). Leiter's linkage of the empirical sciences with "naturalism" (as exemplified by Darwin's theories) is precisely the understanding of "naturalism" that this study will question.

[15] D.H. Monro, *A Guide to the British Moralists* (London: Fontana, 1972), 23.

the objectives of contemporary "naturalism." In that sense, Nietzsche's use of terms such as weak and strong wills, sickness, health, and decadence can be entirely consistent with an overall anti-naturalist stance.

My study is situated between two dominant traditions. On the one hand, many scholars ever since Heidegger have approached his works as "pure" philosophy and have not seriously explored the philosophy's connections to science. As a result, they have neglected to give an adequate explanation for its biological and physiological resonances. Heidegger himself disparagingly referred to "Nietzsche's alleged biologism"[16] in an effort to counter the powerful first wave of reception which prioritized the biological traces in the wake of Darwin's incredible influence at the turn of the century. Nietzsche's thought clearly seemed to coalesce with notions drawn from eugenics and the theories of degeneration and decadence dominating the fin-de-siècle and beyond.[17] Thus, Heidegger's efforts to rescue the "philosophical" core of Nietzsche from a vulgar, one-dimensional "scientism" are to some degree understandable.

Many studies have followed Heidegger's lead. They have approached Nietzsche's works as a complete philosophical system, with his three main concepts – the *Übermensch*, the will to power, and the eternal return – serving as its foundational pillars. Despite these works' valuable insights, they often reveal two core deficiencies: they extract Nietzsche's work from its immediate historical context – though Nietzsche more than most philosophers emphasizes his (antagonistic) cultural contingency; and they tend to ignore, and therefore fail to make sense of, the "scientific" dimension of his thought. In attempting to extract a "pure" philosophical agenda from Nietzsche's disparate texts, they disregard significant components of that philosophy's totality.

On the other hand, a second scholarly lineage *has* taken the scientific dimension seriously. Whereas some interpreters explore how the natural sciences of the time left their traces on his philosophy,[18] others go further. They suggest that Nietzsche's project was "scientific" in its very orientation and it incorporated findings from the sciences to legitimize

[16] The title of a section of Heidegger's influential two-volume Nietzsche study (Martin Heidegger, *Nietzsche* [Pfullingen: Neske, 1961]).

[17] Some recent studies on these late-century cultural currents include: Moore, *Nietzsche, Biology and Metaphor*; Dan Stone, *Breeding Superman: Nietzsche, Race, and Eugenics in Edwardian and Interwar Britain* (Liverpool: Liverpool University Press, 2002); and Richard Weikart, *From Darwin to Hitler: Evolutionary Ethics, Eugenics, and Racism in Germany* (New York: Palgrave Macmillan, 2004).

[18] For example, Moore again; but also the studies by Robin Small, *Nietzsche and Rée* and *Nietzsche in Context* (Burlington, VT: Ashgate, 2001).

its objectives. In their views, his thought does not become more philosophically significant as a result of its isolation from science, but, on the contrary, because it recognizes that it must square with the "higher" truth standards of science.[19] While their approach offsets some of the limitations that arise from the philosophical "purists," it falls short in another regard: it fails to make adequate sense of Nietzsche's explicit *antagonism* toward science.[20] Here, too, this group willfully disregards a major component of his philosophy.

For this reason, my account differs from the most recent work on the subject, John Richardson's *Nietzsche's New Darwinism* (2004). Though Richardson acknowledges Nietzsche's antagonism, he believes that Nietzsche misunderstands specific points of Darwin's arguments – for example, that Darwin retains an implicit teleology, which he, Nietzsche, overcomes with the "will to power."[21] Richardson's study then goes on to show how many of Nietzsche's thoughts merely transfigure Darwin's findings – to the point that Darwin's science, in Richardson's view, becomes the infrastructure for Nietzsche's philosophical project[22] – while he systematically downplays the significance of Nietzsche's objections to Darwin and his theories or criticizes them as misguided or "wrong."[23]

[19] For example, Richardson: "[Nietzsche] prides himself in his naturalism – in his study of contemporary science, and in his philosophy's incorporation of its truths. He claims to know what the science knows – and something else besides" (Richardson, *Nietzsche's New Darwinism*, 4). Maudemarie Clark, *Nietzsche on Truth and Philosophy* (New York: Cambridge University Press, 1990) and Leiter, *Nietzsche on Morality* are also prominent proponents of readings sympathetic to science.

[20] Leiter, referencing Clark (*Nietzsche on Truth*) (22), tries to explain away Nietzsche's numerous skeptical comments regarding "science" (21–22), "causation" (22–23), "materialism" (23–25), and "human nature and essence" (25–26) and asserts that "in his later works, Nietzsche's skepticism vanishes and he repeatedly endorses a scientific perspective as the correct and true one" (Leiter, *Nietzsche on Morality*, 21)! Aside from the fact that there are hardly any indications to back up such an assessment (and Leiter's explanations are unpersuasive), my study will show that, in fact, the modern scientific enterprise becomes one of Nietzsche's most significant polemical targets in the final period.

[21] Richardson, *Nietzsche's New Darwinism*, 23. Richardson believes, however, that Nietzsche still adheres to those teleological assumptions, and he makes much of the preposition "to" in the "will *to* power," as though the concept itself revealed Nietzsche's teleological tendencies: "What can that towardness be, if *not* an end-directedness" (Richardson, *Nietzsche's New Darwinism*, 21)?

[22] "[Nietzsche] sets something distinctively his own *on top of* (explanation by) natural selection. He proposes a kind of selective mechanism – likely nonindividual and largely noncognitive – that operates *over* human societies" (italics mine) (Richardson, *Nietzsche's New Darwinism*, 4).

[23] "Nietzsche's criticisms and amendments are wrong not about Darwin, but about the facts, as we now know them; on these points Darwin has been confirmed, and Nietzsche's doubts carry no weight" (Richardson, *Nietzsche's New Darwinism*, 17). But where is there any indication that Nietzsche truly *cares* about the "facts" of evolution? By failing to detect the radical nature of Nietzsche's implicit critique of natural science, *including* evolution, Richardson continues to judge Nietzsche on the basis of traditional criteria of being "right" or "wrong" about the objective science of Darwinism.

This approach raises some serious questions;[24] but perhaps the most serious one is this: what does one make of, and how does one explain, Nietzsche's explicit later antagonism if that critique is not merely an issue of being "right" or "wrong" about Darwin's theories? In short, what is the purpose behind Nietzsche's "anti-Darwinism" if its "truthfulness" is no longer an issue? Because of his allegiance to the scientific truth standards of Darwin's model, Richardson fails to uncover the truly radical core of Nietzsche's fundamental Darwinian critique.

Finally, I wish to say a word about my "strategy" in regard to the texts. Over the years, scholars have argued about the status and ranking of the texts, more specifically, the role and the value of the unpublished note-books, i.e. the so-called *Nachlass*, much of which his sister, Elisabeth, compiled in a separate posthumous volume entitled the *Will to Power* (*Wille zur Macht*). The latter "work," which Walter Kaufmann subsequently translated into English, has endured a stubborn and influential afterlife in the Anglo-American Nietzsche world despite the fact that it has proven to be an editorial "forgery."[25] Moreover, Heidegger's preference for the "philosophy" of his unpublished notebooks – he famously stated that the "true" Nietzsche resided in the *Nachlass* – has encouraged many scholars to prefer the notes to the published work.[26]

When Giorgio Colli and Mazzino Montinari published their landmark German-language edition of the complete works in 1967, the so-called *KSA*, they not only gave scholarship a critical apparatus of the highest

[24] Why would Nietzsche wish to construct his philosophy on a Darwinian infrastructure if he does not even agree with Darwinian insights? Or, if Nietzsche misunderstands those insights, i.e. gets them "wrong," what philosophical relevance would his enterprise have if it misrepresented "nature" and scientific "truth" in such a fundamental way? Then again, if Nietzsche creatively applies Darwin's findings to his own philosophical project, making it irrelevant that he misrepresents the "facts" of Darwinism, would not that turn him into just another Social Darwinist? Finally, why should we study him as an original thinker at all, and not just as a cultural artifact, if he belongs to that category?

[25] Walter Kaufmann's *Will to Power* (*WP*) translation is still in print and popular (Friedrich Nietzsche, *The Will to Power*, ed. Walter Kaufmann [New York: Random House, 1967]), and Nietzsche scholars in the English-speaking world still readily quote from it. Part of the problem is that Anglo-American scholarship does not yet have access to a complete English translation of the Colli–Montinari edition (Friedrich Nietzsche, *Sämtliche Werke*, 15 vols. [Berlin: de Gruyter, 1980] [from now on, *KSA*]) and must continue to work with citations from *WP*.

[26] Richard Schacht, defending the use of *WP*, argues that working with it is permissible as long as one treats the material therein as having no higher value than anything else in the notebooks (Richard Schacht, *Making Sense of Nietzsche: Reflections Timely and Untimely* [Urbana: University of Illinois Press, 1995], 124). But then the question arises: why draw from the fictional *WP* at all if one can take the citation directly from the notebooks? By "quoting" from *WP*, one supports the illusion that there is a coherent authorial "system" behind a posthumously compiled collection of thought-fragments, i.e. one creates an "author" where there is none.

editorial standard;[27] they also helped demarcate the published works from the unpublished fragments, which now appear in strict chronological order (and not in the form of an illusory separate "work").[28] Their edition demolished the myth of the *Will to Power*. And yet, they did not put the debate completely to rest, for it has since shifted to philological questions such as whether to draw from the notebooks at all or how far to work with the fragments versus the published works. As a result, an author feels compelled to clarify the philological procedure before tackling the subject.

Stated simply, I argue for the priority of Nietzsche's published works, and I will draw almost exclusively from them.[29] Adopting such a practice in no way means that I ignore the *Nachlass* or find it immaterial; when it helps my argument, I will turn to it. But there are two persuasive reasons to emphasize the published work. For one, I believe it is philologically suspect, in Nietzsche's case or any author's, for that matter, to prioritize a writer's notebooks over work he intended to publish – or even to treat them as equal. Although one must consider everything a thinker such as Nietzsche has written when one evaluates his philosophy, one should not disregard the author's very clear intention of introducing only certain of his ideas to the public for a reason. By placing precedence on his published word, one does not "fetishize" the author or treat him as an "idol";[30] one merely wishes to respect the author's distinction between public persona – which is what published works represent – and thought fragments and private jottings, which lack the conscious systematization and coherence of a published oeuvre.[31]

---

[27] "We shall forever be in Mazzino Montinari's debt for his enormous labor of love, which left to us what is likely to remain the best possible presentation of Nietzsche's legacy to us ... He put nearly the whole of Nietzsche's written legacy at our disposal, as faithfully and authoritatively as anyone could" (Schacht, *Making Sense of Nietzsche*, 117).

[28] "What Montinari made available to us, in definitive form and clearly demarcated fashion, is not merely the body of work Nietzsche published or readied for publication, but also that immense and diverse mass of material he left upon his collapse" (Schacht, *Making Sense of Nietzsche*, 117).

[29] Here I differ in methodology from Moore and Richardson, the two most prominent recent interpreters of the Nietzsche–Darwin connection, who draw rather indiscriminately from both published and unpublished works to make their case.

[30] Schacht, *Making Sense of Nietzsche*, 119.

[31] The recent pioneering philological efforts of Marie-Luise Haase, Montinari's former assistant, have rendered excessive reliance on the "notebooks" even more problematic. Her philology, an expansion of Colli–Montinari's, has shown that even the great editors had taken considerable liberties with their compilation of "notebook" entries, which they placed in chronological order and to which they gave a "neater" systematic appearance. As the careful philological work on the manuscripts now reveals, many of these entries were random jottings and marginalia over time, which did not at all exhibit the sense of coherence or chronology that the Colli–Montinari edition seemed to indicate. This "new" evidence should render the published work even *more*

But beyond that, I think the question of publication holds especially true for a writer like Nietzsche – more so, perhaps, than for most published authors.[32] Aside from the significant fact that literary style and the art of rhetorical presentation are paramount for Nietzsche and his meanings, a point to which most scholars now readily accede,[33] I believe that a major part of his philosophy is revealed in the *fact* of publication, that is, in the objectives he pursues *through* publication. As my study will reveal, the polemical, antagonistic character of his late works in particular is inseparable from the "message" of his final philosophy as a whole. To divorce the thoughts from the overt polemical strategy – as well as from the complex personality of its strongly opinionated author – means to *distort* the meanings of that philosophy. Indeed, Nietzsche emphasized the importance of the personality behind the work *throughout* his literary career – namely, the "human, all too human" character concealed behind expressions of "genius" – and he sought to strip away the accretions of interpretation that had collected around flesh-and-blood historical individuals.[34] That rhetorical practice, too, was an extension of hard-won *philosophical* insights.

definitive, being the only "corpus" which Nietzsche himself chose to systematize, sign off on, and publish under his name (and therefore less prone to philological "tampering"). See Stephan Günzel, "Review of Friedrich Nietzsche, *Werke. Kritische Gesamtausgabe*, Neunte Abteilung, *Der handschriftliche Nachlass ab Frühjahr 1885 in differenzierter Transkription*, Vol. 1–3, ed. Marie-Luise Haase and Michael Kohlenbach," *Nietzscheforschung* 10 (2003): 348–53; Renate Reschke, "Review of Friedrich Nietzsche, *Werke. Kritische Gesamtausgabe*, Neunte Abteilung, *Der handschriftliche Nachlass ab Frühjahr 1885 in differenzierter Transkription*, Vol. 4–5, ed. Marie-Luise Haase and Martin Stingelin in Verbindung mit der Berlin-Brandenburgischen Akademie der Wissenschaften," *Nietzscheforschung* 13 (2006): 287–95; and Marie-Luise Haase, "Nietzsche und ...," *Nietzscheforschung* 10 (2003): 17–36.

[32] On this point I disagree with Schacht, who correctly starts by saying: "I readily grant that, as a general rule, in interpreting an author's thought primacy should be given to things the author is prepared to say in things intended for publication"; but then concludes with: "Here, however, as in so many other respects, Nietzsche is a rather special case" (Schacht, *Making Sense of Nietzsche*, 118).

[33] For example, Christopher Janaway: "Nietzsche's way of writing addresses our affects, feelings, or emotions ... I argue that this is not some gratuitous exercise in 'style' that could be edited out of Nietzsche's thought" (Christopher Janaway, *Beyond Selflessness: Reading Nietzsche's Genealogy* [Oxford: Oxford University Press, 2007], 4). Whereas earlier reception often questioned the philosophical value of Nietzsche's writings *because of* their rhetorical brilliance, a new generation of scholars now acknowledges that the "style" of his writings does not detract from the philosophy but, quite the contrary, serves as an integral part of its meanings; see, e.g., Daniel Conway, "For Whom the Bell Tolls," *Journal of Nietzsche Studies* 35/36 (2008): 96–98.

[34] "[W]ho knows if this is not just what has happened in all great cases so far: the masses worshipped a God, – and that 'God' was only a poor sacrificial animal! Success has always been the greatest liar, – and the 'work' itself is a success. The great statesman, the conqueror, the discoverer – each one is disguised by his creations to the point of being unrecognizable. The 'work' of the artist, of the philosopher, is what invents whoever has created it, whoever was supposed to have created it. 'Great men,' as they are honored, are minor pieces of bad literature, invented

Nietzsche's philosophy, I will argue, can only be understood on the basis of his antagonisms, both personal and cultural. One of the most significant in his last phase was his antagonism toward Darwin and his science. To repeat, I do not mean to suggest that Nietzsche builds his entire philosophy around this antagonism alone, since his work develops other significant and productive rivalries – such as with Wagner, Schopenhauer, Plato, Pascal, Spinoza, and Kant, to name but a few. They too reveal key dimensions of his thought. But his ongoing involvement with Darwin led him to develop his innovative theory and practice of polemical philosophy in the first place, which evolved into his signature style in the important final years.

My approach will require us to think differently of what constitutes Nietzsche's "philosophy." While his earlier period developed into a critique of traditional metaphysics based on Darwin-inspired insights, his mature work became what I will refer to as a philosophy of "creative antagonisms." In the end, Nietzsche even includes Darwin and his genealogical practitioners in that polemical circle once he understands how his critical reassessment also implicates them. My study will seek to do justice to Nietzsche's philosophy in its totality; but it will seek to do so by making sense of the undisputed "scientific" components of his thought, particularly its widespread biological and physiological resonances.

after the fact; in the world of historical values, counterfeit *rules*" (*BGE* 269) (reprised in *Nietzsche contra Wagner* "Psychologist" 1).

PART I

Early Darwinism to the "Anti-Darwin"

CHAPTER I

Towards the "Anti-Darwin": Darwinian meditations in the middle period

Nietzsche met George C. Robertson, editor of the quarterly *Mind*, at a resort in the Swiss Alps in the summer of 1877. *Mind* was the premier British journal open to new Darwinian perspectives in philosophy. In an enthusiastic letter to his friend Paul Rée, Nietzsche wrote: "Among the Englishmen staying here with me there is a very genial professor of philosophy at London University College, *Robertson*, editor of the best English journal for philosophy *Mind*, a quarterly review … All the great names of England – Darwin … Spencer, Tylor, etc. – contribute to it … During his discussions on Darwin, Bagehot, etc., it occurred to me again how much I would have liked you to have taken part in this company, the only true philosophical one currently available."[1] Nietzsche's unmitigated praise for "all the great names of England" would later turn into scornful derision – the "English psychologists" of *GM*. Within a span of ten years, Nietzsche gravitated from considering Darwin and his "school" "the only true philosophical company" to writing a scathing indictment of their positions. What had transpired in these ten years? How did Darwin go from being his great inspiration in the 1870s to becoming the target of his "Anti-Darwin" writings of 1888?

Many of the answers to these questions lie buried in the often-neglected middle period of his philosophizing. At that time, Nietzsche entered into a subtle, fascinating, and fruitful dialogue with Darwin-inspired genealogical perspectives. But while scholars almost unanimously acknowledge his turn away from the metaphysical preoccupations of his earliest works towards an interest in the natural sciences in the middle period, they fail to excavate the subterranean cadences in this stage of his career. That is, they do not sense how many of his mature points of critique were already firmly established by the end of the middle period, so that his final

[1] Nietzsche, *Sämtliche Briefe* (Berlin: de Gruyter, 1986), vol. v, 265–66; from now on, *KSB*.

writings represented a change of style and tone from, and a radicalization of, positions already staked out in this time.

SOURCES FOR DARWIN

Nietzsche's first significant exposure to Darwin came through his reading of F.A. Lange's *History of Materialism*. Nietzsche read the work shortly after its publication in 1866. In a letter to his friend Hermann Muschacke, Nietzsche concluded: "The most important philosophical work to appear in the last decades is undoubtedly Lange, History of Materialism, about which I could write reams of praise. Kant, Schopenhauer and Lange's book – that's all I need."[2] In a letter to Carl von Gersdorff of February 1868, more than a year and a half after his initial reading, Nietzsche summarized the list of questions that had interested him in Lange:

At this point I must once again praise the efforts of a man I've already written to you about. If you care to inform yourself about the materialist movement of our age, about the natural sciences with their Darwinist theories, their cosmic systems, their animated [*belebten*] *camera obscura*, etc., but also about ethical materialism and Manchester theory, then I can think of no better work to recommend than the *History of Materialism* by Friedr. Alb. Lange (Iserlohn 1866). It is a work which delivers much more than its title promises; it is a true treasure trove that one would like to return to and read over and over again. (*KSB* II, 257)

Since Nietzsche seems not to have read much of Darwin in the original, it would be fair to assume that he drew a considerable amount of his knowledge from "popular" discussions, as Dennett has suggested.[3] "Darwin's own works," Alfred Kelly writes, "never achieved any mass popularity in Germany. Like most great books, *The Origin* was much discussed but little read. It was only indirectly, through the popular accounts, that the public discovered Darwinism." On the other hand, Kelly concludes, "these were not thirdhand accounts. Actually the public got closer to the 'real thing' because from the beginning professional scientists assumed the burden of popularization."[4]

At the same time, Nietzsche became increasingly interested in the natural sciences in Basle. Here, several prominent scientists were engaged in ongoing Darwinian controversies. For one, there was Ludwig Rütimeyer,

[2] *KSB* II, 184.   [3] Dennett, *Darwin's Dangerous Idea*, 182.
[4] Alfred Kelly, *The Descent of Darwin: The Popularization of Darwinism in Germany, 1860–1914* (Chapel Hill: University of North Carolina Press, 1981), 21–22.

professor of medicine, whose scholarly interests extended to geology, pale-
ontology, zoology, and biology: "It has become impossible to determine
to what extent Nietzsche was personally acquainted with Rütimeyer,
who had become a member of the University of Basle in 1855 through
the efforts of Peter Merian and Wilhelm Vischer. Yet, Nietzsche, always
on the search for true personalities, could not have failed to detect
this man of character."[5] Though he was critical of Darwin, Rütimeyer
ensured that Darwinian issues remained alive and hotly contested during Nietzsche's years in Basle: "During the public academic discussions
in Basle, Nietzsche experienced the entire spectrum of conflict between
Darwin and the opposition, which was well-represented in the figure of
Rütimeyer."[6] Nietzsche had read some of the latter's articles and recom-
mended them to his friend Gersdorff. He even indicated that he favored
Rütimeyer over the more famous Darwinian Ernst Haeckel.[7]

In short, Nietzsche most likely "knew" Darwin from specialized literature, scientific debates, *and* more "popular" accounts. Although the latter
might have given the inevitable distortions, they often presented fairly
accurate synopses of Darwin's scientific principles:

Contrary to what is often said, the popularizers usually did a fairly accurate job
of representing Darwin. Some simplification was inevitable and necessary – few
could follow Darwin's often tortuous qualifications – but charges that popularizers vulgarized or sensationalized come from those who have labeled without bothering to read. These charges do not stand up to close scrutiny. If the
popularizers changed Darwinism – and they did – they did so by going beyond
Darwin's works to philosophize on their own. When Darwinism evolved into
new *Weltanschauungen* in Germany, it usually did so on a sound factual basis; it
was just that the facts often appeared in a context foreign to Darwin's own more
limited perspective.[8]

One should also consider Nietzsche's idiosyncratic means of acquir-
ing information on a host of contemporary issues. Although he had
firsthand knowledge of Wagner, Schopenhauer, and the many ancient
authors whom he had studied as an academic philologist, Nietzsche often
based his understanding of modern thinkers and movements on secondary sources and exchanges with specialists or representatives close to the
respective positions. Not only was Nietzsche practically blind; he suffered

[5] Curt Paul Janz, *Nietzsche* (Munich: Hanser, 1978), vol. 1, 317.
[6] Janz, *Nietzsche*, vol. 1, 320.
[7] Nietzsche: "Does the great fame of the scientist Häckel do any damage to the greater fame-
worthiness of Rütimeyer?" (quoted from Janz, *Nietzsche*, vol. 1, 317).
[8] Kelly, *The Descent of Darwin*, 8.

terrible migraines whenever he had to read longer texts that posed little obstacle for normal readers. It was not unusual, then, for him to depend on a combination of oral readings, exchanges with specialists, and learned summaries for his information on any given contemporary topic.

Finally, one should not underestimate the importance of Nietzsche's training as a classical philologist and his graduate-school investigations into the pre-Socratic philosophers and their natural philosophy. Many studies justifiably recognize and emphasize the importance of Wagner and Schopenhauer in Nietzsche's early intellectual development. But they take less account of how his scholarly interests predisposed him to modern scientific *methods* – all the tools of nineteenth-century *Wissenschaft* and philology – and to an overall scientific-materialist perspective on life and nature.[9] Once one gives this prominent side of Nietzsche's early thought its proper recognition, it becomes easier to appreciate both his predisposition to, as well as his sophisticated understanding of, Darwin and his ideas.

THE *DAVID STRAUSS* ESSAY (1873)

According to Robin Small, traces of Nietzsche's interest in natural science are not very visible in his early published work.[10] Though this assertion is generally true, it does not hold true for Nietzsche's first *Untimely Meditation, David Strauss: The Confessor and Writer (DS)* (1873). In section 7 of this essay, Nietzsche reveals key aspects of what I term his "early Darwinism," i.e. the first signs of his initial sympathy for Darwin. Nietzsche wrote the essay in polemical response to David Strauss's work *The Old and the New Faith*, which had preceded the publication of *DS* by one year.

Kelly gives the following synopsis of Strauss and his work:

Strauss, who had already dismissed the Bible as myth in his *Life of Jesus* (1835) believed that Darwinism had finally cleared the way for a rational religion by proving that man's dignity came from his own efforts, not from God. How much more dignified it was for man to have risen from animals than to have fallen from a state of perfection! For Strauss, such a view led straight to the worship of modern scientific culture. But he brushed aside the need for a formal church, 'as if meditation were only possible in a church, edification only to be

---

[9] "Despite [his] Schopenhauerian and Wagnerian allegiances there was another side to Nietzsche's mind, even before his move to Basle: an active interest in natural science and in the naturalistic tradition within philosophy" (Small, *Nietzsche and Rée*, 4).

[10] Small, *Nietzsche and Rée*, 7.

found in a sermon!' That "New Faith" was an individual declaration of independence from the past. It needed no institutional expression.[11]

In short, Strauss "had accepted science, above all Darwinism, as the sole legitimate path to truth."[12]

In an afterword to his translation of the *Meditations*, Richard Gray writes: "The critical reception of the four *Unfashionable Observations* [Gray's translation of the title] is marked by the paradox that the essay to which Nietzsche himself attached the least importance, *Utility and Liability of History for Life*, is today almost universally recognized as the most significant work in the collection. By contrast, *David Strauss*, the piece that even later in his life Nietzsche most prized, has come to be viewed as an incidental polemic, which, when not completely forgotten, is largely ignored by Nietzsche scholars."[13] Further, "scholarly interest in the *Unfashionable Observations*, when pursued outside the context of general introductions into Nietzsche's life and philosophy, has overwhelmingly concentrated on his study of history, which is credited with advancing a substantial, influential and hence lasting philosophical position."[14] But this assessment begs the question: if the history piece were so intrinsically valuable, why would he then consider his "incidental polemic" *more* relevant, "even later in life?" Was this truly a sign of Nietzsche's "self-delusion," as Gray claims?

One possible explanation for the "history" essay's greater success in terms of critical reception might be that it reflects a more traditional understanding of philosophy, namely, a dispassionate, depersonalized treatment of certain abstract, "eternal" positions. Over time, however, Nietzsche increasingly began to reject this mode of philosophizing. Instead, he began to favor a more personal, direct, and above all opinionated engagement with ideas as well as their historical exponents. In that sense, the Strauss essay's personal polemics were neither incidental nor peripheral to Nietzsche's intentions and ambitions. On the contrary, this polemical response to issues and their representatives eventually developed into his main mode of philosophical expression, particularly in his final works. Nietzsche later become less satisfied with the history piece, one could argue, because he drafted it in the more traditional and abstract style of philosophical discourse, where he ultimately felt the least

---

[11] Kelly, *The Descent of Darwin*, 78.   [12] Kelly, *The Descent of Darwin*, 74.
[13] Friedrich Nietzsche, *Unfashionable Observations*, ed. Richard Gray (Stanford: Stanford University Press, 1995), 408.
[14] Nietzsche, *Unfashionable Observations*, 408.

comfortable, creative, and personally engaged. Perhaps for that reason it "unleashed a crisis in Nietzsche's self-understanding as writer" (Gray).

It is interesting to note that *David Strauss* is the only truly *polemical* piece among the four *Meditations*. At this stage, Nietzsche was still enthralled with idealism and believed in the "virtues" of self-abnegation, devotion to a higher cause, and deference to heroic, creative individuals. Both the "Wagner" and "Schopenhauer" essays were more characteristic of that spirit. On one level, then, the "David Strauss" essay might have appealed to him as unexplored creative terrain: namely, polemics as an original means to express independent philosophical positions. At the same time, the Strauss essay unleashed a deep sense of guilt, anxiety, and anguish,[15] in part because it prioritized personal attack over heroic adulation, at least stylistically. It was only when Nietzsche had later developed and refined his notion of "creative antagonism" that he learned to appreciate the personal antagonist as the perfect vehicle to express all aspects of his philosophical, psychologically attuned position in the most effective and literarily satisfactory manner. The "Strauss" piece could then present itself as the most representative and clearly articulated expression, the unexpected stylistic forerunner, of his preferred philosophical practice: psychological acuity and polemical antagonism wedded to philosophical rigor.

THE *DAVID STRAUSS* ESSAY, SECTION 7

In my analysis of *DS* 7, I will concentrate on five main components of Nietzsche's critique. All five of them reveal a significant feature of his "early Darwinism." In the first example, Nietzsche criticizes Strauss for wrapping himself in the "shaggy cloak" of "our ape-genealogists," i.e. German Darwinists, even while he fails to think through the importance and far-reaching implications of Darwin for traditional metaphysical ethics: "With a certain crude contentment he covers himself with the shaggy cloak of our ape-genealogists and praises Darwin as one of humankind's greatest benefactors – but we realize with consternation that his ethics is constructed independently of the question: 'How do we conceive the world'" (39)? If Strauss had truly understood, appreciated, and agreed

---

[15] Strauss died shortly after the publication of Nietzsche's polemic, and Nietzsche was unsettled by the thought that Strauss might have seen it before his death: "Yesterday they buried David Strauss in Ludwigsburg. I very much hope I didn't make his last moments of life more burdensome and that he might have died without knowledge of me. It has disturbed me a bit" (*KSB* 4, 200).

with Darwin and his ideas, he would need to base his moral code on two essential aspects of his scientific thought: the Hobbesian-inspired *bellum omnium contra omnes* (or in Darwin's terminology: the "struggle for existence"); and Darwin's "survival of the fittest."

Nietzsche, however, does not consider Strauss capable of such a resolute, heroic, and noble love of truth. Instead, Strauss avoids the severe implications of Darwin's findings for morality. In reality, Strauss merely fears to alienate his followers, for whom Darwin has become a vehicle to savage established religion, superstitions, and discredited theological doctrine:

Here was a real opportunity to exhibit natural courage: for here he [Strauss] would have had to turn his back on his "we" and boldly deduce from the *bellum omnium contra omnes* and the privileged right of the strong a moral code for life. To be sure, this moral code would have had to have been born of … a love of truth utterly different from one that always only explodes in angry invectives against priests, miracles, and the "world-historical humbug" of the resurrection. For the same philistine who takes the side of all such invectives would take sides against such a genuine Darwinian ethic that was consistently carried through. (*DS* 39)

Nietzsche's second critique relates to Strauss's vague and facile moral imperative: "All moral activity … is the self-determination of the individual according to the idea of the species [*Gattung*]" (39). Using Darwin-inspired terminology (*Gattung*), Strauss constructs a "morality" on the basis that man is part of a larger, single human species, and he hopes that that knowledge must ultimately stem his individualism. But all this means, Nietzsche rejoins, is to "[l]ive like a human being and not like an ape or a seal" (39). Specifically, Nietzsche criticizes Strauss because he prefers to "preach morality," which is easy, rather than to explain the grounds for morality, which would be infinitely more challenging. Strauss's objective, in fact, should be to determine how one could explain acts of kindness, compassion, love, and renunciation, i.e. morality, on the basis of Darwin's findings:

Strauss has not even learned that a concept alone can never make human beings better and more moral, and that it is just as easy to preach morality as it is difficult to establish it; instead, it should be his task earnestly to explain and derive, on the basis of his Darwinistic premises, the phenomena of human kindness, compassion, love, and self-denial, whose existence one simply cannot deny: in fact, however, Strauss chose instead to flee from the task of *explanation* by making the leap into imperative diction. (*DS* 39–40).

Third, these efforts to "flee explanations" allow Strauss "to skip with ease away from" Darwin's "cardinal principle" (*bei diesem Sprung begegnet es ihm sogar, auch über den Fundamentalsatz Darwins leichten Sinnes hin-wegzuhüpfen*): namely, that existence is based on brutish struggle whereby man constantly forgets that he is part of a larger species while asserting supremacy and securing survival. Strauss's homespun moralizing and loose rendition of Darwin merely sugarcoat the radical implications of his findings, which problematize morality altogether:

> But where does this resounding imperative come from? How can this be innate to human beings when, according to Darwin, the human being is wholly a creature of nature and has evolved to the heights of humanity by adhering to a completely different set of laws; namely, by no other means than by constantly forgetting that other similar creatures possess the same rights, by feeling himself to be the stronger and gradually bringing about the demise of other specimens displaying a weaker constitution. (*DS* 40).

In the fourth example, Nietzsche criticizes Strauss's attempt to project a redemptive message into natural processes and to treat them as reflections of a divine master plan. Nietzsche quotes from Strauss's work: "'[Our God] shows us that chance would be an unreasonable master of the world, and that necessity, that is, the chain of causation manifest in the world, is reason itself'" (41). In true Hegelian fashion – Nietzsche: "in this Hegelian devotion to the real as the reasonable, that is, to the *idolatry of success*" (41) – Strauss interprets natural history as the enactment of God's will in the long causal chain of necessity. For Strauss, this mani-festation of unfolding reason in human history reconciles all past actions (i.e. both examples of great good as well as evil) in the culmination of the present moment.

In this example, Nietzsche criticizes Strauss's ideal from the standpoint of science. He implies that Strauss ignores both the methods and basic principles of modern science, including Darwinism, to which and he and his followers otherwise claim allegiance. But "honest scientists" would in fact reject Strauss's interpretation, for they would consider it both an unacceptable anthropomorphism and an attempt to project ethical cat-egories into an indifferent process guided solely by natural laws: "an hon-est natural scientist believes in the absolute adherence of the world to laws, without, however, making any assertions whatsoever about the ethical or moral claims of these laws: in any such assertions he would recognize the supremely anthropomorphic demeanor of a reason unable to adhere to the constraints of what is allowed" (41). Strauss, on the other hand, "sim-ply assumes without further ado that everything that occurs in the world has the *highest* intellectual value, in other words, that it is ordered in an absolutely reasonable and purposive manner, and hence that it embodies a revelation of eternal goodness itself" (41).

Nietzsche's fifth and final critique elaborates on this point. He accuses Strauss of pouring "soothing oil" into the mechanistic worldview and playing "metaphysical architect." In truth, however, Strauss is alarmed by what modern scientific methodology implies for his and his followers' faith. Instead of embracing science and the theories of natural law *in toto*, Strauss and his adherents dread the "rigid and pitiless mechanism of the worldly machine" and seek refuge and consolation in metaphysics. Strauss lacks the courage to tell his followers that life is nothing but an indifferent mechanism and that they must beware of its crushing wheels: "[Strauss] does not dare tell them honestly: I have liberated you from a compassionate and merciful god, and the 'universe' is nothing but a rigid mechanism; beware lest its wheels crush you! He does not dare: and hence he must resort to a sorceress, namely to metaphysics" (43). In the end, Strauss's philistines prefer Straussian to Christian metaphysics, because at least Strauss can make sense of their reality and conditions, whereas Christianity expects them to believe in miracles, something beyond their limited comprehension.

IMPLICATIONS OF NIETZSCHE'S POSITION

What inferences can one draw from his "early Darwinism?" First of all, Nietzsche clearly understands that Darwin's worldview necessitates a radical overhaul of traditional metaphysics and ethics. He also understands that it is impossible to separate Darwinism as a cultural phenomenon from Darwin's overall naturalist–materialist paradigm. That is, if one adheres to Darwin's naturalist outlook as well as his attempts to explain ethics and morality on the basis of that naturalism, one would have to proceed strictly within the confines of a naturalist framework. The larger issue of morality cannot be separated from the way in which one perceives and examines the natural world.

Nietzsche also reveals his interest in the ethical and materialist implications of Darwin's science, how it affects our understanding of moral behavior and actions, but he concerns himself less with that aspect of Darwinism which received the most popular and controversial attention during his lifetime (and beyond): the theory of the evolution of species as it pertains to human descent. Nietzsche in fact seems to disparage those interpreters, who focus on the evolutionary issue ("our ape-genealogists"), while proceeding straight to the nexus that would dominate his later philosophy: Darwin's impact on ethics and morality. He divides Darwinism into two distinct parts – i.e. Darwin's materialist and genealogical methodology versus his theory of organic evolution *per se* – and this division did not change during the course of his future engagement. Indeed, the gap only widened. For Nietzsche, the genealogical and ethical dimension of Darwin's ideas grew in significance and eventually influenced *GM*. Darwin's theory of evolution and man's origins, on the other hand, continued to receive scant treatment. When Nietzsche mentioned it at all, it would most often be in ridicule.

Another interesting dimension of Nietzsche's position relates to Darwin's impact on religion. Once again, Nietzsche reveals himself to be serious about the materialist implications of evolution. He recognizes, for one, that Darwin's scientific position undercuts attempts to project religious longings into an objective scientific process. As a result, Nietzsche is more critical of religious and scientific popularizers and proselytizers such as Strauss and Haeckel, who extract a monist religion from a loose, inconsistent, and distorted (mis)reading of Darwin. He himself, however, takes seriously the implications of Darwin's findings for religion and traditional morality. Even more significantly, he defends Christianity from those who used Darwin to vent vulgar anti-clerical, anti-Christian sentiments. If one considers his own anti-Christian pronouncements, this might seem unusual. However, it reveals two important features of his thought; these did not change significantly, even in later years. First, he always remained more critical of self-anointed free-thinkers and founders of new religions than of traditional Christians. Second, he does not naturally assume that Darwin's science necessitates the extreme anti-clericalism and anti-Christian fulminations of some of his followers. The latter point is significant for his subsequent engagement, because it implies that he could see Darwin's thought as a positive and conscientious perspective *within* the Christian tradition.

At this formative stage, Nietzsche focuses immediately on a set of problematic issues. These issues preoccupied and animated the moral imagination of Darwin himself. For one, Nietzsche recognizes that the struggle for scarce resources presupposes that man is a "creature of nature" and, as such, is subject to the same natural laws as the rest of organic nature. He also realizes that Darwin's scientific perspective demands us to suspend moral judgment. Traditional Christian categories are not involved or grounded in the evolutionary mechanism. Man evolves because man constantly forgets that "other similar creatures possess the same rights, by feeling himself to be the stronger and gradually bringing about the demise of other specimens displaying a weaker constitution." Evolution has to proceed out of this amoral, entirely this-worldly struggle. Darwin focuses on survival and *not* on the desirability of a specific moral outcome. His adherence to strict scientific methodology and a system of natural laws precludes him from making assertions, moral or otherwise, about natural processes. Such assertions would be unscientific and would reflect "the supremely anthropomorphic demeanor of a reason unable to adhere to the constraints of what is allowed."

Nietzsche's reading also shows that he understands Darwin's theories need not imply a progressive bias in the evolutionary process. Some commentators have critiqued Nietzsche's view of Darwin on this account. They contend that he, like many Victorians, allied with a progressive form of evolution and thus with an inscribed moral bias within evolution. (Indeed, many first-generation Darwinists, especially in Germany, *did* subscribe to such a progressive reading.) Nietzsche's ultimate rejection of Darwin, they argue, was thus premised on a false understanding of his core proposition: he rejected Darwin on the basis of a perceived moral bias in evolution to which, in fact, Darwin did not adhere. As modern Darwinists now believe, Darwin envisioned a non-linear, branching model of evolution: "the coral of life." Unlike his followers, then, he rigorously avoided equating evolution with upward development, or progression.

But a closer examination of Nietzsche's position in this section reveals that he grasps this implication. For one, he recognizes that Darwin concentrates on the process of natural struggle and its outcome; Darwin does not project moral valuations into his scientific analysis. Second, Nietzsche criticizes interpreters who *did* draw perfectionist religious inferences from evolution. He is also highly critical of projecting Hegelian notions into Darwin. Since one can consider Hegel the intellectual bridge to a progressive reading, Nietzsche seems to ally himself here with a strict anti-Hegelian, non-linear model of evolution. Third, Nietzsche recognizes that Darwin's importance resides in his rigorous adherence to scientific standards. No implicit moral or ethical assumptions, no metaphysics – Christian or otherwise – should either be associated with or projected into nature. He does not associate evolution with improvement and higher morality, nor with progressively superior forms, as some continue to assume. He adheres to a strictly functional interpretation of "struggle" and "fitness," concentrating on the implications of natural struggle for the development of the human species and the human mind. But Nietzsche did sense how Darwin's notion of "struggle" disturbed Christianity. To paraphrase his argument in *DS* 7, if only some form of the "fitter," or stronger, survives in the "struggle"; if man, that "creature of nature," "evolved" only by asserting untrammeled individuality against other "weaker specimens"; how could one explain and evaluate those random examples of human goodness, compassion, kindness, self-denial (or morality), "whose existence one simply cannot deny," on the basis of the same Darwinian premises?

Nietzsche here touches upon the cardinal dilemma of Darwin's theses for the issue of man's (moral) development. The entire first section of the *Descent* is devoted to a naturalist explication of this very problem. But unlike Strauss, Nietzsche realizes that an answer to the question of morality and its origins had to be found within scientific Darwinism and on Darwinian terms. One could not simply present a naturalist notion of struggle and then proceed to introduce reason and morality through alternative, non-naturalist processes, i.e. through some form of intellectual/moral *deus ex machina*. The latter type of interpretation, common at the time, *could* be reconciled with a progressive understanding of evolution. Man's "superiority" in terms of reason and the moral sense *could* be explained as the result of a goal-directed, purposeful evolution and could be justified by fortuitous past developments, all leading to the present moment. But these forms of external, non-naturalist (i.e. "moral") explanation were precisely the ones on which the *Origin* casts doubt. Nietzsche grasps this truly original insight. In fact, both their mature systems offer alternative explanations for the same cardinal question: how could morality have arisen on the basis of immanent natural struggle?

IMPLICATIONS FOR NIETZSCHE'S WAGNERISM

At the time of *DS*, Nietzsche was able to reconcile his enthusiasm for his mentor Wagner (and Schopenhauer) with admiration for Darwin. After all, *DS* 7 was a smaller, self-contained piece buried within a longer polemic that as a whole was directed against the self-satisfied middle classes and their negative effects on culture. Strauss and his followers could represent compatible targets for Wagner and Nietzsche, because they both shared contempt for the German *Philister*. But while *DS* criticized first and foremost Strauss's indiscriminate reading, his meshing of contradictory styles, and his ideological eclecticism, Wagner's primary interest was to use Nietzsche's polemic to thwart cultural resistance to his artistic ambitions. When their cultural goals had begun to diverge, Nietzsche could recognize similar harmonizing tendencies and stylistic eclecticism in Wagner. The critique that he once leveled against Strauss – that he invoked Darwin and his science without grasping their wider implications for morality – could now be directed against Wagner's similar efforts to cite Darwin without recognizing his science's threat to Wagnerian metaphysics.

On another level, Nietzsche's youthful ardor sought solace in a Wagnerian "metaphysics of art," whose essential cultural pessimism did not pose a serious threat to Darwin's scientific vision. In fact, Darwin's implications for traditional morality most likely reinforced the need to seek refuge from the painful scientific insights into life and nature. Furthermore, both Schopenhauer and Wagner did not so much directly challenge Darwin as forge individual creative responses where the will was either renounced (Schopenhauer) or redeemed through the absolute artwork (Wagner). Eventually, however, Nietzsche's interest in Darwin's science, his efforts to develop a naturalist paradigm for morality, and his impatience with overarching metaphysical constructs meant that neither a Wagnerian nor Schopenhauerian solution to the problem of the will could prove acceptable. The choice now was not to escape the implications of the naturalized will by fleeing into a personal form of philosophical or aesthetic metaphysics; it was to confront Darwin's biological will in all its dimensions without metaphysical consolation. In *DS*, Nietzsche had not yet made that decision. By 1878, he could find no other choice. He began to sacrifice his once-cherished ideals, including his Wagnerian faith, in order to explain the emergence of morality in purely naturalist terms without recourse to metaphysics, either Christian or aesthetic.

Another point of tension between Nietzsche and Wagner arose from Darwin's naturalist explication for the emergence and evolution of mind. Darwin had a clear psychological orientation. He sought scientific explanations for human institutions, including religion and morality, in man's nature and behavior. Though Wagner too possessed an acute psychological sensibility, he did not approach mind and morality from a psychological perspective; morality was a given. Darwin's paradigm, on the other hand, turned morality itself into an open problem, and it sought to explain human constructs on the basis of scientific naturalism. Darwin started with the biological will and the human mind in order to examine human history and development. He approached man from "beyond good and evil," or better, beyond the desirability of a specific moral outcome.

Five years after the appearance of *DS*, Nietzsche officially broke with Wagner. With the publication of *Human, All Too Human* (*HH*) in 1878, he liberated himself from his former mentor and made a decisive move towards the Enlightenment.[16] At this point, the Frenchman Voltaire, to whom Nietzsche dedicated the work, became Wagner's stylistic and philosophical antipode. Nietzsche later claimed that his public embrace of the Enlightenment tradition as well as its most famous exponent allowed him to recognize and articulate his own philosophical perspectives.[17] In short, at the moment when Nietzsche had decided to engage with Darwin more seriously, he had already allied himself with French and English rationalism and Enlightenment thought, against which Wagner's German art and theories as a whole were directed.

NIETZSCHE, RÉE, AND THE *MORALISTES*

Nietzsche's alienation from Wagner and his ideological circle coincided with his discovery of the French *moralistes* and his friendship with the German Darwinian Paul Rée. In 1875, Rée had published *Psychological Observations*, a book in the style of the *moralistes*, for which Nietzsche had unqualified praise: "Dr. Rée, very devoted to me, has anonymously published an excellent little book, *Psychological Observations*; he is a 'moralist' with the sharpest eye, a most seldom talent among Germans."[18] The latter work, along with personal exchanges with Rée and his reading of the *moralistes*, inspired Nietzsche to embark on the aphoristic style characteristic of his middle period. Nietzsche's own ideas and psychological insights, in turn, helped Rée formulate a work which was to have an even greater influence on Nietzsche ten years later: *The Origin of Moral Sensations* (1877). Nietzsche referred to the latter in the Preface to *GM*, where he claimed it had introduced him to "the back-to-front and perverse kind of genealogical hypotheses, actually the *English* kind" (*GM* "Preface" 4).

Not coincidentally, Rée was influenced by both the French *moralistes*, culminating in the early aphoristic *Psychological Observations*, as well as by the English "genealogical school," which eventually served as the inspiration for his *Origin* essay. Variations of the *moralistes*' insights had worked

---

[16] Nietzsche later stylized the rupture when he recounted how *Parsifal* and *Human, All Too Human* might have crossed paths in the mail: "These two books crossing paths – it was as if I had heard some ominous sound. Didn't it sound as if *swords* were crossing?" (*EH*, "Human, All Too Human" 5).

[17] "The name 'Voltaire' on one of my writings – that was true progress – *towards myself*" (*EH*, "Human, All Too Human" 1).

[18] *KSB* V, 127.

their way into eighteenth-century British philosophy, most prominently into the works of Hume and Smith, thereby influencing the direction of the European Enlightenment in general. Two philosophical traits distinguish the *moralistes*. On the one hand, their outlook was characterized by a fundamental pessimism and skepticism concerning man and human behavior. On the other, the *moralistes* perfected a psychologist sensibility. They dispensed with an explicit form of metaphysics, focused on the passions, and remained wary of the powers of reason. Their intention was to present an "objective" view of man liberated from traditional Christian constraints on the nature of good and evil and born from precise psychological penetration.[19]

The *moralistes* were famed for their polished, urbane style; their masterful use of the aphorism; the clarity and lucidity of their literary expression; and their unblinking evaluation of human behavior and motivation. They also adopted an unconventional attitude toward altruism and egoism, a distinction that figured prominently in eighteenth-century philosophical discourse. Critical of absolute virtue, the *moralistes* focused instead on hidden human motives and drives: "Our virtues are mostly hidden vices" (La Rochefoucauld). Rather than accept the sanctity of Christian ideals, the *moralistes* sought to develop an "objective" assessment of human behavior freed from explicit moral assumptions and value judgments.[20] Typically, the *moralistes* located a single source for human motivation.[21]

DARWIN, THE *MORALISTES*, AND GENEALOGY

On several fundamental levels, Darwin built further on principles previously established by the *moralistes*. For example, Darwin too eschewed metaphysics and focused on observable human emotions and behavior; only they constituted "facts." He clearly worked with a non-idealized, naturalized understanding of "man," considering egoism and self-interest primary human traits. He even postulated a central wellspring of behavior: the instinct of "self-preservation." Nietzsche would later trace

---

[19] Fritz Schalk, *Die französischen Moralisten* (Leipzig: In der Dieterich'schen Verlagsbuchhandlung, 1938), xx.

[20] "He who lives among Germans must consider himself fortunate to find someone free from the kind of idealistic self-deception and colorblindness which Germans love and practically worship as virtue itself. (The French with their Montaigne, La Rochefoucauld, Pascal, Chamfort, Stendhal, are a much purer-spirited nation.) That was my joy when I met Rée: he spoke about morality as far as he knew of it and without having too high an opinion of his own moral instincts" (*KSA* X, 243).

[21] For La Rochefoucauld it was "self-love," whereas Rée concentrated on "envy."

Darwin's understanding of "self-preservation" back to the *moralistes* through its link to Spinoza (*GS* 349). Furthermore, Nietzsche recognized that Darwin, like the *moralistes*, did not treat moral values as absolutes, anchored in a metaphysical realm, but as *relative* distinctions. His theory of evolution could at least explain how socially esteemed values had emerged from their opposites. Traditional metaphysicians, on the other hand, presupposed an absolute moral realm outside of human experience from which morals had miraculously sprung.

Darwin's theories relativized the valuation of human behavior. As a result, he could appreciate human actions and motivations with a greater sense of sophistication and nuance. "Altruism" and "selfishness" were, at closer inspection, not *ipso facto* opposites but were intertwined to such a degree that one value merely represented a finer gradation of the other. Darwin's influence on Nietzsche, filtered through Nietzsche's general sympathy for the *moralistes* at the time, left distinct traces on the opening lines of *HH*:

[H]ow can something originate in its opposite, for example rationality in irrationality, the sentient in the dead, logic in unlogic, disinterested contemplation in covetous desire, living for others in egoism, truth in error? Metaphysical philosophy has hitherto surmounted this difficulty by denying that the one originates in the other and assuming for the more highly valued thing a miraculous source in the very kernel and being of the "thing in itself." Historical philosophy, on the other hand, which can no longer be separated from natural science, the youngest of all philosophical methods, has discovered in individual cases (and this will probably be the result in every case) that there are no opposites, except in the customary exaggeration of popular or metaphysical interpretations, and that a mistake in reasoning lies at the bottom of this antithesis: according to this explanation there exists, strictly speaking, neither an unegoistic action nor completely disinterested contemplation; both are only sublimations. (*HH* I, 1)

Darwin broke with conventional metaphysics. If there were no recourse to absolute moral standards, current moral standards must in fact have *evolved* into their present state. Consequently, natural history, and not biblical sources, could reveal how certain moral standards had achieved dominance and supplanted others over time. Darwin was fascinated with origins. Interest in origins was not tangential to his system; it was embedded in its core. If primitive history were no longer the dark prelude to Christian revelation, man's genealogical history needed to be reconfigured and situated within nature. Present moral values would have to have had their origins in more primitive, pre-moral behavior patterns. Darwin's historical-materialist perspective paved the way for a thorough-going materialist analysis of human institutions and religions, with variations of this approach finding their way into the works of his many followers and imitators. A scientific-materialist examination of historical origins purged from a metaphysical bias would not reveal "moral" inspirations but the contribution of all-too-human passions, ambition, error in the establishment of the most sacred and moral institutions.[22]

Finally, Darwin's empiricism allowed for a naturalistic analysis of individual motivation and behavior. Eschewing religious explanations and concentrating on the biology of the will, Darwin recognized the primacy of instinct. Darwin did not discredit moral motivations as such; rather, he presented a picture of a naturalized man composed of both moral aspirations and immoral impulses. The latter were vestiges of primitive human states and instincts; the former represented behavior patterns that had evolved over time and had begun to assume authority and autonomy in the hierarchy of the human will. Once again, Darwin rejected a metaphysical basis for morality and reduced moral actions to instinctual behavior; he treated the moral sense itself as an extension of evolved instincts. Darwin then projected this emphasis on the biological will into his greater vision of struggle within nature. Human morality was not static; it had evolved, because individual wills with more powerful, refined moral instincts had proven more successful in this-worldly, natural struggle. Morality had been *selected*, because variations with a more highly developed moral sense could replace more primitive competitive types over time.[23] The success of more moral wills, not morality as such, had ensured the rise of (moral) institutions.

To summarize, the three following constituents define Darwin's scientific materialism – and they define the parameters of Nietzsche's middle-period philosophy as well: the denial of a transcendent moral universe and the belief in the relativity of values; the emphasis on naturalism and genealogical origins; and the concentration on individual biological wills and their struggle *within* nature. If one were to highlight these surface similarities between them and recognize the Darwinian association between Nietzsche's *moraliste* and genealogical preoccupations (mediated, in part, through Rée), then one could easily conclude that Nietzsche's

---

[22] Nietzsche would later express this early Darwinist bias within his earlier work when he wrote: "where *you* see ideal things, *I* see – human, oh only all too human!" (*EH* "Human, All Too Human" 1).

[23] "[A]t all times throughout the world tribes have supplanted other tribes; and as morality is one element *in their success*, the standard of morality and the number of well-endowed men will thus everywhere tend to rise and increase" (italics mine) (Darwin, *Descent*, 166).

philosophy was essentially compatible with Darwin – in short, an expression of "higher Réealism."[24] But one must also examine the subtle ways Nietzsche reconfigured these general premises and offered creative variations. While some of his thoughts would subvert Darwin's key assumptions, others would radicalize his ideas and take them to their logical conclusion. These revisions had started as responses *within* Darwinism; they would ultimately place his philosophy *beyond* Darwinism.

NIETZSCHE'S TERMINOLOGICAL CRITIQUE

Nietzsche's first major revision represented a terminological critique of Darwinian categories. Darwin's genealogical method proceeded from an approval of altruism, a historical excavation of the altruistic instincts, and a philosophical appreciation of the altruistic instincts for mankind's development. Here too Darwin was an heir to eighteenth-century debates surrounding altruism and egoism.[25] To Darwin, the distinction presented itself in the following manner: if Christian morality could no longer be posited *a priori* – that is, through recourse to a transcendent Truth – natural science needed to explain how a sense of morality, or altruism, might have arisen. More significantly, it would have to explain how morality benefited the species if, as natural selection otherwise indicated, only actions that helped the individual (egoism) ensured survival. The tension between altruism and egoism, or selfless and self-interested motivation, was by no means peripheral; it was shorthand for the question of morality. It stood too at the heart of Darwin's theory of human development. In fact, Darwin recognized the dilemma of selfless versus selfish behavior, and his conscience wrestled with it his entire life.

It is not difficult to understand why. If one takes the radical standpoint on the question of self-preservation – as Social Darwinists have always done – the question of morality becomes, at best, problematic. Confronted with the choice of personal survival or altruism leading to

---

[24] Nietzsche complained that some commentators treated his thoughts in *HH* merely as a "higher" form of Rée's (*höherer Réealismus*) (*EH* "Human, All Too Human" 6).

[25] I do not mean to suggest that Darwin was Nietzsche's primary source for the altruism–egoism discussion; he surely derived much more information and material concerning this question from more explicit treatments in Herbert Spencer and Eugen Dühring, for example. But that is the point I wish to make: that Nietzsche recognized how the question of altruism–egoism was central to the philosophical debates of his times and that Darwin, in turn, did not distance himself from that discussion but uncritically worked its suppositions into his theoretical framework. In that sense, altruism–egoism became further validated through its grounding in Darwinian *science*; in his theories, the dichotomy reached its apotheosis.

individual extinction, the Social Darwinian solution is unequivocal: survival is best secured by self-preservation, at whatever cost. In order to resolve this dilemma theoretically, a model consistent with natural selection would need to explain the emergence and utility of un-egoistic (i.e. altruistic) behavior. Otherwise the effects of unrestrained egoism and selfishness would lead to societal anarchy and disintegration.

Here, Nietzsche's increasingly differentiated reading of the *moralistes* informed his critical awareness toward the English materialists, including Darwin. Enlightenment thinkers, to reiterate, built further on the terminology and insights of the *moralistes*, but they overlooked the Christian temperament and moral fervor that had inspired and colored their investigations; for it was a rigorous Christian understanding of (moral) virtue that had motivated them to dissect human behavior in the first place. On the basis of this notion of Christian virtue, they then judged man's actions according to an inherent and absolute standard of morality. Though they did not resort to an *explicit* metaphysical context in their exploration of human nature, their psychological penetration was motivated by *implicit* transcendental, static, and absolute standards of "morality" and "virtue," though now increasingly abstract, secularized, and internalized. This acceptance of moral standards and actions, this vestige of Christian moralism, allowed them to formulate an "objective" evaluation of man.

The exemplary case of La Rochefoucauld, the *moraliste* Nietzsche most admired, illustrates Nietzsche's growing critical awareness.[26] Though he had originally praised La Rochefoucauld for his superior knowledge of human behavior and his keen psychological penetration, he eventually began to expose the Christian moral skepticism behind La Rochefoucauld's psychological talents. "Christianity represents *progress* in greater psychological penetration: La Rochefoucauld and Pascal. [Christianity] understood the *essential equality* of human actions and their equal value on the whole (– all *unmoral*)."[27]

La Rochefoucauld's approach to (moral) actions, according to Nietzsche, conflicted with the code of chivalry in which he, as an aristocrat, was born and bred. Instead of recognizing the *sui generis* value of noble behavior, La Rochefoucauld's skepticism made him deprecate nobility and insinuate ulterior motives behind noble actions:[28] "La Rochefoucauld represents the awareness of the motivation behind nobility – and an evaluation of

---

[26] In this case, the notebooks become the best place to pursue Nietzsche's distancing from the *moralistes*.
[27] *KSA* XII, 488. [28] See also *GS* 122.

it darkened by a Christian perspective."[29] His Christian moralism prevented him from recognizing the *simultaneous* existence of *distinct, non-tangential* moral codes. Instead, he measured human actions against a *single* and *absolute* moral standard. As a result, he remained pessimistic toward human behavior because man's actions *had* to fall short of his absolute "moral" code: "La Rochefoucauld erred only in the sense that he ranked those motives he deemed the actual ones lower than the other, alleged ones: that is, *he still believes in* the other motives and bases his *standard of measurement* on them: he denigrates man in that he believes him incapable of certain motives."[30] Instead, he should have taken the ultimate step of denying the validity of "evil" actions after refuting the possibility of "good" ones: "[H]e denied the 'good' qualities in man – he should have denied the bad ones as well."[31] Wedded to a moral perspective, he grounded his judgments on absolute moral standards *even after* questioning the possibility of pure "moral" actions.

While Nietzsche recognized the spiritual continuity between the *moralistes* and the eighteenth-century materialists and *philosophes*, he also emphasized an interesting distinction. The latter resided in the *moralistes'* Christian motivation. Nietzsche saw this motivation as the hidden source for their cynical assessment of human behavior. But despite his ultimate critique of the *moralistes*, Nietzsche continued to have greater respect for their philosophical depth, purity, and psychological self-awareness (which explains his sustained ambivalence towards Pascal, Spinoza, and La Rochefoucauld) than for the scientific materialists and *philosophes* that followed them. The reason for this ambivalence: the *moralistes* had at least attempted to embody the difficult, inherently contradictory, and ultimately impossible Christian ideals. The scientific thinkers of the eighteenth century and beyond inherited the terms and adopted the outer manifestations of their insights without sensing the strong sense of faith – or even *awareness* of that faith – that had animated their predecessors.

Darwin continued with their pessimistic assessment of man and human behavior; but he too did not challenge its Christian provenance. The result was that the moral inferences of the newly secularized terms – e.g. the assumptions of man's "self-interest," the notion of an inherent "egoism," man's instinct of "self-preservation" – could become theoretically embedded within a materialist–secular worldview: a complete *system* of nature. By assuming that self-interest, egoism, and self-preservation were

---

[29] *KSA* XI, 61.   [30] *KSA* IX, 441–42.
[31] *KSA* X, 67.

primary, even *instinctual*, rather than interpretations of personal behavior projected *into* nature – i.e. theoretical offshoots of a rigorous Christian understanding of (moral) virtue – Darwin and his followers could allow individual moral valuations to become the building-blocks of an "object-ive" scientific perspective. In that sense, the need to explain "altruism" in accordance with natural selection did not merely serve as a corrective to a radical understanding of "egoism." The entire notion of "egoism" as *essentially* "human" (rather than being an individual evaluation of human behavior) presupposed an awareness of its "opposite," "altruism." Once Darwin operated with these categories, he had invested in a theoretical framework that compelled him to locate the source and explanation for their alleged opposites.

NIETZSCHE'S UNDERSTANDING OF (MORAL) TYPES

Nietzsche's terminological critique paralleled a second major revi-sion, which can be termed *a critique of morality from a psychological–physiological perspective*. It can be expressed in the following way: if moral terms were no longer anchored in an inviolable transcendent (moral) realm and no longer expressed *absolute* truths about man and human nature, as Darwin's theories had implied, if they were mere *interpretations*, as Nietzsche began to believe, then moral categories and values had to express something else: namely, individual states of consciousness – or the mind reflecting on *perceived* psycho-physiological states. This conclusion emerged from Nietzsche's critique of Darwin's terminological categories, but it also proved his *indebtedness* to Darwin, for the latter's theories had focused attention on the human will as the source for the moral imagin-ation in the first place.

From the earliest sections of *HH*, and well into the middle period, Nietzsche started to develop his own Darwin-inspired, though increas-ingly independent notion of individual biological *types* and the world of interpretations they fashion for themselves. These early entries were the first intimations of his crystallizing notion of the "will to power": the will's attempt to understand and seek mastery over its instincts and then to project that power through the force of interpretation. In a section entitled "How appearance becomes being," he gives one of the earliest signs of the *priestly* type. He describes him as a born hypocrite who even-tually *becomes* the type through the force of his internal nature: "The hypocrite who always plays one and the same role finally ceases to be a hypocrite; for example priests who are usually conscious or unconscious hypocrites, finally become natural, and then they really are priests without any affectation" (*HH* I, 51). In the chapter "The Religious Life," he examines the priestly type and the holy man; his point of entry is their instinctual life and its relationship to their interpretation: "It is not what the saint *is*, but what he *signifies* in the eyes of the non-saints, that gives him his world-historic value. Because he was mistaken for what he was not, because his psychological states were interpreted falsely and he was set as far apart as possible from everyone else as though he were something altogether incomparable, strange and supra-human: that is how he acquired the extraordinary power with which he was able to dominate the imagination of whole nations and whole ages" (*HH* I, 143).

In a chapter titled "From the Souls of Artists and Writers," Nietzsche deconstructs metaphysical belief in the "genius" and sketches the *artist/writer* as a type who creates a world of illusion based on his own metaphysical needs. In "Achilles and Homer," he distinguishes between the writer *of* the experience and the character *with* the experience. The "genius" (Homer) can only extrapolate from the experience of his own life and project his own reality into the "hero" (Achilles) and his action; he has no access to a "higher" reality or truth as such: "It is always as between Achilles and Homer: the one *has* the experience, the sensation, the other *describes* it. A true writer only bestows words on the emotions and experiences of others, he is an artist so as to divine much from the little he himself has felt. Artists are by no means men of great passion but they often *pretend* to be, in the unconscious feeling that their painted passions will seem more believable if their own life speaks for their experience in this field" (*HH* I, 211). Or: "The task of painting *the* picture of life, however often poets and philosophers may pose it, is nonetheless senseless: even under the hands of the greatest of painters-thinkers all that has ever eventuated is pictures and miniatures *out of one* life, namely their own – and nothing else is even possible" (*HH* II, 19).

Nietzsche even develops his first critical awareness of the *Freigeist* (free spirit), foreshadowing the (ascetic) *scientist* in *GM* III. Rather than accept unconditionally the *Freigeist* as a purveyor of a higher "truth," Nietzsche presents him as a (biological) type, who has distanced himself instinctually from the "community of believers" (*gebundenen Geister*) and who then tries to dislocate their traditional faith through another *relative* truth ("Free spirit a relative concept"): "what characterizes the free spirit is not that his opinions are the more correct but that he has liberated himself from tradition" (*HH* I, 225). He argues that not only is the metaphysical world an illusion based on one's personal experience; but the conventional manifestations of morality – the related feelings of guilt, the sense of compassion, and the bad conscience – represent expressions of biological inadequacy, impotence, and frailty projected outward onto others and "nature"; these then become externalized and fashioned into a complete metaphysical interpretation of existence.

Once again, Nietzsche provided glimpses of his later, more developed positions in his earlier works. In a section entitled "The desire to be just and the desire to be a judge," he writes: "The error lies not only in the feeling 'I am accountable,' but equally in that antithesis 'I am not, but somebody has to be'" (*HH* II, 33). Writing against traditional philosophers (here, specifically, Schopenhauer), Nietzsche begins to fashion his notion of the *philosopher* as type:

This, approximately, is how [the philosophical heads] go on: "What, is no man accountable? And is everything full of guilt and feeling of guilt? But someone or other has to be the sinner, if it is impossible and no longer permissible to accuse and to judge the individual, the poor wave in the necessary wave-play of becoming – very well: then let the wave-play itself, becoming, be the sinner: here is free will, here there can be accusing, condemning, atonement and expiation: then let *God be the sinner and man his redeemer*: then let world history be guilt, self-condemnation and suicide; thus will the offender become his own judge, the judge his own executioner." (*HH* II, 33)

In *Daybreak* (*D*), Nietzsche develops the notions with even greater precision and self-confidence. In his portrayal of St. Paul ("The First Christian"), he narrates how the "first Christian" succeeded in dislodging the antique world through the metaphysical construction of an alternative reality born from the labyrinth of his own tortured soul. The phenomenon of morality that Paul *invented*, Nietzsche argues, distracted him from the crippling awareness that he could not fulfill ancient customs:

Paul had become at once the fanatical defender and chaperone of this God and his law, and was constantly combating and on the watch for transgressors and doubters, harsh and malicious towards them and with the extremest inclination for punishment. And then he discovered in himself that he himself – fiery, sensual, melancholy, malevolent in hatred as he was – *could* not fulfill the law, he discovered indeed what seemed to him the strangest thing of all: that his extravagant lust for power was constantly combating and on the watch for transgressors and goad. (*D* 68)

And in a later, more epigrammatic summation:

The delusion of a moral world-order. There is absolutely no eternal necessity which decrees that every guilt will be atoned and paid for – that such a thing exists has been a dreadful and to only a miniscule extent useful delusion – : just as it is a delusion that everything is guilt which is *felt as such*. It is not *things*, but opinions *about things that have absolutely no existence*, which have so deranged mankind. (*D* 563)

In contrast, Darwin never challenges morality as such. Much more cautiously, and less radically, he questions only that it exists in a separate, inviolable realm. He seeks a *naturalist* explanation for how morality had evolved out of the biological instincts (specifically, the *social* instincts) over time. Here, he gives precedence to the "instinct of sympathy," which forms the "natural" source of what he calls man's "moral sense" ("the all-important emotion of sympathy," he argues, "is distinct from love"). Though other animals display the "sympathetic sense," man alone extended it consistently to his fellow men, allowing for its greater cultivation and its dispersal throughout the community. "Natural selection" selected those tribes where the sympathetic sense was most developed:

With mankind selfishness, experience, and imitation probably add ... to the power of sympathy; for we are led by the hope of receiving good in return to perform acts of sympathetic kindness to others; and there can be no doubt that the feeling of sympathy is much strengthened by habit. In however complex a manner this feeling may have originated, as it is one of high importance to all those animals which aid and defend each other, it will have been increased, through natural selection; *for those communities, which included the greatest number of the most sympathetic members, would flourish best and rear the greatest number of off-spring.*[32]

In this manner, Darwin could posit both that man's moral development proceeded from social instincts shared with other animals, thereby arguing for a natural origin for morality, *and* imply that man alone could have developed a higher "moral sense." "It may be well first to premise," he qualifies in the *Descent*, "that I do not wish to maintain that *any* strictly social animal, if its intellectual faculties were to become as active and highly developed as in man, would acquire exactly the same moral sense as ours" (italics mine).[33] Whereas Nietzsche, in response to Darwin, challenges morality altogether and sees it as a symptom of individual consciousness processing and making sense of unique physiological states, Darwin holds on to belief in the moral self and the moral sense. He merely seeks a natural origin for morality's inception and subsequent development.

---

[32] Darwin, *Descent*, 82; italics mine.   [33] Darwin, *Descent*, 73.

In the end, Darwin not only fails to break new ground with his understanding of "morality" (he relies on conventional notions developed by earlier and contemporary moral philosophers and moralists such as Kant, Bain, Lecky, Mill, the Utilitarians, Aurelius, Lubbock); but his evolutionary hypotheses concerning morality merely seek to "naturalize" and "originate," to *embed*, those very same notions: "This great question [of the moral sense or conscience] has been discussed by many writers of consummate ability; and my sole excuse for touching on it is the impossibility of here passing it over, and because, as far as I know, *no one has approached it exclusively from the side of natural history*" (italics mine).[34]

NIETZSCHE'S CRITIQUE OF THE "SELF"

Finally, Nietzsche's critique of the altruism–egoism dichotomy and his concurrent elaboration of a theory of independent biological wills, or types, led him to challenge the notion of the "self." Part of this conclusion emerged, once again, from his ongoing critical engagement with the *moralistes* and their cardinal assumptions. For example, La Rochefoucauld had developed his insights about human nature by assuming man's essential egoism and vanity. Nietzsche, however, began to postulate that there could be no "egoism" – the "ego" was everything. "Egoism" had arisen from a philosophical misperception of "altruism" as a distinct category. For Nietzsche, there could be no behavior deemed disinterested, selfless, or altruistic as such: "The Christian moroseness in La Rochefoucauld, who pointed to [egoism] and thought by that he had *reduced* the value of things and of virtues. I tried to challenge this at first by trying to prove that there *could* be nothing other than egoism."[35]

For the *moralistes* and their followers, the concept of "vanity," or self-love, was contingent on their understanding of the "self." Because they had rejected traditional "moral" categories and their bases in a "higher" inviolable morality, they could only see human behavior deriving from "lesser" motivations. Consequently, vanity and self-interest had to be behind every action, even the most "moral." While Nietzsche had aligned himself with this genealogical perspective in the early middle period, he began to work out a new and independent variation. He no longer treated "vanity" as an absolute "objective" assessment of human behavior but associated it instead with a certain "type" – a *lesser* man who had needed to adapt and dissimulate in the face of a higher, over-powerful

[34] Darwin, *Descent*, 71. [35] *KSA* XII, 319.

authority: a fuller human being. This "lesser" type (i.e. the "man" of the *moralistes*) had lost sight of the original historical reference point and now could no longer recognize how its understanding of "self," its *sense* of "self," was secondary and derivative, constructed and passed down in response to values and categories previously established by more power-ful, nobler wills. Whereas the "self-esteem" of the higher type was entirely "natural," the "vanity" of the lesser type resulted from a *lack* of natural egoism and self-valuation:[36]

Vanity is perhaps one of the most difficult things for a noble person to compre-hend: he will be tempted to keep denying it when a different type of man will almost be able to feel it in his hands. He has difficulty imagining creatures who would try to inspire good opinions about themselves that they themselves do not hold – and consequently do not "deserve" either –, and who would then end up *believing* these good opinions. (*BGE* 261)

Nietzsche took his critique of the "self" beyond its terminological basis in the philosophy of the *moralistes* and examined the question from a physiological standpoint. He began to argue that the traditional understanding of the "self," or "ego," expressed a false perception of wholeness and integrity based on the notion of an independent, autono-mous "mind" evaluating and reacting to certain underlying drives and instincts.[37] But Nietzsche argued that the existence and understanding of these drives and instincts as separate and distinct from "conscious-ness" was an illusion. "Consciousness" was an *extension* of them – a "blind tool" of competing random, chaotic drives, each seeking indi-vidual mastery and expression: "[T]hat one *desires* to combat the vehe-mence of a drive at all, however, does not stand within our own power; nor does the choice of any particular method; nor does the success or failure of this method. What is clearly the case is that in this entire procedure our intellect is only the blind instrument of *another drive* which is a *rival* of the drive whose vehemence is tormenting us" (*D* 109).

---

[36] In *GS*, Nietzsche already begins to map out what will develop more widely and fully into his "two-fold history of morality" in *GM*. He distinguishes between the actions of higher, or noble, types on the one hand, and those of more "common natures" on the other; these two typologies will never understand each other's motivations: "For common natures all noble, magnanimous feelings appear to be inexpedient and therefore initially incredible: they give a wink when they hear of such things and seem to want to say, 'Surely, there must be some advantage involved; one cannot see through every wall.' … In comparison, the higher nature is more *unreasonable* for the noble, magnanimous, and self-sacrificing person does in fact succumb to his drives; and in his best moments, his reason *pauses*" (*GS* 3).

[37] Nietzsche also argued that consciousness was a late "development" (and an inferior one) in rela-tion to the instincts; in fact, if it hadn't been for the underlying stabilizing force of the instincts, humanity would have already perished from the errors of "consciousness" (*GS* 11).

Consequently, there could be no "true world," no objective world of knowledge, separate from instinctual reality; that too was chimerical: "The habits of our senses have woven us into lies and deception of sensation: these again are the basis of all our judgments and 'knowledge' – there is absolutely no escape, no backway or bypath into the *real world*" (D 117). It would not be possible for one to remove oneself from the nature one described or give ultimate, "objective" assessments about nature, for nature acted through the totality of the instincts. The belief that one could make independent "objective" judgments stemmed from a delusion that a "consciousness" existed independent from instinct.[18]

Nietzsche's rejection of the "self" of the moralists, as well as his belief that the individual biological will was inextricable from overall necessity, demanded that he deny "free will." For Nietzsche, "free will" was a chimera based on the notion of a "mind," or self, acting on a free (moral) choice between two alternative realities: a realm of "moral" freedom on the one hand and natural "egoism" on the other. But this physiological state merely reflected the instincts in conflict with one another as well as the naïve belief that any "self" could make a decision *against* its instincts. While an individual might make a ("moral") decision based on his *belief* in that decision's inherent moral superiority – and might even "choose" to act against specific instincts according to "moral" criteria – this choice did not make the action inherently more "moral" or more "free." It simply proved that the individual's delusion of free will, or retrospective interpretation, had cast an interpretative sheen on a choice not free at all but contingent on the underlying instincts. Nietzsche later used the term

---

[18] For an example of how Nietzsche turns Darwin on his head – while still seeming to articulate Darwinian principles – see "Origin of the logical" (*GS* 111). On the one hand, Nietzsche says that the origin of logic is based on *mistaken* assumptions (e.g. treating things as equal when they are only similar – "an illogical disposition, for there is nothing identical as such"), but that such behavior might still have helped earlier creatures survive, since it led them to make quicker decisions. On the other hand, innumerable beings who made inferences different from ours (because they were more cautious in making judgments and evaluations) were favored with a lesser probability of survival and therefore perished – *even if "they might have been closer to the truth."* Nietzsche here argues for the naturalist origins of logic and how it succeeded in Darwinian struggle, but he then goes on to show that (1) that logic is based on false inferences; and (2) has led to the entrenchment of an error, even while it might have led to the success of certain types who practiced such "logic." Thus, even if the "fitness" of human logic is proven in Darwinian terms, i.e. because it has "survived," it still remains an error in Nietzschean terms, because pure survival is not his evaluative standard. Furthermore, Nietzsche's argument reveals that the practice of logic does not reflect a superior form of reasoning as such, but actually derived from the survival requirements of a particular human type. This type's "consciousness" has allowed his form of logic to "survive," even if it is built on a *false* understanding of nature.

"decadence" to describe the will's "conscious" choice to decide against itself and its underlying instincts ("the will to nothingness").

Judging the "ego" to be a part of overall necessity, Nietzsche rejected definitive claims about "nature" as such. "Nature" could not be grasped in human terms at all; it was elusive, forever inaccessible to human knowledge, logic, or intuition: "The total character of the world ... is for all eternity chaos, not in the sense of a lack of necessity but a lack of order, organization, form, beauty, wisdom, and whatever else our aesthetic anthropomorphisms are called" (*GS* 109). Illusionary were also the "laws of nature": they could only represent individual interpretations projected *into* "nature," they could never be extrapolated *from* "nature": "[The universe] has no drive to self-preservation or any other drives; nor does it observe any laws. Let us beware of saying that there are laws in nature. There are only necessities: there is no one who commands, no one who obeys, no one who transgresses" (*GS* 109).

Darwin, on the other hand, assumed the centrality and the integrity of the "self." Natural selection premised a "struggle for existence" in which individual biological types with "fitter" modifications would be "selected." It *acted on* the "self"; the "self" figured as the key catalyst for evolutionary change. Furthermore, Darwin never doubted that a single, all-encompassing explanation for man's development could be found; nor did he doubt that the "state of nature" offered the framework in which that development could be explained. Morality might have evolved; but natural selection could give a complete scientific explanation for its origins and evolution. But for Nietzsche, the relevant question was now not how morality had evolved. It was how *belief* in morality had originated; how a moral interpretation could have superseded other possible interpretations; and what morality revealed about the instincts.

CONCLUSIONS

In his earlier published writings, specifically in *DS* 7 and *HH*, Nietzsche began to experiment with genealogical hypotheses. His developing internal debate about the question of morality (its value and its origins) and his attempt to find a naturalist source for morality's existence predisposed him to Darwin's genealogical outlook; it also caused him to question his allegiance to Wagnerian metaphysics. No longer willing to accept that morality was anchored in an inviolable transcendental realm, as Wagner did, Nietzsche now approached morality as a factor of "human, all-too-human" experiences. This "genealogical" angle coincided with his turn away from the German tradition and towards the French *moraliste* legacy of the seventeenth century and the English moralist–psychologist schools of the eighteenth and nineteenth. Both these traditions believed in the importance of human psychology and motivation as the linchpin for human institutions; shared a critical, almost cynical estimation of character as driven by "lesser," amoral drives and instincts; held an objective view of the "self" freed from moral pretensions; and esteemed the "natural" (i.e. amoral, "real") world of human passions, struggles, and endeavors.

During the middle period, there existed strong and significant parallels between Nietzsche and Darwin. This compatibility is neither coincidental nor surprising. Darwin too built his own system of naturalist explanation from the bricks and mortar of previous "naturalist" philosophizing. Far from rejecting the terminology and worldview of his moralist predecessors, Darwin had absorbed their view of human behavior and nature, *even if* these earlier thinkers had ultimately used that terminology towards different ends or had arrived at different conclusions. Some of the assumptions Nietzsche and Darwin shared at this juncture were: a belief in the relativity of (moral) values; the rejection of a transcendent (moral) universe; a concentration on biological wills and their struggle in nature; and the attempt to find genealogical explanations for human institutions and development.

At the same time, Nietzsche had begun to excavate original points of difference. He navigated around these pivotal points in the middle period and expanded on them in later works. One key area of distinction was Nietzsche's increased skepticism towards the altruism–egoism distinction, a major constituent of his middle-period philosophy. Though Nietzsche saw this distinction reflected in the worldview of the *moralistes*, he saw how it had made its way into the terminological arsenal of subsequent "genealogical" philosophers and had colored their understanding of "human behavior." He also recognized how unchallenged Christian moral values had inspired the *moralistes*, but that future thinkers merely elaborated on this foundation without a critical appraisal of the genesis of their terms.

Nietzsche subscribed early on to Darwin's central notion that discrete biological wills struggle within nature ("struggle for existence"); and that this struggle expressed an entirely this-worldly, immanent clash of wills. Like Darwin, he did not believe that a "moral" outcome was inscribed into this process or that it reflected any plan, progress, improvement, or upward movement – in short, any teleology. Morality was a product of human struggle and an outgrowth of conflicting human physiological needs and drives. On this point, Darwin and Nietzsche agreed. One could even argue that Nietzsche's philosophy merely elaborates further on just how "morality" emerges from man's natural struggle in nature.

But this perspective would fail to recognize Nietzsche's original – in fact, *crucial* – deviation from Darwin. While the *Descent* sought to explain how human "morality" had evolved based on natural selection, Nietzsche sketches out his contrary theory of self-contained "moral" types. Not only is morality not inscribed into "nature"; it is an entirely human, psychologically based construct reflecting a specific constellation of instincts and drives and their complex relationship to one another. For Nietzsche, morality becomes an interpretation projected onto – or, alternatively, arising out of – a cluster of conflicting emotions, instincts, and drives peculiar to specific types. For that reason, he is not interested in establishing how "morality" had emerged or grounding it in "nature"; he is intent on examining the phenomenon of distinct "moral" wills in order to decode what their (moral) *interpretations* reveal about their underlying instinctual reality. His future works would merely expand on and deepen this key distinction.

CHAPTER 2

Overcoming the "man" in man: Zarathustra's transvaluation of Darwinian categories

Thus Spoke Zarathustra (*Z*) appeared at a critical juncture in Nietzsche's life. Focusing on the biographical context, Mazzino Montinari has explained Nietzsche's *Übermensch*, introduced for the first time in *Z*, as a form of psychological compensation for the personal humiliations he had suffered at the hands of Lou Salomé and his friend Paul Rée. According to Düsing, Montinari's interpretation helps to counterbalance the uncomfortable impression that Nietzsche had intended the *Übermensch* to represent the prototype of a master race.[1] Such a straightforward biographical explanation, while comforting and persuasive on the surface, fails on two important counts. First, it implies that *Z* reflected psychological debility and a quest for compensation when in fact it embodied a sense of wholeness and completeness unique to his writings. Second, it ignores the work's relationship to Nietzsche's successful transvaluation of Darwinism in the middle period – a great personal victory on his part requiring a visionary literary and stylistic expression.

Nietzsche's problem by the end of the middle period was twofold. He had not only rejected the conception of "man" presented in the works of the great moralists, philosophers, and scientists. He had also lost confidence in the terminology used to characterize that conception. After undermining the altruism–egoism distinction at its core (rather than merely valuing the one over the other) and exposing the type of "man" he wished to overcome, Nietzsche needed a new terminological platform and storehouse of metaphors that could affirm his higher, fuller human type: the *Übermensch*. That new metaphoric language had to breach the polarities and dichotomies critiqued in his middle period and had to conjure up a world of wholeness, richness, and completeness that could only be poetic, metaphoric, and allusive, not prosaic and descriptive. Commentators have difficulties with *Z* precisely because of its poetic qualities. They neglect or

---

[1] Düsing, *Nietzsches Denkweg*, 306.

47

marginalize the work, downplay its significance, or use it to gloss other texts.[2] But the work's literary self-expression *is* the message, and it affirms a world beyond traditional philosophizing. As such, it stands at the perfect tipping-point between the philosophical probing of his middle period and the polemical antagonism of his last works.

THE LANGUAGE OF DARWIN AND NIETZSCHE CONTRASTED

Darwin's presentation and accumulation of facts in an orderly, inductive manner, which point to the "preservation of favored species in the struggle for life," undermine Christian assumptions about man's place in a moral universe, religion based on miracles and faith, and theological arguments of evolution based on design. Darwin sanctioned and legitimized various heterogeneous strands of Enlightenment thought by channeling them into an impressive, powerful, theoretical system: a complete *vision* of nature. At the same time, he tapped into the undiminished metaphysical needs of his core audience during a period of waning Christian faith through a cautious use of evocative images and metaphors.[3]

In some ways, his narrative works at cross purposes. While the scientific "facts" of natural selection disturb religious assumptions about man's centrality in the universe, the *Origin*'s metaphors, images, and general narrative voice offer metaphysical solace and resignation in the face of a law-bound evolution of life, where "endless forms most beautiful and most wonderful have been and are being evolved":[4] "[Darwin] can be shown to preach a naturalist reconciliation of the sublime and the beautiful. When he lifts up the vision of a natural world created and finely balanced by selection, he captures the heightened religious emotions of a doxology and appeals to a spirituality dislocated by the Victorian crisis."[5]

---

[2] "Nietzsche scholarship has generally approached Nietzsche's works as philosophical texts, where 'philosophical' is understood in a relatively narrow sense as a term of categorization. This approach tends to focus on the arguments and propositions that can be abstracted from the text, and it tends to underplay any significance that might inhere in the work's literary form" (Kathleen Higgins, *Nietzsche's Zarathustra* [Philadelphia: Temple University Press, 1987], xiii).

[3] A.N. Wilson sees deep-felt religious uncertainty and the loss of Christian faith as the hallmarks of the age: "Nineteenth-century unbelief seldom limits itself to an expression of specific uncertainty about, let us say, the literal truth of the Bible, or the existence of angels. It accompanies wider symptoms of disturbance, a deep sense (personal, political, social) of dissolution" (A.N. Wilson, *God's Funeral* [New York: W.W. Norton, 1999], 11).

[4] Darwin, *The Origin of Species*, ed. Gillian Beer (Oxford: Oxford University Press, 1996), 396.

[5] David Kohn, "Darwin's Ambiguity: The Secularization of Biological Meaning," *British Journal for the History of Science* 22 (1989), 234.

Despite his efforts to stabilize their implications, Darwin's metaphors have a suggestive quality that remain in the memory far more than the "facts" of evolution: "[i]t is the element of obscurity, of metaphors whose peripheries remain undescribed, which made *the Origin of Species* so incendiary – and which allowed it to be appropriated by thinkers of so many diverse political persuasions. It encouraged onward thought: it offered itself for metaphorical application and its multiple discourses encouraged further acts of interpretation. The presence of *latent meaning* made *the Origin* suggestive, even unstoppable in its action upon minds."[6]

Walter Cannon suggests Darwin "never found an over-all metaphor, or guiding image, which he was willing to affirm." He worked with a host of diverse images: "a tree, a bank, Dame Nature, a struggle, a chain, a beehive." In relation to the vast diversity of life, these single metaphors "were all too simple to be taken seriously." But then Cannon refers precisely to the kind of overall vision, which each of Darwin's metaphors appears to evoke and his readers intuitively grasped: "a vision of the whole world with all things that have ever lived moving over it in space and all time in a complex pattern of intuitively comprehensible principles."[7] It was not the effect of any single metaphor, or range of images, but how those metaphors combined together to inspire a creative reinterpretation of nature truly ambitious in its scope.

The *Origin* pursues another narrative strategy. While it emphasizes the bleakness of nature – war, famine, death, extermination – the text as a whole suggests a unifying thread of existence, which brings together everything into a transcendent and ultimately redemptive picture: "from the war of nature, from famine and death, the most exalted object which we are capable of conceiving, namely the production of the higher animals, directly follows."[8] Even though one encounters dissension, pain, anguish, and struggle everywhere, one can find consolation in the greater "wisdom" of evolution. At the same time, Darwin suggests that one cannot attain that wholeness and perfection in the here and now but can only comprehend it through the faculty of human *reason*: "the most exalted object which we are capable of *conceiving*" (italics mine).

Nietzsche, in contrast, does not emphasize the mind or the faculty of reason, but physicality. He does not just hold out the promise of a future

---

[6] Gillian Beer, *Darwin's Plots: Evolutionary Narrative in Darwin, George Eliot and Nineteenth-Century Fiction* (London: Routledge & Kegan Paul, 1983), 100.

[7] Walter F. Cannon, "Darwin's Vision in *On the Origin of Species*," in *The Art of Victorian Prose*, ed. George Levine and William Madden (New York: Oxford University Press, 1968), 172.

[8] Darwin, *Origin*, 396.

higher human type, but suggests its imminent attainability. This type cannot be *described* in prose; its superior well-being can only be *conjured* through poetic affirmation. It is an entirely self-contained, outer-directed will unaffected by ruptures within the soul and able to expend its super-abundance on its surroundings:

The most encompassing soul, which can run and stray and roam farthest within itself; the most necessary soul, which out of joy plunges itself into chance – the soul that loves being, but submerges into becoming; the having soul that *wants* to rise to willing and desiring – the soul that flees itself and catches up to itself in the widest circle; the wisest soul which folly persuades most sweetly – the one that loves itself most, in which all things have their current and recurrent and ebb and flow. (*Z* "Old and New Tablets" 19)

On the other hand, Nietzsche uses the negative images of the "flea-beetle," the "herd" and "poison" to describe the antithesis of the *Übermensch*, the "last man." In the Prologue to *Zarathustra*, he departs from Darwin in two ways. First, he equates "reason" with the last man and his particular *form* of existence and life-choices;[9] his inability to attain higher spiritual awareness; and his hatred of all superior things.[10] Second, he does not distinguish "reason" as an essential human faculty as such but as characteristic of specific wills and the life-world they create for themselves; he forges a connection between the thought and the instinctual reality of the thinker. Whereas the *Übermensch* embodies a more whole physiological awareness, which can only be expressed through poetic images of plenitude, overflowing, and richness, the "last man" exhibits hatred of self and psychic disruption. By exposing its negative connection to specific biological wills and their instinctual realities, Nietzsche under-mines our traditional faith in "reason."

EVOLUTIONARY READINGS OF THE *ÜBERMENSCH*

Numerous accounts have interpreted the *Übermensch* as some form of "higher" biological type and a product of Darwinian evolution, despite the fact that Nietzsche had ridiculed such efforts as early as 1888 (*EH* "Books" 1). Certainly, the *Übermensch* is the Nietzschean concept that resonates most conspicuously with the theory of evolution, and both

---

[9] "One is clever and knows everything that has happened, and so there is no end to their mock-ery. People still quarrel but they reconcile quickly – otherwise it is bad for the stomach" (*Z* "Prologue" 5).

[10] "'What is love? What is creation? What is longing? What is a star?' – thus asks the last human being, blinking" (*Z* "Prologue" 5).

scholars and the general public alike have made that facile association. Many are convinced that Nietzsche accepted Darwin but adapted the latter's findings to his own project of human transfiguration and transcendence. Whereas Darwin had discovered the *fact* of evolution (though trying hard to avoid speculation about human development), Nietzsche's main interest all along was man and how he could use Darwin's insights to express his personal goals for humanity.[11]

One can divide attempts to interpret the *Übermensch* along Darwinian lines into two camps.[12] While one group sees Nietzsche's vision primarily in "scientific" terms – the *Übermensch* representing a "fitter" biological type in the literal sense of evolution – the other interprets the relationship more figuratively. Here, the *Übermensch* represents a *symbolic* transcendence of modern man and "evolution" expresses a "higher" dialectical stage. Though interpretations often reflect a hybrid of these two positions, common to both is an implied *progression* along an evolutionary continuum to a superior stage of human development.

The first generation of readers – the one to which Nietzsche responded with such derision in *EH* – adhered to a fairly narrow version of the "scientific" evolutionary interpretation. Enamored of Darwinian "science," its applicability to society and its problems, and the "promise" of eugenics, these readers envisioned a "superior" human type, which could be bred. Nietzsche's translators into English, August Tille (1895) and Raoul Richter (1903), were important exponents of the latter. One could see how that strand culminated in the eugenicist fantasies of the Nazis. More recently, scholars have moved away from such a one-dimensional assessment and have promoted a broader, more balanced understanding. Though they recognize an evolutionary underpinning to Nietzsche's concept, they interpret the *Übermensch* as a vision of human transcendence. Such views often still mediate between Nietzsche and Darwin, and they prioritize biology and natural selection as constituent parts of Nietzsche's "evolution."[13] For example, "evolution is for Nietzsche primarily a process of progressive individuation that is as much moral as it is biological in

---

[11] Understood in that way, one could say that Nietzsche was one of the most prominent figures, along with the Social Darwinists, who applied Darwin's theories to address specifically human concerns and objectives.

[12] Practically all accounts of Nietzsche deal in some way with the *Übermensch*, which is perhaps his most famous notion, and most commentators refer to a connection to Darwin.

[13] Examples of this position – all three of the most significant recent scholarly accounts of the Nietzsche–Darwin connection: Moore, *Nietzsche, Biology, and Metaphor*; Richardson, *Nietzsche's New Darwinism*; and Düsing, *Nietzsches Denkweg*.

character: the *Übermensch* is by definition a solitary figure who has left the herd behind him at an earlier stage of his development."[14]

Other interpretations downplay "scientific" evolution and interpret Nietzsche's "evolution" as a higher level of humankind: "The whole sense of the philosophy which produced the superman makes it clear that what is being held up here as a new 'image of man' to stand against the growing nihilism of modern Europe – a man who is no longer animal; and it is suggested that the 'goal' of mankind is to 'produce supermen' – that is, to transform itself into the no-longer-animal."[15] Nietzsche's biographer Rüdiger Safranski echoes a similar assessment.[16] As for Annemarie Pieper, she dismisses a strict Darwinian reading.[17] For her, the *Übermensch* represents a stage of development, where man transcends the historical body–soul duality.[18]

ZARATHUSTRA'S PROLOGUE: AN ANTI-EVOLUTIONARY READING OF THE *ÜBERMENSCH*

Against the above set of interpretations, I suggest a contrary one. While I believe the *Übermensch* was inspired by Darwin's findings and clearly emerges from Nietzsche's engagement with his ideas in the middle period, the work ends up not in agreement with them, but rather engages them in a creative dialectic. Expressed in another way, Darwin's theories are the foil for Nietzsche's *alternative* vision of the *Übermensch*. A closer look at the Prologue will help explain this.

After ten years in the mountains, Zarathustra descends into the valley below to share with the people the wisdom gained from his solitude (*Z* "Prologue" 1). After encountering a holy man, he arrives at a nearby town. In the marketplace, Zarathustra declares: "*I teach you the overman.* Human being is something that must be overcome. What have you done to overcome him?" (*Z* "Prologue" 3). His subsequent words evoke Darwin:

All creatures so far have created something beyond themselves; and you want to be the ebb of this great flood and would even rather go back to animals than

---

[14] Moore, *Nietzsche, Biology, and Metaphor*, 136.
[15] R.J. Hollingdale, *Nietzsche: The Man and His Philosophy* (Cambridge: Cambridge University Press, 1999), 163.
[16] "Nietzsche's Übermensch is the consummate realization of human potential and, in this sense, is also a response to the 'death of God'" (Rüdiger Safranski, *Nietzsche: A Political Biography* [New York: W.W. Norton, 2002], 271).
[17] Annemarie Pieper, *Ein Seil geknüpft zwischen Tier und Übermensch: philosophische Erläuterungen zu Nietzsches erstem Zarathustra* (Stuttgart: Klett-Cotta, 1990), 48.
[18] Pieper, *Ein Seil geknüpft*, 63.

overcome humans? What is the ape to a human? A laughing-stock or a painful embarrassment. And that is precisely what the human shall be to the overman: a laughing stock or a painful embarrassment. You have made your way from worm to human, and much in you is still worm. Once you were apes, and even now a human is still more ape than any ape. (*Z* "Prologue" 3)

"Mankind is a rope," he continues, "fastened between animal and over-man – a rope over an abyss. A dangerous crossing, a dangerous on-the-way, a dangerous looking back, a dangerous shuddering and standing still. What is great about human beings is that they are a bridge and not a purpose: what is lovable about human beings is that they are a *crossing over* and a *going under*" (*Z* "Prologue" 4).

According to Zarathustra, it seems that the *Übermensch* will one day represent a higher stage of humanity. Man in his current state will then appear "like a laughingstock or painful embarrassment," just as apes now are to man. Zarathustra reinforces this Darwinian association with the metaphor of the tightrope, or bridge, straddling the abyss between beast–man-*Übermensch*. Even if Zarathustra's words suggest a "false" reading of Darwin, in that he introduces a sense of upward progression into the evolutionary process, he clearly references Darwin.

At this point, three important things should be kept in mind. First, Nietzsche "the writer" should not be confused with Zarathustra "the character." Zarathustra plays a role in the writer's "story" in the Prologue: his role as a mouthpiece for a particular "message" – a higher stage of humanity, according to a particular reading of Darwinian evolution – is overshadowed by his function in the development of the "story" as a whole. Second, Zarathustra speaks in the role of prophet; but, by the end, Zarathustra will come to reject the prophetic stance. Finally, Zarathustra speaks to the people in the *marketplace*, a fact that dictates the style and content of the message. The first point concerning Nietzsche as author of the text *Zarathustra* should seem obvious, and yet many readings continue to assume that Zarathustra's voice must be Nietzsche's. The latter has led some to believe that Zarathustra merely articulates Nietzsche's view of the *Übermensch* as a higher stage of humanity in an evolutionary sense. But Zarathustra plays the role of a literary figure in a narrative, and his speech in front of the marketplace is less important for its own sake than for its position in the trajectory of the overall plot.

Let us resume the narrative. Following his speech, the townspeople clamor for the last man rather than hold out for the *Übermensch*. Speaking to his heart, Zarathustra says: "They do not understand me. I am not the mouth for these ears. Too long apparently I lived in the mountains, too

much I listened to brooks and trees: now I speak to them as to goatherds"
(*Z* "Prologue" 5). Zarathustra suddenly realizes that he has had to compromise his vision in order to reach the widest possible number. To communicate his ideas to the people in the marketplace, he has had to "speak
to them as goatherds." Here, Nietzsche makes a subtle psychological
point that connects with his notion of the will to power: the unique self-
imposed conditions of the recluse – isolation from humanity and solitary communion with nature on the mountaintops – have produced the
standard pose of the prophet. The need to reconnect with humanity and
communicate one's innermost thoughts after years of isolation produces
the specific will to power of the prophetic type.

At that point, the tightrope walker begins his act. He reaches the middle of the course and is suddenly pushed from the rope by "a colorful
fellow resembling a jester." In his dying words, the shattered man says: "'I
lose nothing when I lose my life. I am not much more than an animal
that has been taught to dance by blows and little treats.'" "'Not at all,'"
Zarathustra responds. "'You made your vocation out of danger, and there
is nothing contemptible about that. Now you perish of your vocation, and
for that I will bury you with my own hands.' When Zarathustra said this,
the dying man answered no more, but he moved his hand as if seeking
Zarathustra's hand in gratitude" (*Z* "Prologue" 6). Zarathustra searches
far and wide for an appropriate burial ground after the gravediggers of
the town refuse to bury the corpse, and he finally lays it to rest in a hollow tree in the wild to "protect him from the wolves" (*Z* "Prologue" 8).

This episode represents a turning point. The death of the tightrope
walker occurs after Zarathustra "the prophet" has begun to question his
mission. Scorned by the masses, Zarathustra is suddenly moved by the
plight of a single human being. His admiration for the courage and selflessness of the tightrope walker, in contrast to the callous behavior of the
masses, humanizes him and inspires him to the noble and humane ges-
ture of burying the corpse of a stranger. He now realizes that it is not
the clamoring masses who carry the seeds of the *Übermensch*, but solitary individuals like him: "It dawned on me: I need companions, and
living ones … It dawned on me: let Zarathustra speak not to the people,
but instead to companions!" (*Z* "Prologue" 9). This "new truth" will be
addressed to other individuals and companions who separate from the
herd and learn to write "new values on new tablets": "They shall be called
annihilators and despisers of good and evil" (*Z* "Prologue" 9).

Zarathustra the "prophet" proclaimed his initial message as a common vision for humanity. But he tailored it to his audience. In order for

it to be understood, the message had to be couched in a language and embellished with images that the marketplace could understand. For the *Übermensch* to become a universal goal, it had to be encapsulated in a standard evolutionary narrative. In short, the *Übermensch's* message of transcendence could only succeed if it chimed in with the audience's vulgar perceptions of Darwinian evolution. But his painful experience with the marketplace and his revelatory one with the tightrope walker cause him to reject the *Übermensch* as a common evolutionary goal. In addition, the death of the noble tightrope walker humbles him, making him realize that the vision of the *Übermensch* should inspire only isolated individuals.

The above reading does not *require* conflict with Darwin. One could counter that Nietzsche rejects only the progressive *interpretations* of evolution common at the time, not the scientific *fact* of evolution. In that account, Zarathustra's repudiation of his original message would signal Nietzsche's critique of the masses' vulgar Darwinism. It need not imply that he questioned Darwin's scientific account of evolution as such or that the *Übermensch* is incompatible with Darwin. But I will argue that the *Übermensch did* represent a transvaluation of Darwin and that it had emerged as an alternative precisely because he *had* come to question the fundamentals of Darwinian science.

DARWIN'S NATURAL SELECTION IN RELATION TO "MAN"

As one might expect from an all-encompassing cosmological theory, Darwin could never exclude man from the overall theory of natural selection. He initially attempted to skirt the problematic issue of man's origins and development, and the *Origin* presented his theory of natural selection in general, non-anthropomorphic terms.[19] But as his early notebooks reveal, Darwin wrestled with the problem of man from the beginning.[20] Based on the general theory of evolution outlined in the *Origin*, Darwin's theory of man's development is essentially (1) *mechanistic*; and

---

[19] At the *Origin's* conclusion, Darwin famously (and somewhat coyly) wrote that "in the distant future ... light will be thrown on the origin of man and his history" (Darwin, *Origin*, 394).

[20] In a letter he sent to Wallace two years before the *Origin*, he wrote: "You ask whether I shall discuss 'man'. I think I shall avoid the whole subject, as so surrounded with prejudices; though I fully admit it is the highest and most interesting problem for the naturalist" (John R. Durant, "The Ascent of Nature in Darwin's *Descent of Man*," in *The Darwinian Heritage*, ed. David Kohn [Princeton: Princeton University Press, 1985], 284).

(2) primarily focused on *external factors* of adaptation. His theory of speciation and development can be reduced to a straightforward formula: the number of variations rises through natural increases in population and those variations with more favorable modifications for survival (i.e. the "fittest") will prevail. Less successfully adapted variations will disappear over longer stretches of time.

Darwin, interestingly, does not emphasize individual will within his equation. Though he often hedges on this question, occasionally praising the "virtue" of dogged persistence in the "struggle for existence," his theory ultimately relativizes individual contribution: the "fittest" are simply specimens that produce the most offspring – and thus greater pool of variation – on which selection can perform. The concentration on fecundity, variation, and natural selection means that Darwin focuses primarily on *external factors*. In the *Origin*, survival implies the successful adaptation of a chance variation to changed environmental conditions. Darwin works with a dynamic system. Stasis is not the rule; constant change is. Evolution occurs at the interstices between stasis, i.e. input of fixed biological material, and flux, i.e. the constant oscillation of environmental conditions. The focus on environmental conditions and subsequent adaptation reinforces the insignificance of human will; for the direction of evolution is not determined by the existence of a specific quality or virtue – or even the will to obtain that quality or virtue – but the success of a *relative* "virtue" or characteristic in relation to changed environmental circumstances. Darwin had famously rejected Lamarck's notion of will and theory of the inheritance of acquired characteristics in favor of his own model of disinterested natural selection.

The latter point has developed into a controversy within Darwinism. It centers on whether Darwin subscribes to a progressive notion of evolution, as many in the late nineteenth century assumed, or to a more decentered, constantly branching model of diversifying speciation – "the coral of life" – as many biologists now hold. In truth, Darwin works with *both* paradigms, particularly in relation to the controversial issue of man's development. He understands *successful* modifications to be instrumental in the formation of "higher," i.e. better-adapted forms. He is unequivocal on this point: "It may metaphorically be said that natural selection is daily and hourly scrutinizing, throughout the world, every variation, even the slightest; rejecting that which is *bad*, preserving and adding up all that is *good*; silently and insensibly working whenever and wherever opportunity offers, at the *improvement* of each being in relation to its organic and inorganic conditions of life" (italics mine).[21] Or even more explicitly: "as natural selection works solely by and for *the good of each being,* all corporeal and mental endowments will tend *to progress toward perfection*" (italics mine).[22]

If one accepts the *Origin* on this point, then Darwin sees evolution as *linear in its most basic requirements* – with each successive stage representing an "improvement" over the previous one and with "good" modifications being selected and passed to subsequent generations. Even though Darwin tried his utmost to avoid progressionist language in the articulation of his theory, this effort proved insurmountable and often led to tortured logic: "I entirely reject, as in my judgment quite unnecessary, any subsequent addition of 'new power and attributes and forces': or any 'principle of improvement', except in so far as every character which is naturally selected or preserved is in some way an advantage or an improvement, otherwise it would not have been selected."[23] Indeed, any additions were "quite unnecessary," because he had enshrined the "law of improvement" within the theory of natural selection. He simply assumes that the improvement is a progression and even states that an example of an inherited modification shown to be detrimental to the organism would "prove fatal to my theory." The evolutionary tendency to "higher," i.e. more complex forms, is fundamental to the theory – regardless if one interprets or evaluates the modifications functionally (more successfully adapted to the environment) or morally (possessing inherently superior qualities deserving to be selected).[24]

To summarize: Darwin focuses on *process*. In relation to any organism, individual will matters next to nothing; evolution concerns itself only with the objective mechanism of natural selection, which "selects" superior modifications over time. Crucial are survival and greater fecundity, leading to an increase in chance variations, and the organism's ability to adapt better to changes in environment.

CHARACTERISTICS OF THE *ÜBERMENSCH*

The *Übermensch*, in contrast, is predicated on *internal* factors. Once again, Nietzsche ignores the process and focuses on the psycho-physiological

---

[21] Darwin, *Origin*, 70. [22] Darwin, *Origin*, 395.

[23] Bert J. Loewenberg, "The Mosaic of Darwinian Thought," *Victorian Studies* 3 (1959), 15.

[24] Darwin had no problem applying this notion of evolutionary perfectability to man. In the *Autobiography,* he stated that to those people who believed in the possibility of man's future perfection, as he did, the thought of total annihilation would be far worse than to those who believed in the immortality of the human soul (Charles Darwin, *The Autobiography of Charles Darwin,* ed. Nora Barlow [New York: W.W. Norton & Co., 1993], 92).

components that comprise the totality of the individual biological self. Within his theory, psychological and physiological terms are tightly interwoven, and Nietzsche sees the self and its perception being the sum product of the internal coordination of the instincts, of their relationship to one another. For Nietzsche, the *Übermensch* does not exhibit superior mind or the faculty of "reason," but a "higher" body. In fact, the *Übermensch* is *all* body, a more profound physicality in which instincts and drives are harmoniously coordinated and active energy emanates from heightened instinctual coordination.[25] This higher self's actions, its affirmative, outer-directed energy, are never mere (*re*)actions or adaptations to external conditions in a Darwinian sense; rather, its actions emerge directly from a more complete, fuller existence: "a new beginning, a game, a wheel rolling out of itself, a first movement" (*Z* "On the Three Metamorphoses"). This fuller being actively creates and forms its *own* reality and external conditions.

Another characteristic is *self-overcoming* (*Selbstüberwindung*). Nietzsche often stresses the dangers and higher probability that the higher type can perish (*zugrunde gehen*). The complexity of its will is so great that the smallest irritation, incident, or affront to its system can irreparably damage the tightly wound, perfectly calibrated physiological "machine," which the higher type represents. These dangers need not be major events or calamities, but could be minor personal misfortunes, interferences, or failures that might be difficult to "digest" and could thus "poison" the organism as a whole – against the self and against life. Nietzsche remarked that one of his major objections to the eternal return was always his mother and sister – two people who could wound him during his "highest" moments when he did "not have the strength to resist poison worms" (*EH* "Why I Am So Wise" 3). In his injunctions to "higher men" (*Z* "On the Higher Man" 14), those to whom the promise of the *Übermensch* is directed, he warns them not to despair of existence because something has gone "wrong" *for them*.

In sum, Nietzsche's *Übermensch* embodies *Wohlgerathenheit*, or the condition of being instinctually "well-turned out." In some senses, it is Nietzsche's variation on Darwinian "fitness." But this fitness is not the outcome of a process – the organism's relative success in a random "struggle for existence" – but reflects a superior state of being and a higher

---

[25] "[T]he awakened, the knowing one says: body am I through and through, and nothing besides; and soul is just a word for something on the body" (*Z* "On the Despisers of the Body").

awareness emerging from the will's successful mastery of the instincts and practice of *self*-selection and *self*-hygiene:

And basically, how do you know that someone has *turned out well*? By the fact that a well-turned-out person does our senses good: by the fact that he is cut from wood that is simultaneously hard, gentle, and fragrant. He only has taste for what agrees with him; his enjoyment, his desires stop at the boundary of what is agreeable to him. He works out how to repair damages, he uses mishaps to his advantage; what does not kill him makes him stronger. He instinctively gathers *his* totality from everything he sees, hears, experiences: he is a principle of selection, he lets many things fall by the wayside. He is always in his *own* company, whether dealing with books, people, or landscapes: he honors by *choosing*, by *permitting*, by *trusting*. He reacts slowly to all types of stimuli, with that slowness that has been bred in him by a long caution and a willful pride, – he scrutinizes whatever stimulus comes near him, he would not go to meet it. He does not believe in "bad luck" or "guilt": he comes to terms with himself and with others, he knows how to *forget*, – he is strong enough that everything *has to* turn out best for him. (*EH* "Wise" 2)

Nietzsche's emphasis here is on internal conditions; he remains indifferent to external circumstances or realities. Whatever this "higher man" experiences in his connection to the "world," both good and ill, is successfully converted to something good – for himself: from injuries and ill chances he derives advantage; from random sensory impulses he creates his sum; he leaves out much, because he selects what he wishes to incorporate; he approaches outside stimuli with in-bred caution and skepticism. In short, external conditions matter little; rather, the successful type projects *its* meanings onto the random experiences of life.

The *Origin*, on the other hand, defines "fitness" in terms of objective survival: the organism's success in the "struggle for existence" and its subsequent ability to pass its modifications on to successive generations. The latter will have the advantage in future competition over others: "[As] natural selection acts through one form having some advantage over other forms in the struggle for existence, it will chiefly act on those which already have some advantage; and the largeness of any group shows that its species have inherited from a common ancestor some advantage in common."[26] The *Übermensch* embodies the opposite: he courts risks and danger and embraces adventure and the very real possibility of extinction. It is not survival he craves; it is maximum self-affirmation and expression regardless of external conditions and obstacles. In fact, the *Übermensch* is the *least* likely to survive in the Darwinian "struggle for existence" and to

[26] Darwin, *Origin*, 103.

propagate. Zarathustra points instead to the higher type's need to expend itself to the detriment of personal survival (*Z* "Prologue" 4).

In contrast, the opposite of the *Übermensch*, the "last man," is a caricature of Darwin's "man" – one who avoids danger and seeks comfort, base personal gratification, individual survival, and the hope for a long and uneventful life: "[The last men] have abandoned the regions where it was hard to live: for one needs warmth. One still loves one's neighbor and rubs against him: for one needs warmth" (*Z* "Prologue" 5). These types survive not on account of any superior modification, but because they do not have sufficient energy and the higher will to squander themselves in pursuit of creative self-affirmation. They consider their "survival" – in actuality, their *inability* to "live dangerously" and their *avoidance* of struggle – a "virtue" rather than a direct expression of their instinctual reality and personal life-choices. Zarathustra even includes a subtle jibe against Darwin's principle of fecundity. Whereas fecundity creates greater speciation on which natural selection can act, the "last man's" longevity and fecundity are a horrifying prospect for Zarathustra, for it means that he can overrun the earth in his terrible mediocrity, clogging the outlets for the singular *Übermensch*: "the earth has become small, and on it hops the last human being, who makes everything small. His kind is ineradicable, like the flea beetle; the last human being lives longest" (*Z* "Prologue" 5). Thus, nothing "higher" results from "survival" except the greater preponderance of a specific mediocre type.[27]

THE "INSTINCT OF SELF-PRESERVATION"

If an organism's fitness is measured in terms of its survivability, it also holds true that it "wills" to survive, that it is naturally programmed to preserve itself and procreate. Procreation and fecundity, once again, are central ingredients of natural selection. In the *Descent*, Darwin even speaks of an "instinct" of self-preservation.[28] Without such an instinct, there could be no raw material on which nature could select. Of course, this does not mean that every organism as such survives; it just ensures

---

[27] "People who are more alike and ordinary have always been at an advantage; while people who are more exceptional, refined, rare, and difficult to understand will easily remain alone, prone to accidents in their isolation and rarely propagating" (*BGE* 268).

[28] "[A]lthough some instincts are more powerful than others, thus leading to corresponding actions, yet it cannot be maintained that the social instincts are ordinarily stronger in man, or have become stronger through long-continued habit, than the instincts, for instance, of self-preservation, hunger, lust, vengeance, &c" (Darwin, *Descent*, 89).

natural variation of the species and competition, which determines each organism's "fitness" or "unfitness" for survival.

Through numerous images and poetic allusions, Zarathustra expresses the vision of an *Übermensch*, who does not care about preserving, but rather expending himself. By courting risk and danger and neglecting caution, he minimizes his chances of survival and procreation in Darwinian terms. Indeed, it would be hard to project an "instinct of self-preservation" into this type at all or to envision any future *Übermenschen* being "selected" according to the basic laws of evolution: "[The genius's] instinct for self-preservation gets disconnected, as it were; the overwhelming pressure of the out-flowing forces does not allow for any sort of over-sight or caution" (*TI* "Skirmishes of an Untimely Man" 44).

But Zarathustra merely states in poetic terms what Nietzsche had already begun to question, and would continue to question, in his published writings as well as in his notebooks – and, on occasion, with specific references to Darwin and his followers. In the fifth book he added to *The Gay Science* in 1887, Nietzsche summed up his thoughts on "self-preservation":

The wish to preserve oneself is a sign of distress, a limitation of the truly basic life-instinct, which aims at *the expansion of power* and in so doing often enough risks and sacrifices self-preservation. It is symptomatic that certain philosophers, such as the consumptive Spinoza, took and indeed had to take just the so-called preservation instinct to be decisive – they were simply people in distress. That today's natural sciences have become so entangled with the Spinozistic dogma (most recently and crudely in Darwinism with its incredibly one-sided doctrine of the "struggle for existence" –) is probably due to the descent of most natural scientists: in this regard they belong to "the people", their ancestors were poor and lowly folks who knew all too intimately the difficulty of scraping by. English Darwinism exudes something like the stuffy air of English overpopulation, like the small people's smell of indigence and overcrowding. As a natural scientist, however, one should get out of one's human corner; and in nature it is not distress which *rules*, but rather abundance, squandering – even to the point of absurdity. The struggle for survival is only an *exception*, a temporary restriction of the will to life; the great and small struggle revolves everywhere around preponderance, around growth and expansion, around power and in accordance with the will to power, which is simply the will to life. (*GS* 349)

Here, again, Nietzsche links the interpretation (the "instinct of self-preservation") to the life-experiences and life-conditions of a specific human type. According to this perspective, self-preservation is not a "truth" but only a symptom of specific wills –"individuals in conditions of distress" (in Spinoza's case, also a symptom of his physiology: he was "a consumptive"). For such types, life has to appear like struggle and express self-preservation, for that is the way they experience it. However, the natural scientist should see beyond the confines of his world, work against his instinctual tendencies, and break through to a higher awareness of nature. There the struggle for existence will appear but "an exception, a temporary restriction of the will of life." He will realize that individuals do not "instinctually" want to preserve themselves but to grow and achieve greater power and superiority.

Nietzsche's notebooks prior to *Z* (and later as well) are ripe with thoughts on this issue. In one representative entry from fall 1880, Nietzsche emphatically denies the existence of a self-preservation instinct within the species: "*there is neither an instinct of self-preservation, nor an instinct of species-preservation.*"[29] The biological sciences, he believes, had not shaken off their metaphysical vestiges, and he questions the implicit teleology built into the species concept, as though nature somehow were interested in "species" and its preservation. In the following year, he writes: "It is a wrong point of view: *in order to* preserve the species, countless specimens must be sacrificed. Such an 'in order to' does not exist! Just as there is no such thing as a species, only numerous different individual types! And therefore there can be no sacrifice, no wastefulness! And thus also *no irrationality* in the process! – Nature does not wish to 'preserve the species'!"[30] Over and over again, Nietzsche critiques efforts to project goals, direction, or intentionality into the instincts. The drives and instincts in no way work in service of the species, its preservation, or any other goal. He stated that one could also not explain the existence of species on the basis of any fundamental drives such as the "instinct of preservation" or so-called "sexual instinct":

There is no such thing as the "instinct of preservation" – the search for that which is pleasurable, the avoidance of that which is unpleasurable, explains everything necessary about that drive. There is also no instinct to preserve oneself through the species. That's all mythology ... Generation is a matter of pleasure: its consequence is procreation; i.e., without procreation, this form of pleasure – and pleasure itself – would not have been preserved. Sexual lust has nothing do with the procreation of the species! (*KSA* IX, 234)[31]

---

[29] *KSA* IX, 226.   [30] *KSA* IX, 508.

[31] Compare Nietzsche's view of the "sexual instinct" here to that of the British eugenicist James Marchant, in *Birth-Rate and Empire* (1917), where Marchant argues that his aim was "to accustom the young to regard the sex instinct as a 'racial instinct', as something which exists, as it in reality does, not primarily for the individual but for the race. It is a trust for posterity ... the racial act is for the race" (quoted in Stone, *Breeding Superman*, 118).

Günter Abel argues that Nietzsche's critique of the instinct of "self-preservation" represents one component of his larger anti-teleological challenge to the scientific–mechanistic paradigm of cause and effect, which stands at the heart of modern science. On the basis of his alternative theory of the will to power, which can be explained in neither teleological nor mechanistic terms, Nietzsche believed that the will impresses its form and meaning onto something less powerful.[32] "[E]very purpose and use is just a *sign* that the will to power has achieved mastery over something less powerful, and has impressed upon it its own idea [*Sinn*] of a use function" (*GM* II,12). The theory of the will to power does unsettle the cause-and-effect paradigm, as Abel suggests; but Nietzsche's challenge to the Darwinian worldview goes further. Not only can there be no inscribed "direction" or goal in the evolutionary process – "the 'development' of a thing, a tradition, an organ is therefore certainly not its *progressus* towards a goal, still less is it a logical *progressus* taking the shortest route least expenditure of energy and cost" (*GM* II, 12) – but "evolution" itself, Nietzsche implies, is just one of the many possible interpretations of nature symptomatic of a distinct type impressing *its* will onto natural phenomena.

THE ROLE OF BREEDING (*ZÜCHTUNG*) AND SELECTION

The opening chapter of the *Origin*, "Variation under Domestication," introduces breeding as the dominant means by which Darwin conveys his theory of natural selection. His theory is drawn from insights into the breeding process, scientifically revolutionized in nineteenth-century Britain, and the notion of breeding serves him as far more than an analogical device. For Darwin, natural selection is the method of breeding writ large. It is a "natural," objective means of selection, one at the highest level:

I have called this principle, by which each slight variation, if useful, is preserved, by the term of Natural Selection, in order to mark its relation to man's power of selection. We have seen that man by selection can certainly produce great results, and can adapt organic beings to his own uses, through the accumulation of slight but useful variations, given to him by the hand of Nature. But Natural Selection, as we shall hereafter see, is a power incessantly ready for action, and is as immeasurably superior to man's feeble efforts, as the works of Nature are to those of Art.[33]

---

[32] Günter Abel, "Nietzsche contra 'Selbsterhaltung': Steigerung der Macht und Ewige Wiederkehr," *Nietzsche Studien* 10/11 (1981/82), 375.

[33] Darwin, *Origin*, 52.

On the other hand, Nietzsche's discussions of *Zucht* and *Züchtung*, sometimes in relation to the *Übermensch*, have often produced eugenic readings, most notoriously in National Socialism, but in other critical assessments of his philosophy as well. Darwin's insights into selection supposedly inspired Nietzsche's fantasy that a physiologically and biologically higher type, or *Übermensch*, could be "bred." Many scholars, therefore, see this question of breeding as a strong indicator that Nietzsche adhered to Darwin's theory of natural selection. But here, too, it pays to take a closer look at Nietzsche's thoughts on the subject, and such an examination will reveal that significant differences exist. In earlier writings, Nietzsche seems to have entertained the possibility that one could create the optimal environmental conditions conducive to a higher type and that such a type could be "bred."[34] These passages seem to overlap with Darwin's ideas on breeding and selection.

But by the time of *Z*, and even more in later writings, Nietzsche had moved away from this point of view. Whereas previously he had lamented the cruel randomness of nature and wished to curtail the effects of chance, he from then on rejoices in capriciousness: "My formula for human greatness is *amor fati*: that you do not want anything to be different, not forwards, not backwards, not for all eternity. Not just to tolerate necessity, still less to conceal it – all idealism is hypocrisy towards necessity – but to *love* it" (*EH* "Clever" 10). Life's necessities must be endured, even loved, and the precondition for higher existence is the successful mastery of chance as well as the conversion of all the misfortunes into personal advantages: "[The higher type] works out how to repair damages, he uses mishaps to his advantage.... [H]e is strong enough that everything *has to* turn out best for him" (*EH* "Wise" 2).

Nietzsche stresses the immediate, open-ended, and non-goal-oriented nature of this experience. As a result, one cannot fashion the *Übermensch* into an objective goal or human ideal for others; for he reveals his superiority over time in his actions, his unselfconscious assurance, and his instinctive ability to make the "right" choices. These choices are only recognized and validated *in retrospect* when the instinctual superiority of the higher type has manifested itself in its more perfect creations.[35] This

---

[34] See e.g. *HH* I, 24.

[35] Compare this notion to Nietzsche's famous discussion of the "blond beasts," whose entirely spontaneous, unselfconscious actions in the wild leave behind something more perfect – a higher state formation: "What they do is to create and imprint forms instinctively, they are the most involuntary, unconscious artists there are – where they appear, soon something new arises, a structure of domination [Herrschafts–Gebilde] that *lives*" (*GM* II, 17).

notion of unselfconscious creation as well as the absence of intentionality explains why Nietzsche, in his effort to prove his own superior nature, claims not to have known anything about the development of his special skills or talents; they just appeared to him one day, perfectly formed: "the *higher protection* [of my instinct] manifested itself so strongly that I had absolutely no idea what was growing inside me, – and then one day all my capabilities suddenly *leapt out*, ripened to ultimate perfection" (*EH* "Clever" 9).[36]

Nietzsche points this out not to prove his singularity, but to suggest that the higher type must be an immediate extension of a perfectly structured and balanced instinctual life, regardless of external conditions: "Rank order of abilities; distance; the art of separating without antagonizing; not mixing anything, not 'reconciling' anything; an incredible multiplicity that is nonetheless the converse of chaos – this was the precondition, the lengthy, secret work and artistry of my instinct" (*EH* "Clever" 9). Any conscious effort at "breeding" with a specific end, goal, or objective in mind, any form of utility and planning or any conscious struggle between the instincts ("you will not detect any trace of *struggle* in my life") would not be considered *übermenschlich*: "To 'will' anything, to 'strive' after anything, to have a 'goal', a 'wish' in mind – I have never experienced this" (*EH* "Clever" 9). Purposeful breeding would have little impact on his success, because the *Übermensch* only defines and proves himself, *in retrospect*, through mastery of the concrete, spontaneous situation.

Nietzsche's version of *Züchtung* relates to internal criteria, more specifically, to the heightening of the individual type based on a successful realignment of the instincts and drives. For Nietzsche, *Züchtung* became infused with the ideals of self-control, self-mastery, and discipline but, above all, with self-overcoming or *Selbstüberwindung*. The opposite of the latter is decadence and "letting-oneself-go," or *laissez-aller* (*sich gehen lassen*).[37] *Züchtung* presupposes a superior, autonomous will that distinguishes between and selects specific instincts based on a deeper awareness of health. In contrast to the model of Darwinian breeder, who might select certain traits which he wishes to draw out over time based on their utility, Nietzsche's higher type acts internally and selectively on his drives,

---

[36] This notion is strongly linked to the sudden, unexpected appearance of the "ripe fruit" of the "sovereign individual" after the long, hard work of the morality of mores has made him predictable. See my discussion of the opening sections of *GM* II in Chapter 5.

[37] "[The quality of] 'not-letting-oneself-go' [*das 'Sich-nicht-gehen-lassen'*], Nietzsche repeatedly emphasizes, is one of the characteristics of noble types, beginning with the Greeks" (Gerd Schank, *Rasse und "Züchtung" bei Nietzsche* [Berlin: de Gruyter, 2000], 275).

but according to a *transfigured* valuation – namely, with the will to select *out* (re)active impulses. The latter are expressed most fully in man's transcendental tendencies when the spirit of *ressentiment* becomes isolated from its derivation in the instincts – i.e. in the physiological weakness, illness, and fatigue of degenerating health – and becomes transposed into a complete metaphysical ordering of existence.[38]

In Nietzsche's view, the higher man requires the great strength and the sublime health (*die grosse Gesundheit*) to undertake such a transvaluation, but on the level of the instincts. He reassesses the "evil" instincts – specifically, all active, spontaneous, outer-directed impulses – and establishes them as the new foundation for his own good. At the same time, he recognizes the so-called "good" instincts – those impulses which lead him to de-emphasize the drives and prioritize non-worldly, ascetic values – as symptoms of his decline and weakness:

For too long, man has viewed his natural inclinations with an "evil eye", so that they finally came to be intertwined with "bad conscience" in him. A reverse experiment should be possible in *principle* – but who has sufficient strength? – by this, mean an intertwining of bad conscience with *perverse* inclinations, all those other-wordly aspirations, alien to the senses, instincts, to nature, to animals, in short all the ideals which up to now have been hostile to life and have defamed the world. (*GM* II, 24)

In Darwin's system, nature acts the breeder. Nature "selects" the "fittest," i.e. the variation better adapted to the changed environmental conditions.

---

[38] Richardson posits that Nietzsche believes in breeding on a grand scale, but with a scientific awareness, newly derived from the theory of natural selection, that will allow "philosophers of the future" for the first time to become "conscious" breeders. Whereas earlier "breeders," the priest and the philosopher, did not know what they were doing and sought to "tame" man, we now have insight into natural selection and "evolution can today be self-willed, self-guided" (Richardson, *Nietzsche's New Darwinism*, 194–95). Richardson here again conflates Darwin with Nietzsche and simply assumes that Nietzsche agrees with, and philosophizes on the basis of, Darwin's categories of natural selection without offering any evidence to support his position: "I think there is overwhelming evidence [!] that Nietzsche does think of drives as (at least in part) products of selection. However, this evidence does not include many explicit statements of these points (though it does include some) [!]. This is partly due, I think, to how thoroughly Nietzsche absorbed this Darwinian way of explaining things: he uses its logic, without thinking of himself as explaining 'by Darwinian selection'" (Richardson, *Nietzsche's New Darwinism*, 37). What Nietzsche does, indeed, argue about "breeding" is that it requires the individual to work on the instinctual level, namely, by prioritizing active instincts and selecting out (re)active ones. This spirit of personal self-mastery, however, is *not* based on any insight into natural selection; as I have argued, he does not even believe that such a resulting higher type will survive, nor is that a concern of his. *Züchtung* instead has the potential of creating an individual higher type that can transcend the "morality" of the herd at any given time. In that sense, the process is not a "going-forward," but rather a "returning-back" to the naïve "animal" instincts covered over and confused by two thousand years of Christian morality.

Though he tries to avoid anthropomorphic imagery and terminology, Darwin's use of the breeding analogy makes it difficult *not* to conceive of "nature" in the role of "active" selector.[39] This dilemma is revealed in his use of language: "Nature *acts on* the organization"; "in the preservation of favored individuals and races ... we see the most powerful and *ever-acting* means of selection"; "natural selection is daily and hourly *scrutinizing ... rejecting ... preserving ... working ...*" (italics mine). Even if one regards such expressions as limitations imposed on the language, particularly one still informed by the earlier perspectives of natural theology, one would have to agree that Darwin focuses on *result* – namely, the survival of specimens.

Nietzsche is indifferent to survival; therefore, his *Züchtung* is inconsistent with purposeful breeding,[40] that is, the creation of a superior modification. The heightening of the type does not lead to a greater chance of survivability; indeed, it makes the specimen even more vulnerable to extinction. For him, "nature" is supremely indifferent to the outcome of *Züchtung*. Nothing (genetically) superior comes out of it; the great individual, indeed, is an "end":[41] "A great human being is an end ... Genius – in works and deeds – is necessarily wasteful and extravagant: its greatness is in *giving itself away*" (*TI* "Skirmishes" 44). In effect, Nietzsche sees no connection whatsoever between the outcome of his brand of *Züchtung* and the evolution of a "superior" species within nature as a whole.

THE WILL TO POWER, THE "STRUGGLE FOR EXISTENCE,"
AND THE SPIRIT OF THE *AGON*

Nietzsche's famous dictum that "all life is will to power" has led some prominent commentators to treat the will to power as his brand of metaphysics. Nietzsche, it is held, replaced God with just another mono-causal explanatory paradigm: the will to power. The philosopher's sister, Elisabeth, furthered this perception by publishing his unsystematized

[39] As Robert Young observes: "In moving from artificial to natural, Darwin retains the anthropomorphic conception of *selection*, with all its voluntarist overtones" (Darwin's Metaphor, 455). And: "Anthropomorphic, voluntarist descriptions of natural selection occur throughout *On the Origin of Species* ... It will help to sharpen our sense of how remarkable this is if it is recalled that the rules of scientific explanation which were developed in the seventeenth century had banished purposes, intentions, and anthropomorphic expressions from scientific explanations" (Darwin's Metaphor, 462).

[40] See Schank, *Rasse und "Züchtung,"* 284.

[41] Compare this to something in one of his "Anti-Darwin" passages: "The short moment of beauty, of the genius, of Caesar, is sui generis; such a type does not get inherited" (*KSA* XIII, 317).

thoughts from the notebooks under the title *Will to Power* after his death. In so doing, she hoped to associate her brother's philosophy with a larger "metaphysical" project and thereby secure his reputation. Heidegger built further on this legacy. He drew primarily from Nietzsche's non-existent "magnum opus" and exaggerated the primacy of the concept in his philosophy as a whole. Thanks to painstaking philological research, Karl Schlechta and Mazzino Montinari have demolished this stubborn twentieth-century myth:[42] "Just the thought of a 'magnum opus' – in any systematic sense – misunderstands Nietzsche's way of thinking and his style of philosophy … One can not speak of the will to power as his actual teaching, his systematic major work. What we have are merely literary remains, typical literary remains, nothing more!"[43]

Nietzsche's "will to power" should be purged of its metaphysical accretions and brought into conjunction with Darwin. Through his exposure to Darwin, Nietzsche had questioned traditional metaphysics and Christian belief in a moral universe and had analyzed actions from the perspective of their underlying instincts and drives. According to his final views, each biological entity does not seek stability, stasis, adaptation, or balance of power – though that might express a temporary option, a "restriction" – but the maximum projection of "power." From this point of view, morality was not a higher equilibrium, or the expression of a larger, static "moral universe," but an interpretation from the limited perspective of a specific physiological will seeking to project its own outer-directed energy.

By deconstructing traditional metaphysics from a biological perspective – more specifically, as an example of how "moral" wills distort individual conflict into a grand metaphysical struggle between "good and evil" – Nietzsche undermines efforts to establish a single cosmology. Nietzsche does not postulate that "Life is Will to Power," with capital letters. His examples instead suggest clashing "*wills* to power" – namely, a decentralized, open-ended clash between self-contained biological types, each of which seeks to promote its power along with its own interpretation of existence. The historical interpretation of life that prevails at any moment in time, then, is a result of the particular constellation

---

[42] Brobjer attempts to prove that Nietzsche intended to write a "Hauptwerk" (*magnum opus*) and that this intention should be considered when approaching his late thinking. And yet, even if one accepts his evidence, one is still left with the *fact* of Nietzsche's intact, final works, meant for publication, versus the *intention* of a planned "major work," which remained unfulfilled (Thomas H. Brobjer, "Nietzsche's *magnum opus*," *History of European Ideas* 32 [2006]: 278–94).

[43] Karl Schlechta, *Der Fall Nietzsche* (Munich: Hanser Verlag, 1959), 74–75.

of predominant wills, the underlying physiological correspondence of like-willed types. Unlike Darwin, Nietzsche does not believe anything emerges from such a clash of wills; it does not produce a "fitter" type. "Struggle" between types is merely the clash of two or more biological entities projecting their own brand of power.

Inspired by Malthus's essay on overpopulation, scarcity, and competition, Darwin argues that changed environmental conditions result in a struggle between various types of the same species, as well as other species, leading to the success of a favored variation. Nietzsche, however, questions the existence of just such a struggle. His theory of the will to power suggests that each biological type projects power according to the instinctual requirements of its own will. By necessity, all organic wills *must* be outer-directed – either active and self-affirmative (strong) or (re)active and directed against a perceived threat or opponent (weak). "Competition" is an interpretation projected onto a situation by weak wills who wish to legitimize opposition, allowing them to assert (re)active power in "good conscience." In creating competition from what is a *neutral* situation, weak wills release their brand of energy. This discharge of (re)active energy converts negative sentiments – envy, suspicion, general feelings of weakness and impotence – into a force strong enough to compete in "good conscience" against wills perceived as stronger.

Instead of competition, Nietzsche the classical philologist promotes the ancient *agon*, a formalized contest between superior types. Nietzsche's reflections on the subject were inspired by his colleague Jakob Burckhardt, professor of ancient Greek history in Basle.[44] Burckhardt, who incorporated the chapter "The Colonial and Agonal Man" into his *History of Greek Civilization*, held seminars on ancient history, which Nietzsche attended. In *TI*, Nietzsche called Burckhardt "the most profound expert on Greek culture now alive" (*TI* "What I Owe the Ancients" 4) and "my most esteemed friend" (*TI* "What the Germans Lack" 5). Burckhardt treated the *agon* as a fascinating artifact of ancient Greek culture now no longer possible in the modern era; it could only appear in the debased form of nineteenth-century economic competition. Though Nietzsche shared Burckhardt's negative assessment of the modern age and his positive estimation of antiquity, he saw the *agon* as a still viable humanistic enterprise worthy of revival. In his view, one could enter into the *agon* with the great

---

44 Campioni argues that Nietzsche's reception of Burckhardt's conception of Greek society, characterized by the *agon* and the plurality of higher types, helped him develop his critique of Wagner's notion of the tyrannical genius with absolute authority (Giuliano Campioni, *Der französische Nietzsche* [Berlin: de Gruyter, 2009], 91).

figures of the past and present at all times, despite the breach of centuries and the cultural limitations of modern society.

For Nietzsche, the spirit of the *agon* is not specifically directed against an opponent or competitor, nor does it require the existential elimination of that opponent, though that might tangentially ensue. Rather, the *agon* is the ritualized means by which superior wills assert active power. It creates a controlled, formal setting, one in which two or more strong wills can project power, but as a positive, outer-directed expression of will to power. Instead of incurring competition and the build-up of negative energy with emphasis on survival and elimination of the opponent, the *agon* channels potentially destructive, outer-directed force, resulting from the will's need to assert and project itself, into a socially accepted forum. In the *agon*, the superior type never foists unwanted competition onto a rival, for the goal is not competition as such. It is to locate an equal that one can challenge on equal, established terms so that power can be directed outward. The *agon* establishes the rules and conditions whereby such power projections occur.[45]

For Darwin, survival connotes "fitness" and relative superiority, while life itself *is* "struggle for existence." But Nietzsche's *agon* should not be taken as a metaphor for life. The *agon* is not "nature"; it is a step *outside* nature. It removes traces of ill-will, malice, rivalry, which could undermine or destroy the community, and creates the institutional outlet for strong types to project power outwardly, assertively, and affirmatively.[46] Without such a neutral zone of power-assertion, the destructive animosities that result from overpowerful wills randomly clashing might tear the community asunder: "If we were to take the *agon* out of Greek life, we would stare immediately into that pre-Homeric abyss: the horrible savagery of hate and lust for extermination" (*HC*).

The scene with the tightrope walker in the Prologue of *Z* presents an interesting allegory. The tightrope act indicates the natural parameters of the *agon*: a neutral zone of higher endeavor outside the social constraints in which a higher being can release its outer-directed energy and prove its superiority. Though the tightrope walker does not directly clash with another will, he needs to prove his skill, dexterity, and courage in relation to the act's inherent risks. By entering into this formalized arena, he has already overcome the "man" in man, e.g. the natural instinct of fear and

---

[45] For the *agon*, see also Christoph Cox, *Nietzsche: Naturalism and Interpretation* (Berkeley: University of California Press, 1999), 233.

[46] "The core of the Hellenic concept of the *agon*: it scorns the rule of the one and fears its dangers; as *protection* against the genius it requires – a second genius" (*HC*).

the challenge of gravity, which could send him to his death. He does not compete against anyone but must still embody a mastery of instincts at the highest level. He becomes pure outer-directed affirmative energy.

Suddenly, a jester-like competitor, whom Nietzsche paints in blatantly negative tones, rushes over and pushes him from the tightrope. This "jester" represents the spirit of negative "competition." He does not officially enter into the contest with the tightrope walker, but targets him as a competitor and attempts to eliminate him. But to represent the true spirit of the *agon*, the jester should first accept the rules of the "game." Both must stand on equal footing within the *agon* before one can be considered superior. Instead, the jester channels (re)active energy, the spirit of malice and base competition – that which the *agon* is meant to banish – against a superior type in order to seek cheap advantage. In a Darwinian sense, he has demonstrated himself to be the "fittest" – he has survived; the tightrope walker has perished. But for Nietzsche, he has simply proven that he is not a higher type.

THE ETERNAL RETURN

The most extensive articulation of the "eternal return" occurs in *Z*. Nietzsche introduced his "highest possible formula of affirmation" (*EH* "Thus Spoke Zarathustra" 1) towards the end of his preceding work, *GS* 341, though it only fully emerged in *Z*, which followed. The thought of the eternal return figures most prominently in the sections "The Vision and the Riddle," "The Sleepwalker's Song," and "The Convalescent," but I will concentrate on the latter in my subsequent analysis.

In "The Convalescent," Zarathustra suddenly awakens "like a madman" and announces the arrival of his most "abysmal thought." Calling it up from his depths and almost choking, he abruptly falls down as though dead. He regains his senses but refuses to eat and drink. After seven days, during which his animals remain by his side, he raises himself and eats a rose apple brought to him by an eagle. The animals around him decide it is now time to speak, and Zarathustra is happy to hear their light-hearted chatter. The animals then recite *their* version of the eternal return. Zarathustra listens respectfully; but replies at the end: "O you foolish rascals and barrel organs! … How well you know what had to come true in seven days – and how that monster crawled into my throat and choked me! But I bit off its head and spat it away from me. And you – you have already made a hurdy-gurdy song of it? Now I lie here, weary still from this biting and spitting out, sick still from my own redemption. *And you looked on at all of this?* Oh my animals, are you also cruel? Did you want to watch my great pain the way people do? For human beings are the cruelest animal." He continues with examples of man's cruelty and declares himself sickened by the thought of man:

My great surfeit of human beings – *that* choked me and crawled into my throat ... A long twilight limped ahead of me, a tired to death and drunk to death sadness that spoke with a yawning mouth. "Eternally he returns, the human of whom you are weary, the small human being" – thus my sadness yawned and dragged its foot and could not fall asleep ... Naked I once saw them both, the greatest human and the smallest human: all too similar to one another – all too human still even the greatest one! All too small the greatest one! That was my surfeit of humans! And the eternal recurrence of even the smallest! – That was my surfeit of all existence! (*Z* "The Convalescent" 2)

The animals bid him to be silent, then again launch into their rendition of the eternal return. Zarathustra admonishes them not to convert his words into a hurdy-gurdy song, but they ignore him and complete their version of his most "abysmal thought." Then "[they] fell silent and waited for Zarathustra to say something to them: but Zarathustra did not hear that they were silent. Instead he lay still, with eyes closed, like someone sleeping – even though he was not sleeping. Indeed, at this moment he was conversing with his soul. The snake and the eagle, however, finding him silent in this manner, honored the great stillness around him and cautiously slipped away" (*Z* "The Convalescent" 2).

In interpreting the eternal return, one should keep three things in mind. First, Nietzsche's eternal return is neither a new faith, nor a cosmology, nor a metaphysical doctrine, but an *anti*-faith.[47] Second, there is a "scientific" dimension to the eternal return, which is connected to an altered understanding of "reality" and the physical world beyond Darwinism. Finally, Nietzsche's theory has a crucial *subjective* dimension; as such, it is essentially impossible to express it in theoretical or descriptive terms,

---

[47] Discussions to what extent the eternal return is meant to be a cosmological insight or a subjective one dominate the literature on the subject. My anti-Darwinian reading here should make clear why I come out, in general, on the side of the "anti-cosmologists." I will include two more basic objections to the cosmological theory. First, Nietzsche calls Zarathustra the great skeptic and claims that all great thinkers are skeptics. Why should he then have Zarathustra proclaim yet another all-encompassing cosmological doctrine? Why should a "great skeptic" even want to believe in that? Second, Zarathustra several times calls the doctrine his most abysmal thought and claims that it will divide the weak from the strong. But the cosmological version that he presents to the dwarf in the "Vision and the Riddle" can hardly be termed "abysmal" or terrifying; indeed, it is almost comforting, and Zarathustra narrates it with great calm and equanimity.

because it gives voice to a mood reserved for the heightened awareness of an *Übermensch*.

Alexander Nehamas argues that Zarathustra's disavowal of the animals is crucial for understanding the passage: "But what is even more important is that Zarathustra himself, who affectionately yet condescendingly calls his animals 'foolish rascals and barrel organs' and accuses them of turning his thoughts into a 'hurdy-gurdy song,' remains totally silent and does not once acknowledge the idea his animals attribute to him."[48] Nietzsche had consistently repudiated similar versions of banal cosmic repetition.[49] Nehamas continues: "Nietzsche does not once allude to the specific cosmological view with which the recurrence is usually identified. He is interested only in the realization that the world will continue to be more or less as it has always been so long as it exists, that no final state will redeem those who have gone before."[50] "What is at issue here," Nehamas concludes, "is clearly only the thought that the universe is not progressing in any way, that there is nothing specific toward which it tends, and that it will continue as it is now indefinitely – not the view that the very same individual events will be eternally repeated."[51]

Although I essentially agree with Nehamas, I believe that there is another crucial dimension – and it is a result of Nietzsche's perspective beyond Darwinism. Radicalizing Darwin's premises, Nietzsche had concluded that notions of progression, improvement, cause and effect, teleology, were not *ipso facto* intrinsic to nature, but in fact projections *into* nature from the point of view of particular biological wills. These notions could reveal nothing about "nature" as such; at most, only something about the type of will that espoused them, in other words, about the "nature" of that will. In fact, there was nothing but individual will. Man, like all animals, was indivisible from nature; like nature, he was an immediate expression of will to power. There could be no position *outside* nature from which to reflect on nature, because that too would just be an expression of nature: a falling-away from nature, the perverse phenomenon of nature contemplating itself. The latter would be an intellectual chimera; still worse, it would be a symptom of instinctual decline. For that reason, Zarathustra calls for a "higher" type that *is* nature in nature's own "immoral" totality (*EH* "Why I Am a Destiny" 5).

---

[48] Alexander Nehamas, *Nietzsche: Life as Literature* (Cambridge, MA: Harvard University Press, 1985), 147.

[49] Nehamas, *Nietzsche*, 47–48.   [50] Nehamas, *Nietzsche*, 145.

[51] Nehamas, *Nietzsche*, 145.

By challenging the idea that "man" could make ultimate "object-ive" statements about nature itself, Nietzsche paved the way for his own "higher," "scientific" awareness: that there could be no transcendence, only wills constantly projecting their will to power (with and through their interpretations) and clashing against others in the eternal here and now. The type's interpretation of existence was an intrinsic part of its entire instinctual reality, which (like all will) needed to be directed outward. But nothing "higher" resulted from the random assertion of will; human activity merely reflected the type of energy projected by that particular type of will. Ultimately, Nietzsche distinguished between two major types of will: active, strong wills, who realized their brand of will having rec-ognized the essential "immorality" of nature; and (re)active, weak wills, those who could only become active by embodying a "moral" perspective outside of nature that they can then direct against the perceived "immor-ality" of nature (including other "immoral" wills). Nietzsche's insight into nature's supreme indifference towards human struggle, as well as his belief that nothing "higher" emerges from the clash of wills, produces a sense of nihilistic dread and disgust – that "eternally recurs the man of whom you are weary, the small man." Instead of progression or hope for the possibility of a higher humanity, Zarathustra had to accept that this life, *his* life, is all that there is; which also meant accepting that the "small man," the "last man," is not only essential to (t)his life, but would eter-nally return.

Furthermore, Zarathustra's awareness of the dark, hidden origins and secret motives of morality only heightens his disgust with man; for it makes him see behind all so-called "great men," who now appear "small" and "all-too-human" in the blinding light of his deeper insight: "Naked I had once seen both, the greatest man and the smallest man: all-too-similar to each other, even the greatest all-too-human. All-too-small, the great-est! – that was my disgust with man." Whereas his knowledge of the pre-ponderance of the "last man" had first led him to propose the *Übermensch* as a form of compensation and human transcendence of that reality, the eternal return now meant accepting that "man" could not be transcended but had to be accepted as a necessity both in one's own life and in all eternity. It was a reality that even had to be *affirmed*. For Nietzsche, the affirmation of the eternal return – knowing that the small man returns eternally, as will one's disgust, nausea, and *ressentiment* as part of a con-tinuous, endless cycle, with no possibility of final redemption – becomes the new hallmark of the *Übermensch*: "Zarathustra, the advocate of life, the advocate of suffering, the advocate of the circle." The eternal return determines if man is strong enough to accept his (re)active instincts and to achieve the great health to transcend his own recurring *ressentiment* and still to embrace *his* life, his one and only life, unconditionally.

But beyond that, he must do more: he must also accept that he will become the target of "lesser" types, those who will misunderstand the "immoral" nature of the *Übermensch* and will brand him as dangerous and "evil":

> Zarathustra leaves no doubt about this: he says that knowledge of the good, of the "best", is precisely what terrifies him about humanity in general; *this* was the revulsion that gave him wings "to glide off into distant futures", – he does not conceal the fact that *his* type of person – a type that is an overman in comparison – is an overman specifically when compared to the *good*, that the good and just would call his overman *devils*. (*EH* "Destiny" 5)

He must not fight against that recognition or the revulsion that it brings, but must affirm it in the spirit of *amor fati*: "[T]hat you do not want anything to be different, not forwards, not backwards, not for all eternity" (*EH* "Clever" 10). Nietzsche's greatest test for the *Übermensch*, therefore, represents affirmation of the eternal return, for in that affirmation, he has recognized the biological foundations of all metaphysics, has overcome his own *ressentiment*, and has learned to affirm the totality of life as is and as always will be.[52]

We can now re-examine Zarathustra's behavior in the "Convalescent." The thought of the eternal return hits him when he is *vulnerable*: it contributes to his "illness" and need for convalescence. Only after seven days of "going-into-himself" can he speak again about the essence of the eternal return: the horrible thought that "man" cannot be transcended but instead recurs endlessly. During his illness – a result of the nausea, disgust, and *ressentiment* that accompanies his insight – Zarathustra is still healthy enough not to speak about his condition or to act on his resentment. When Zarathustra later hears, however, that the animals had observed him during his "illness," he rebukes them for their "cruelty": they are as cruel as that other "cruelest" animal, man, who runs to those

---

[52] There are, I believe, three other important and related inferences one can draw from the eternal return: one, the fact that there is no morality, and no morally redemptive message, means that you must create your own tablets, your own destiny and greatness, a burden that will crush "lesser men"; second, that you will have to live with all your actions, and be able to affirm every single one of them, because now you no longer have any comforting excuses or metaphysical justifications and thus will be held directly accountable for all your actions; and third, that you will have to live with your failures and the repercussions of your great risks and gambles, and not let that destroy you – and yet still be able to say "once again!"

suffering and calls it his "pity." Instead of respecting his need for solitude and appreciating his form of convalescence, the animals reveal their own self-interest, masked as pity, which once again only intensifies his disgust with life.

Their version of the eternal return, with which they attempt to cheer him up, has nothing to do with his own deeper insight. They offer him a cosmological worldview, a type of creed or religion that is linked to a "scientific" understanding of how the universe functions. But that is something outside the self, whereby Zarathustra believes: "how should there be an outside-myself? There is no outside." In the end, Zarathustra does not even respond to their cosmology, does not even listen to them, but simply remains silent and converses with his soul. For at this point, he has already found his own method of recuperation and has recovered his equanimity and repose.

The animals, however, fail to understand the nature of the eternal return, which is expressed in Zarathustra's *subjective* response to his most "abysmal thought" in the moments he converses with his soul. He has revealed his higher nature in that he can digest his terrible insight and "spew out its head," i.e. overcome his *ressentiment*. During his illness, he has invented his own form of "cure": the healing awareness that one day he must sing again. His intrinsic health lies in his ability to *instinctively* devise the right treatment during recurring bouts of *ressentiment* and still to affirm his life in its totality – even in its worst moments. Singing then becomes the apotheosis of higher health regained .

CONCLUSIONS

In *EH*, Nietzsche linked specific stages in his creative development with specific physiological conditions. Whereas he associated the period before *Z* with personal debility,[53] he claimed that *Z* came as the unexpected product of "great health" and higher inspiration.[54] If we leave aside the question of how much this assessment reflects literary self-stylization, we can say that Nietzsche contrasts two human potentialities within a single identity – decadence and its opposite.[55] While as a decadent, he claimed to

---

[53] "I hit the low point in my vitality, I kept on living, but without being able to see three steps ahead of me" (*EH* "Wise" 1).

[54] "All of this is involuntary to the highest degree, but takes place as if in a storm of feelings of freedom, of unrestricted activity, of power, of divinity (*EH* "Zarathustra" 3).

[55] "Granting that I am a decadent, I am the opposite as well" (*EH* "Wise" 2).

possess a "dialectician's clarity," a "finger for nuances," and a psychology of "looking around the corner," he recognized from a position of higher health that absolute "truths" were only relevant as symptoms of underlying physiological realities; that the need for "truth" was just another expression of decadence; and that the ability to see all sides of a question expressed instinctual decline. In short, he recognized how perspectives on life reflected the instinctual circumstances of individual wills.

For Nietzsche, Zarathustra's great health and excess of vitality represents a position beyond "truth." The higher type does not serve the interest of a superior "truth" – "truth" after all is symptomatic of a decadent will; Zarathustra is a "skeptic" – but is itself truth-creating, value-creating. The *Übermensch* represents a "higher" individual will. He is a distinct physiological type from the mere "dialectician," embodying a will outside the realm of "nature" as described by Darwin. He *is* nature itself. This fuller human type can never serve as an objective for a higher humanity, for it presents a higher potentiality for an individual human type within humanity as a whole. Though Nietzsche knows he cannot completely embody this type, his deeper sense of health allows him to project himself into its potentiality at least temporarily, allowing him to recognize how it might transcend the standard moral and metaphysical awareness of existence.

Nietzsche cannot describe the concrete outer contours of this type; he can only give voice to its internal state of wholeness and plenitude. For that reason, he stresses how his metaphors came to him unmediated during the composition of *Z*: they were direct extensions of his own temporarily heightened physiological awareness.[56] While for him the *Übermensch* was still only an imaginative potentiality, he hoped that it could possibly become a self-contained, constant type – an ever-active will "beyond good and evil" and decadence, with a tragic, not pessimistic, spirit.

The latter point brings up a final interesting distinction, that between a tragic and a pessimistic philosophy. Whereas Darwin's worldview reflects for Nietzsche a pessimistic understanding – with its emphasis on survival, extinction, and struggle – Nietzsche instead promotes a tragic awareness characterized by a Dionysian spirit.[57] The Dionysian spirit does not seek

---

[56] "The most remarkable thing is the involuntary nature of the image, the metaphor; you do not know what an image, a metaphor, is any more, everything offers itself up as the closest, simplest, most fitting expression" (*EH* "Zarathustra" 3).

[57] "I have the right to understand myself as the first *tragic philosopher* – which is to say the most diametrically opposed antipode of a pessimistic philosopher" (*EH* "Birth of Tragedy" 3).

anything "higher" in the processes of nature – for example, an ultimate explanation for struggle and extinction – but accepts the inscrutability and the chaotic and random necessity of nature at it is: "Saying yes to life, even in its strangest and harshest problems; the will to life rejoicing in its own inexhaustibility through the *sacrifice* of its highest types – *that* is what I call Dionysian" (*EH* "Birth of Tragedy" 3).

In short, the tragic represents an overcoming of the spirit of pessimism. Nietzsche recognizes that higher types will perish and there is no consolation in this fact; indeed, accepting this tragic awareness is the prerequisite for the *Übermensch*. Darwin's vision, on the other hand, accentuates the "terror" and the "cruelty" of life. Simultaneously, he seeks metaphysical solace in the "struggle for existence" and in the "wisdom" of the evolutionary process. This process attempts to give meaning to the fact that life, in the here and now, might evade moral certainties, but evolution still holds out the promise that something "higher," "more perfect" might arise from seemingly indifferent struggle.

Nietzsche's overhaul of Darwinism culminates in this final distinction between the tragic and the pessimistic. Though it might appear a minor difference, Nietzsche's entire philosophy hinges on the value he places on the Dionysian – with its tragic awareness and affirmation of the eternal return– and his rejection of the pessimistic.[58] Certainly, Nietzsche recognizes the explanatory power and the suggestive force of the Darwinian worldview – but also the need to transcend it. He does not present the tragic vision as a natural opponent to pessimism. Rather, he sees it as a *reward* for the continuous psycho-physiological overcoming of the spirit of *ressentiment* and pessimism.

---

[58] "(Dionysian wisdom) The highest power, *to feel* all incompleteness and suffering as necessary (*eternally worthy of repetition* [*ewig-wiederholdenswerth*]), based on a surcharge of creative power" (*KSA* XI, 214).

CHAPTER 3

Nietzsche agonistes: *a personal challenge to Darwin*

In the final years after *Zarathustra* (*Z*), Nietzsche revised his stance toward Darwin yet again. His position at this stage resulted both from his critical reappraisal of Darwin's genealogical perspectives in the middle period and his attempt in *Z* to define the parameters of an affirmative, anti-metaphysical vision beyond Darwinism. If one were to characterize his last productive years, one could say that they were defined by an increased *personalization* of his opposition. While Darwinian perspectives had always been the unspoken reference point in his two earlier periods, Darwin and his followers became his targets in the three major works of his maturity, *Beyond Good and Evil* (*BGE*), *On the Genealogy of Morals* (*GM*), and *Twilight of the Idols* (*TI*). This final approach reflected the rhetorical strategy laid out in *EH* for works written after *Z*: "After the yea-saying part of my task had been solved it was time for the no-saying, *no-doing* half: the revaluation of values so far, the great war, – summoning a day of decision" (*EH* "Beyond Good and Evil" 1).

In this chapter, I will examine the overall polemical strategy Nietzsche deploys in the final period, and I will argue that part of it resulted from insights he had gained from exploring Darwinian perspectives in the middle period. This last phase was not so much different in content, but in *style*, and many of his insights were now honed and ready to be directed against his cultural rivals. Whereas many of his key differences with Darwin had lain unnoticed in the middle-period works, he now tried to bring out those distinctions by taking his ideas directly into the playing field of the "genealogists," i.e. into their "natural history" of moral origins. Obviously, the key work in this regard was *GM*, and its importance as an anti-Darwinian work cannot be overestimated. Thus, the entire second part of the book will be dedicated to a close reading of that text and each of its three essays. There, I will relate each essay to central concepts within Darwinism, and I will show that Nietzsche's strategy of replacing "the improbable with the more probable and in some circumstances to replace one error with another" (*GM* "Preface," 4) ends by hollowing out Darwinism at its core.

REFERENCES TO DARWIN, 1886–1888

Nietzsche's first prominent references to Darwin and thinkers sympathetic to him occur in *BGE*, published in 1886. The work followed the poetic and enigmatic *Z*, where his critical interaction with Darwin had proceeded at a more indirect, conceptual level:

There are truths best known by mediocre minds, because they are best suited to mediocre minds; there are truths that have a charm and seductive allure only for mediocre spirits. We are coming up against this perhaps unpleasant proposition right now, since the spirit of worthy but mediocre Englishmen – I mean Darwin, John Stuart Mill, and Herbert Spencer – is starting to come to prominence in the middle regions of European taste ... [W]hen it comes to scientific discoveries of a Darwinian type, a certain narrowness, aridity, and diligent, painstaking care – in short, something English – is not a bad thing to have at your disposal. (*BGE* 253)

Nietzsche's critique even went beyond Darwin to incorporate an entire "English" philosophical tradition that dated back to the seventeenth century: "This is not a philosophical race – these Englishmen. Bacon signified an *attack* on the philosophical spirit in general; Hobbes, Hume, and Locke indicated a degradation and a depreciation in value of the concept 'philosopher' for more than a century" (*BGE* 252). The so-called "English school" merited only minor passing references in *BGE*. Yet, Nietzsche now no longer engaged with Enlightenment currents at an abstract level but singled out the most significant exponents of those ideas, which reflected a personalization of his critique.

The following year Nietzsche published *GM*. Considered by many to be his seminal work,[1] the text was a full-length study devoted to the "English psychologists" and their genealogical method, and it expanded

---

[1] *GM* is often considered the most important of Nietzsche's texts, and it is the one that has most beguiled scholars. Four new commentaries were published in 2008 alone, "a testimony to how prominent the text has become in scholarship and college courses" (Lawrence Hatab, "How Does the Ascetic Ideal Function in Nietzsche's *Genealogy*?" *Journal of Nietzsche Studies* 35/36 [2008], 106). And yet, there is nothing to suggest that Nietzsche gave precedence to this particular text. If one considers *GM* a polemic, as its subtitle suggests, then it should be treated more like *Antichrist* (even granted that is richer and more wide-ranging). In my opinion, *GM* has found such favor because it seems to dovetail well with current interest in evolutionary ethics and epistemology.

on the constellation of ideas only hinted at in *BGE*.[2] *GM* became his most systematic, thorough, and far-reaching analysis of the theories of Darwin and their followers. By dedicating an entire study to them, he announced that the school of Darwinism had assumed fundamental importance for his philosophical project. Darwin had become an exemplary aspect of the larger problem of modernity and the broader, interrelated problems of nihilism and decadence.

In 1888, Darwin's significance grew even further, and he became the subject in *TI* of an exclusive mid-length passage, the "Anti-Darwin" (*TI* "Skirmishes" 14). Nietzsche also expanded on his theoretical differences in two notebook entries, similarly titled, from the same year. These latter passages were more extensive and detailed in their objections to Darwinian "science" and were experimental forerunners for the version published in *TI*. Nietzsche had now begun to focus on the person of Darwin. What had caused this "sudden" transition to a more personal style of critique? More important, why did he decide to foreground Darwin rather than just his followers, like he had a year before in *GM*?

ON THE WAY TO THE "ANTI-DARWIN"

In a challenge to Darwin's notion of "struggle," Nietzsche's notion of the will to power posited that separate wills, by physiological necessity, must clash in their attempt to exert power – though he did not interpret this process as a "struggle." From an organic point of view, each will had to be *outer-directed*, thereby creating the best conditions for its *own* survival and propagation; the "species" itself was irrelevant. Based on this understanding, it was a "Darwinian" will that recognized life as struggle; that accepted self-preservation as primary instinct; and that saw a higher form of "fitness" emerge from struggle. For these factors could give adequate description of a life defined by incessant struggle, survival, and self-preservation. In this context, Nietzsche repeatedly stresses the environment as a determinant factor – and not because a specimen best adapted to the environment survives, but rather because the environment mirrors a certain type's instinctual reality; it is the "world" such a type creates for itself.[3]

---

[2] In *GS* 345, he wrote: "These historians of morality (particularly, the Englishmen) do not amount to much: usually they themselves unsuspectingly stand under the command of a particular morality and, without knowing it, serve as its shield-bearers and followers."

[3] "[Natural scientists] belong to 'the people', their ancestors were poor and lowly folks who knew all too intimately the difficulty of scraping by. English Darwinism exudes something like the

Nietzsche's attempt to personalize his differences at this stage did not arise from any animosity he had begun to feel toward Darwin. His position was a logical by-product of his theory of the will to power. His assessment that theoretical pronouncements could never be binding for everyone, but only symptomatic of a particular form of existence, meant that Darwin's theories themselves reflected a certain type of will – a "Darwinian" will. When Nietzsche began to single out Darwin, then, it was no longer on the level of theory or interpretation; it was on the level of personal wills. This was not presumption; it stemmed directly from his recognition that no individual could have singular access to ultimate "truth" and that disagreements were a result of clashing types projecting will to power according to their instinctual requirements.

Nietzsche had challenged Socrates and Plato on the same basis. According to Nietzsche, Plato had wanted to step outside the *agon*, even to abolish its foundations, by promoting the notion of the solitary "genius" with access to a single metaphysical truth-claim.[4] Instead of tolerating multiple perspectives and geniuses, Socrates and Plato had sought to undermine the early Greek institution of the *agon*, which encouraged the multiplicity and natural rivalry of individual strong types: "That is the kernel of the Hellenic idea of competition: it loathes a monopoly of predominance and fears the dangers of this, it desires, as *protective measure* against genius – a second genius" (*HC*).

By reconfiguring his opposition on a personal level, Nietzsche suggested a further insight, one related to the eternal return. Nietzsche accepted the necessity of Darwin's position; in fact, it was the inevitable consequence of a particular physiological type and its interpretation. Nietzsche's eternal return allowed for the simultaneous existence of all human types within the broader scope of life. Indeed, the challenge of the eternal return was, precisely, to accept all existence as necessary; and, what is more, to be able to affirm the return of *the same* in eternity.[5] With his focus on Darwin in this last stage, Nietzsche downplayed the relevance

---

stuffy air of English overpopulation, like the small people's smell of indigence and overcrowding" (*GS* 349).

[4] "The true world attainable for a man who is wise, pious, virtuous, – he lives in it, *he is it*. (Oldest form of the idea, relatively coherent, simple, convincing. Paraphrase of the proposition 'I, Plato, *am* the truth.')" (*TI* "How the True World Finally Became a Fable").

[5] "If this thought gained power over you, as you are it would transform and probably crush you; the question in each and every thing, 'Do you want this again, and innumerable times again?' would lie on your actions as the heaviest weight! Or how well disposed would you have to become to yourself and to life *to long for nothing more fervently* than for this ultimate eternal confirmation and seal" (*GS* 341).

and validity of metaphysical constructs (particularly in their concealment of the biographical and the personal) and focused attention on the individual *behind* the ideas: the "human, all too human" provenance of all thought-systems. In that regard, the "anti-Darwin" perspective did not signify Nietzsche's version of truth in place of Darwin's science. It meant, quite literally, the person of "Nietzsche" who could coexist with a person named "Darwin": but not as a Darwinist.

Three characteristics distinguish Nietzsche's transition to the "anti-Darwin" phase of his final writings. They also relate to his other "larger-than-life" rivals, Schopenhauer and Wagner, and, earlier in his career, to a popular author like David Strauss. They are summed up in his "practice of warfare" (*Kriegspraxis*) (*EH* "Wise" 7). First of all, Nietzsche used these figures to analyze, interpret, and critique broader cultural trends. Through them, he could "magnify" significant contemporary undercurrents in exemplary fashion: "I never attack people, – I treat people as if they were high-intensity magnifying glasses that can illuminate a general, though insidious and barely noticeable, predicament" (*EH* "Wise" 7). In that sense, "Darwin" became the means to target the entire historical phenomenon of "Darwinism." Second, by turning "Darwin" into the shorthand for Darwinism, he could distance himself from personal motivations and limit feelings of empathy for the individual; he could attack the "idol" without concern for harming the "person":[6] "I only attack things where there is no question of personal differences, where there has not been a history of bad experiences" (*EH* "Wise" 7). This form of "attack" would allow active, outer-directed energy to be expended against a rival, ensuring that resentment, antipathy, or animosity would not enter into the higher spiritual exchange:[7]

The task is *not* to conquer all obstacles in general but instead to conquer the ones where you can apply your whole strength, suppleness, and skill with weapons, – to conquer opponents that are your *equals* ... Equality among enemies – first presupposition of an *honest* duel. You *cannot* wage war against things you hold in contempt; and there *is* no war to be waged against things you can order around, things you see as *beneath* you. (*EH* "Wise" 7)

Finally, Nietzsche recognized that the sum total (i.e. "Darwin") was greater than the parts ("the Darwinists"); in other words, the figures that

---

[6] For this reason, Nietzsche emphasizes that his philosophical opposition to Christ and Christianity is not based on negative personal experiences: "I have the right to wage war on Christianity because I have never been put out or harmed by it" (*EH* "Wise" 7).

[7] The *agon* reflects the desire to release one's own affirmative energy without tearing the other down in direct confrontation (*GS* 321).

succeeded in bundling (re)active energies into a larger historical movement were superior to the undercurrents they embodied. By singling them out for critique, Nietzsche acknowledged their superior will and their unique "genius" as well as their ability to captivate and direct the attention and minds of "lesser," though essentially compatible wills. For this reason alone, they deserved respect as well as serious attention and study.

THE MASTER WILL VERSUS THE COLLECTIVE WILL

As a classical scholar, Nietzsche recognized in the relationship between Darwin and his followers a fairly standard one between master and philosophical disciple. After the master had presented a complete and coherent vision of life and nature, the disciples were left behind to convert the thoughts of the solitary individual, the "genius," into a recognizable philosophical platform. The disciples would continue to offer perspectives from that exclusive angle and would engage in battle against rival schools. However, a crucial distinction existed between the philosophies of the pre-Christian era and the "science" of the modern Darwinists.[8] The ancients had implicitly understood that the philosophy of the master could never be absolute but could only *suggest* a means of virtuous living and seeking a fuller, more complete life. Alternatively, it could represent the "reward" for such a complete life lived. Thus, its attraction for others

---

[8] Clark judges his "positive" references to "science" in his later works (particularly in *A*, where he discusses science in antiquity) as evidence of his return to a position consonant with the empirical sciences (Maudemarie Clark, "The Development of Nietzsche's Later Position on Truth," in *Nietzsche*, ed. John Richardson and Brian Leiter [Oxford: Oxford University Press, 2001], 66–67). But Nietzsche nowhere equates the two "sciences" (i.e. ancient "science" versus modern empiricism), but uses the word "science" in relation to the ancient world with a completely different awareness. The "science" of the Roman empire had arisen from an affirmative spirit; it was not premised on an absolute notion of "truth" – (for Nietzsche) a legacy of Christian asceticism. On the other hand, modern notions of "truth" suspect the importance of personal instincts, even if Clark suggests that empiricism claims to be based on the senses. For modern science believes that man can determine an ultimate, "true" perspective on reality, *independent* of the *individual* will's instincts; and furthermore, that this single perspective must be binding for *all*. But Nietzsche believes one cannot develop any notion of ultimate truth beyond, or against, the dictates of one's own instincts, and instead, that one should acknowledge and affirm them as the basis for one's own individual "truth" (*GM* II, 11). Thus, the best minds of the ancients developed a notion of science which did not question or suspect the role of the instincts, but recognized that a complete affirmation of them was the prerequisite for a deeper understanding of reality (*der Tatsachen-Sinn*, as Nietzsche refers to it), despite the fact that such an understanding could never crystallize into "Truth" for everyone. (The "science" of the ancient world, indeed, grew out of the "immorality" of the noble master lineage, not out of the genealogy of Christian ["moral"] asceticism.) In response to Clark, why would Nietzsche lament the loss of the ancient "sciences," if he felt confident that modern science and empiricism, as best exemplified by Darwin's project, fulfilled the original promise of the ancients?

did not reside in the details of the "system," but in the "virtue" of the master's life. The thoughts were just "natural" extensions of that higher spiritual awareness.[9] At that stage, one could become all "active" energy – with no need to negate – and could transcend the distinction between active and (re)active, becoming outer-directed and affirmative.[10]

The Darwinist position, on the other hand, continued to reflect metaphysical aspirations and thus the spirit of (re)action. Not content with reflecting a single outlook or philosophical school, "Darwinism" could become active only by becoming exclusionary, reacting against its existential opponent, Christianity. But belief in total "objectivity" and exclusive truth was another sign of weakness within the metaphysical imperative. While an active, affirmative will can coexist with other active wills – in fact, *needs* those wills in order to affirm itself – (re)active wills must first subvert and eliminate others in order to define their position.[11] For Nietzsche, "truth" was merely a perspective and an exclusive claim to truth revealed an inherently unstable will. That individual will had to ground itself in a concrete position, the "Truth," with which it could identify and through which it could assert ([re]active) energy against "untruthful," competitive claims. This particular notion of "truth" was a legacy of the Western philosophical tradition that had originated in the ascetic practices of degenerating priestly types.[12]

---

[9] Nietzsche contrasts Buddhism positively with Christianity on this score. Though he considered Buddhism a form of *décadence*, he argued that it emerged from a specific way of life and not as a result of a fundamental reinterpretation of existence (*A* 42). Its active hygienic measures to curtail the depression and fatigue of the will further distinguished it from Christianity, which exacerbates instinctual weakness by stoking and overstimulating the (re)active sentiments (*A* 20–21).

[10] Nietzsche's depiction of Christ and his followers reflects this insight. His famous dictum that "there was really only one Christian, and he died on the cross" (*A* 39) means that only the practice of actually living like Christ could be considered Christian: "only the *practice* of Christianity is really Christian, *living* like the man who died on the cross" (*A* 39). This was "[*n*]ot a believing but a doing, above all a *not*-doing much, a different *being*" (*A* 39). The *belief-system* following the crucifixion, on the other hand, became a narrative of *ressentiment* based on Christ's followers' inability to comprehend his death (*A* 40–41). Becoming a Christian from then on meant believing in the *system* of thought, i.e. the master-narrative of death and resurrection. See also Raymond Geuss, *Morality, Culture, and History: Essays on German Philosophy* (Cambridge: Cambridge University Press, 1999), 9. Though Geuss touches upon the notion of the master versus the collective will, he suggests the phenomenon is primarily a religious one, existing above all in Christianity (Geuss, *Morality, Culture, and History*, 14). But the process of projection and interpretation occurs equally in all fields, such as science, philosophy, and the realm of politics, and not only in religions (though perhaps it is the most pronounced there).

[11] I am indebted to Gilles Deleuze's explication of active–(re)active in *Nietzsche and Philosophy* (New York: Columbia University Press, 1983).

[12] "The earliest philosophers knew how to give their life and appearance a meaning, support and setting which would encourage people to learn to *fear* them: on closer inspection, from an even more fundamental need, namely in order to fear and respect themselves" (*GM* III, 10).

For Nietzsche, Darwin's "genius" resided in his "normalcy"; his instinctual correspondence to like-constituted wills ("the spirit of respectable but mediocre Englishmen"); and his ability to construct a complete system which could resonate with the predominant instinctual reality around him. Through this system, these wills not only had a coherent and totalizing metaphysics that could made sense of and give meaning to their instinctual reality; more important, they had found a vehicle with which to articulate and actualize their will. Darwin had become a "world-historical" force, then, by giving institutional momentum to an inchoate instinctual reality which, until then, had lacked a resounding single paradigm to consolidate and direct disparate interpretative wills.

This theory of the master will and the collective will expressed the psychological and physiological correspondence of historical figure and followers and was a corollary to the will to power.[13] He had developed the notion throughout his career, and it gained in rhetorical force and sophistication in his final years. By 1888, Nietzsche had shed his theoretical caution and entered into the *agon* against "world-historical" figures that he felt had rallied the wills to power of lesser, "decadent" types against higher forms of culture. This strategy represented a clear shift in purpose, though it was entirely consonant with, and had grown out of, previous ideas and practices. In *D*, Nietzsche had used St. Paul to probe the psychological depths of the "first Christian." In *A*, he then expanded on this and created a physio-psychological correspondence between Paul and his followers:[14] Paul's instincts of decadence resonated with individuals in the ancient underworld and he was able to direct their wills against Roman political institutions through the combined will to power of Christian religion (*A* 42).[15]

---

[13] "The religion-founder must be psychologically infallible in his knowledge of a certain average breed of souls who have not yet *recognized* one another as allies. He is the one who brings them together" (*GS* 353).

[14] According to Geuss, Nietzsche sees Christianity as a movement representing a conglomeration of wills impressing their meanings onto the "facts" of Christ's life and teachings, with Paul's interpretation being historically the most decisive: "Once Pauline theology has penetrated Christian practice, modified it, given it a certain direction and a particular kind of coherence, etc., any non-Pauline will which tries to impose a new interpretation on Christianity (as thus constituted) won't encounter, as it were, just a tabula rasa, but a set of actively structured forces, practice etc. which will be capable of active resistance to attempts to turn them into other directions, impose new functions on them, etc." (Geuss, *Morality, Culture, and History*, 12–13). Nietzsche's crucial insight is into the master will, or "genius," the one who can appreciate and instrumentalize like-willed types and direct them in the service of both his and their greater will to power. Without the (political) "genius" of Paul, for example, the disparate early Christians would have gone unrecognized and would not have expressed a world-historical destiny.

[15] Also, "Jesus (or Paul), for example, discovered the life of the small people in the Roman province, a humble, virtuous, depressed life: he explained it, he put the highest meaning and value

In *TI*, Nietzsche suggested the physio-psychological interdependence between Socrates and his followers. Socrates proved successful, because he understood *his* will and recognized how it resonated with the instinctual degeneration of the Athenian upper classes: "[Socrates] looked *behind* his noble Athenians; he understood that *his* case, his idiosyncrasy of a case was not an exception any more ... [o]ld Athens was coming to an end. – And Socrates understood that the world *needed* him, – his method, his cure, his personal strategy for self-preservation" (*TI* "The Problem of Socrates" 9). In *CW*, Nietzsche showed how the "Master" expressed the will to power of like-constituted types: "[The admirers of Wagner] are united by the same instinct, they see their highest type in him; he ignited them with his own embers, and since then they have felt transformed into a power, a great power even" (*CW* 11). Nietzsche then did the same with Darwin and his followers. But while the leader of the "movement" had become the centerpiece of his attack in 1888, the "English psychologists" were still his polemical target one year earlier in *GM*. In the one important case of Darwin, that is, Nietzsche divided up his attack and singled out the followers first.

THE "ENGLISH PSYCHOLOGISTS" AND THE THEORY OF *RESSENTIMENT*

Zur Genealogie der Moral (1887),[16] subtitled "a polemic" (*eine Streitschrift*), references a target both specific and elusive. At times, Nietzsche identifies the "English psychologists" or "English school"; at others the "historians of morals." Yet, these titles suggest the same characters, and both terms – "English psychologists" and "historians of morals" – are shorthand for a similar genealogical mode of thinking about human nature and man's early history, including the natural origins of morality. If we are to take the complete title of the text seriously (and both title and subtitle signify

---

into it – and thereby also the courage to despise every other way of life, the silent Moravian brotherhood fanaticism, the clandestine subterranean self-confidence that grows and grows and is finally ready to 'overcome the world' (i.e., Rome and the upper classes throughout the empire)" (*GS* 353).

16 Kaufmann explains why "*Zur*" in the German title must be translated as "On," though it could be rendered as "Toward" (Friedrich Nietzsche, *On the Genealogy of Morals*, trans. Walter Kaufmann [New York: Vintage Books, 1968], 4–5). (A more apt rendering might be "Concerning.") This is a crucial distinction, since it indicates that Nietzsche meant his text to be a (critical) discussion of the genealogists and their historical method, *not* a contribution to their studies. A further proof (not mentioned by Kaufmann) is that if Nietzsche had intended it as "Toward," he would have titled it *Zu einer Genealogie der Moral*: using the "*Zu*" with the definite article ("*Zur*") in the sense of "toward" makes little sense.

a work's basic thrust and intentions), then the author unambiguously intended his text to be *a polemic*. It is the nature of polemic to attack, discredit, and unsettle a historical–cultural opponent.[17]

In fact, he could just as easily have titled his work *On the Genealogists of Morals*. Its opening sentence sets the tone: "These English psychologists, who have to be thanked for having made the only attempts so far to write a history of the emergence of morality, – provide us with a small riddle in the form of themselves; in fact, I admit that as living riddles they have a significant advantage over their books – *they are actually interesting!*" (*GM* I, 1). Curious about these scientific investigators' possible motives and intentions, he asks: "[W]hat is it that actually drives these psychologists in precisely *this* direction"? Nietzsche then attempts to answer his own question by listing a series of motivations: "Is it a secret, malicious, mean instinct to belittle humans, which it might well not admit to itself? Or perhaps a pessimistic suspicion, the mistrust of disillusioned, surly idealists who have turned poisonous and green? Or a certain subterranean animosity and *rancune* towards Christianity (and Plato), which has perhaps not even passed the threshold of consciousness" (*GM* I, 1)?

But who *are* the "English psychologists," against whom the text is directed? Nietzsche's opposition ranges further than is often assumed. It extends well beyond his contemporaries and their positions, tackling a much broader, more formidable tradition. His critique implicates, among others, the Hobbesian naturalism of the seventeenth century as well as the sensualist and psychologist programs of Hume and Locke in the eighteenth. Above all, it polemicizes against the materialist–scientific thinkers of the nineteenth century – Spencer, Mill, Darwin, as well as Darwin's many followers and imitators, including the *German* Darwinian and former friend of Nietzsche, Paul Rée.[18]

---

[17] The fact that the text was intended as a polemic *against* the "genealogists" (and *not* as a furtherance of their cause) escapes commentators. Jacqueline Stevens claims that many scholars have misunderstood and fetishized the concept of "genealogy" as a result of the influence of French theorists (Foucault, Deleuze). She argues that Nietzsche does not practice genealogy, but history; that he criticizes the genealogists for doing "genealogy," not history ("they lack the historical sense"); that the word "genealogy" was not even common in German usage at the time; and that when Nietzsche did use the word in this text (rarely), it was to mock their very own practices (Jacqueline Stevens, "On the Morals of Genealogy," *Political Theory* 31 [2003]: 570–72). I also credit Stevens for pointing out how Nietzsche twice uses the term "*Arten*" in a single reference to Rée's work (*GM* "Preface" 4), a sly and witty reference to Rée's kinship with Darwin and his main text (translated into German as *Die Enstehung der Arten*) (Stevens, "On the Morals of Genealogy," 571).

[18] Clark believes that the collective "English psychologists" refers only to Nietzsche's "intellectual ancestors," above all David Hume (Maudemarie Clark, "Introduction," in Friedrich Nietzsche,

Behind the theories of the "English psychologists," Nietzsche detected the spirit of *ressentiment*. The latter concept, most fully articulated in *GM*, is central to his philosophy and is closely allied with his notion of active and (re)active will. Whereas the higher type transcends active versus (re)active instincts, becoming pure, affirmative, outer-directed momentum, *ressentiment* arises when a weak will is hindered from asserting its power. Though all wills by necessity need to be active in some form, weak wills distort situations and create conflict, *moralize* conflict, in order to feel "good" about projecting power. Even if every human will can feel resentment – namely, any time its power is crossed and it is hindered in projecting outer-directed energy – a strong will quickly shakes off resentment and may even forget the offense:

> When *ressentiment* does occur in the noble man himself, it is consumed and exhausted in an immediate reaction, and therefore it does not *poison*, on the other hand, it does not occur at all in countless cases where it is unavoidable for all who are weak and powerless. To be unable to take his enemies, his misfortunes and even his *misdeeds* seriously for long – that is the sign of strong, rounded natures with a superabundance of power which is flexible, formative, healing and can make one forget. (*GM* I, 10)

The spirit of *ressentiment* is of a different breed. It emerges when the feelings of lingering, festering resentment that grow out of the biology of the will become a world-historical force by crystallizing into a complete interpretational apparatus. This bundled energy gives the *incidental* sentiments of impotence, inadequacy, malice, or envy that an individual feels a directed, self-perpetuating institutional momentum. *Ressentiment* then becomes the "active" energy of weak wills; seemingly isolated from the instincts, it becomes disembodied and enshrined *as* interpretation; it becomes "creative." Behind the theories of the "English psychologists," Nietzsche detected the spirit of resentment and biological (re)action. This spirit was best expressed in three interrelated areas: in the genealogists' general *pessimism*; in the nature of their *scientific explanations*; and, finally, in their *personal relationship to Christianity*.

On the Genealogy of Morality [Indianapolis: Hackett Publishing Co., 1998], xxiii), and ignores the fact that the term applies even more to his contemporaries, who continued with a sensualist paradigm in science and philosophy. Clark needs to make this distinction for the sake of her argument, because she sees Darwin's evolutionary perspective as different in kind as well as superior to the more rudimentary arguments on the basis of utility which Hume and his followers supported (Clark, "Introduction," xxiv). However, Nietzsche views Darwin's arguments as neither distinct from nor superior to theirs, and he repeatedly includes Darwin in his numerous references to "English" philosophy.

RESSENTIMENT AS PESSIMISM

Most fundamentally, *ressentiment* was expressed in the genealogists' pessimism, which colored all their evaluations and made them focus attention in a certain direction. If nature was a "cruel, wasteful, blundering low and horribly cruel" place, as Darwin insinuated, then that perspective revealed the subjective bias of his will. One could easily say, and with equal legitimacy (as Nietzsche in fact did), that life was full of exuberance, of an endless giving-forth and superabundance (*TI* "Skirmishes" 14). There could never be an "objective," disinterested vision of nature *per se*, only interpretations from the perspective of particular individual wills:

Judgments, value judgments on life, for or against, can ultimately never be true: they have value only as symptoms, – in themselves, judgments like these are stupidities. You really have to stretch out your fingers and make a concerted attempt to grasp this amazing piece of subtlety, that *the value of life cannot be estimated*. Not by the living, who are an interested party, a bone of contention even, and not judges; not by the dead for other reasons. (*TI* "Socrates" 2)

To focus on the dark and gloomy sides of "nature," on its alleged struggles, extinctions, and competition, was to paint nature with the shades of one's *ressentiment*. But how does Nietzsche come to associate pessimism with *ressentiment*? And what further conclusions does he draw from the association?[19]

Nietzsche's central point about (re)active wills, as opposed to active, life-affirming ones, is that (re)active wills must first demonize opponents before they can release power. What distinguishes *ressentiment* from the individual expression of temporary resentment is that the former signifies a perpetual state in which negative sentiments have congealed. Instead of overcoming oppositional energy through quick and spontaneous release (which signifies the natural behavior of strong wills), the person of *ressentiment* dams up that (re)active energy and converts it into an elaborate world-historical, friend–enemy polarity. Unreleased negative energy then transfigures life and nature into a ceaseless battlefield of negative, confrontational force. While strong wills seek out other active wills to release affirmative energy, weak wills avoid greater conflict altogether. That unreleased energy then serves as the fermenting ground for a broad, constant hostility, which in turn breeds a metaphysical interpretation of existence.

---

[19] Another of Nietzsche's strategies was to implicate the genealogists' environment and their life-practices as contributing factors in their inherent pessimism. See *GS* 134.

To feel "good" about these (re)active instincts and to able to own up to them and release them in "good conscience," these types must first reconfigure the world as a battleground of contentious, ever-threatening hostile wills and eternal enemies. Pessimism is the inevitable consequence of the *underground* struggle on the part of the forces of *ressentiment*.

RESSENTIMENT AS MODERN SCIENCE

Nietzsche was puzzled by the fact that the "English psychologists" were always drawn to impersonal mechanistic forces – such as natural laws and *verae causae* – in order to ground their explanations:

You always find them at the same task, whether they want to or not, pushing the *partie honteuse* of our inner world to the foreground, and looking for what is really effective, guiding and decisive for our development where man's intellectual pride would least wish to find it (for example, in the *vis inertiae* of habit, or in forgetfulness, or in a blind and random coupling and mechanism of ideas, or in something purely passive, automatic, reflexive, molecular, and thoroughly stupid). (*GM* I, 1)

Rather than realize how personal curiosity or other human motivations stood behind their perspectives ("[W]hat is it that actually drives these psychologists in precisely *this* direction?"), the Darwinists objectified their individual perspectives and converted them into the basis for an unimpeachable science. What is more, they always grounded what was supposedly decisive for man's "development" in the least noble, most banal aspects of his character or in a single passive, impersonal, mechanical, or causal force, operating seemingly beyond human control or influence.[20]

Nietzsche, rejecting attempts to prioritize impersonal forces, wishes to foreground actual *active* energy – aggressive, outer-directed, and dominant human traits ("the actual *active* emotions such as lust for mastery,

---

[20] His study of Herschel and Whewell was the basis for Darwin's attempt to make his science correspond to nineteenth-century standards: "Herschel argued that one must aim to base one's reasonings on *verae causae*, and Darwin was desperately keen to show how evolutionary reasonings were based on a *vera causa*, natural selection ... Darwin, who thought of natural selection as a force, realized that he had an absolutely identical situation in biology. We have in natural selection, *a force directly perceived and caused by us*; hence, analogically, given the struggle and given wild variation, it cannot be denied that there is a natural force of selection making different organisms. In Herschel's own terms he had definitive proof that natural selection is a *vera causa*" (Michael Ruse, "Darwin's Debt to Philosophy: An Examination of the Influence of the Philosophical Ideas of John F.W. Herschel and William Whewell on the Development of Charles Darwin's Theory of Natural Selection," *Studies in History and Philosophy of Science* 6 [1975], 175–76). Natural selection could thus become that single identifiable force which could explain organic development according to nineteenth-century theories of science.

greed and the like" [*GM* II, 11]) – and convert those into the basis for a future evaluative standard. He wants to achieve a transvaluation of values that would allow long-proscribed "immoral" instincts to assume evaluative superiority. This transition in modes of evaluation, he argues, would involve both critiquing the (re)active values ("hatred, envy, resentment, suspicion, *rancune* and revenge") that had become enshrined within nineteenth-century scientific standards and reassessing modern science's *instinctual* prejudice against active, spontaneous energy:

All I want is to point out the fact that this new nuance of scientific balance (which favours hatred, envy, resentment, suspicion, *rancune* and revenge) stems from the spirit of *ressentiment* itself. This "scientific fairness" immediately halts and takes on aspects of a deadly animosity and prejudice the minute it has to deal with a different set of emotions, which, to my mind, are of much greater biological value than those of reaction and therefore truly deserve to be *scientifically* valued, highly valued: namely the actual *active* emotions such as lust for mastery, greed and the like. (*GM* II, 11)

Nietzsche interpreted this nineteenth-century "scientific" bias as an expression of the will to power of *ressentiment* forces. Since this collective will could not admit to open struggle with the forces of opposition in "good conscience," it affected cool objectivity and disinterestedness. At the same time, it presented its own negative, (re)active instincts as a supposedly "objective" assessment. These negative sentiments of *ressentiment*, by-products of unleashed (re)active energy, transformed "nature" into a close-knit, competitive, and selective environment that allowed behavior long-proscribed by Christianity to be vented. In the process, such wills transformed *random* individuals into "natural" competitors, thus allowing weak wills to feel "good" about the discharge of (re)active instincts. The "results" of this "competition" (which never even took place, in Nietzsche's eyes) were then interpreted in a "disinterested" way as part of a "selective" evolutionary process working itself out in "nature" over time.

RESSENTIMENT AS ANTI-CHRISTIAN BIAS

Finally, Nietzsche recognized *ressentiment* in Darwin's and his followers' stance towards Christianity. Darwin's perspective on Christian religion was complex and cannot be reduced to a single position. He often vacillated on this issue and wished at the very least to minimize friction between his theories and Christian institutions. Darwinist opinions on religion and the Church also varied widely (and still do) – from Thomas

Huxley's rabid anti-clericalism on the one hand to Asa Gray's more cautious attempts to reconcile faith and Darwinism on the other.[21]

More important, his emphasis on struggle, competition, and extermination shook Christian faith in a more benign pattern of life. Whatever his unarticulated position toward religion was, Darwin knew that his ideas would unleash a very public struggle against central nineteenth-century institutions. That conflict did not occur over the heads of the Church establishment but engaged them on their own exclusive terrain. Above all, Darwin assumed a neutral (or, at least, equivocal) stance toward human behavior long censured or suppressed by official Christianity.[22] Indeed, he not only gave allowance for such "immoral" instincts; he recognized in them a force for *improvement*: out of the brutish "struggle for existence," the "fittest" emerged.

Based on his theory of the will to power, Nietzsche recognized in the genealogical position an underground struggle for supremacy. Because Darwin did not wish to be associated publicly with radical materialist and anti-Christian currents for fear of reprisal, social ostracism,[23] and familial pressures,[24] he had to channel his (re)active energies into a broad, protracted offensive, one that undermined the institutional

---

[21] Darwin's interment in Westminster Abbey can be seen as one of the great ironies of history, the final step in the curious series of events leading from the broadest vilification of Darwinism to its ultimate sanction at the highest level: "[I]n Westminster Abbey the Church not only reclaimed its erstwhile son; it acknowledged Nature, as Darwin had, to be an authority above itself, and interpreters of Nature to be the mediators of God's will to humankind" (J.R. Moore, "Darwin of Down: The Evolutionist as Squarson Naturalist," in Kohn, ed., *Darwinian Heritage*, 476).

[22] Darwin responded diplomatically to Edward Aveling, a prominent Darwinian "free-thinker," who wished to dedicate his work to him: "though I am a strong advocate for free thought on all subjects, yet it appears to me (whether rightly or wrongly) that direct arguments against christianity & theism produce hardly any effect on the public; & freedom of thought is best promoted by the ['gradual' added] illumination of ['the' deleted, 'men's' added] minds', which follow from the advance of science. It has, therefore, been always my object to avoid writing on religion, & I have confined myself to science. I may, however, have been unduly biased by the pain which it would give some members of my family, if I aided in any way direct attacks on religion" (quoted from Ralph Colp, Jr., "The Contacts between Karl Marx and Charles Darwin," *Journal of the History of Ideas* 35 [1974], 335).

[23] Desmond and Moore describe Darwin's sobering experience as a young Cambridge student with the social and political persecution of Richard Carlisle and Robert Taylor, two radical itinerant free-thinkers who dared challenge the Church establishment of Cambridge: "In later years [Darwin] would remember Taylor as the 'Devil's Chaplain,' fearing that he himself might be similarly reviled, an outcast from respectable society, a terror to the innocent, an infidel in disguise" (Adrian Desmond and James Moore, *Darwin* [New York: W.W. Norton & Co, 1991], 73).

[24] Emma Darwin could never reconcile her strong Christian beliefs with her husband's theories, and Darwin worked hard to avoid offending her sensibilities. The extent of the family's bitter reactions to his perceived irreligion is revealed in their responses to the publication of the *Autobiography*: "The family was, in fact, divided concerning the publication of some of the passages relating to Charles Darwin's religious beliefs. Francis, the editor, held the view that complete publication was the right course, whilst other members of the family felt strongly that

power and prerogatives of the Church at the deeper level of theory or doctrine. Darwin thereby bundled the *same* potent anti-Christian, anti-Establishment sentiment into a more sophisticated theoretical challenge to the Church, thus enlisting disconnected and disaffected individual wills into a more directed, historically effective will to power against established Christianity.

Nietzsche opposed the doctrines of the Church and Christianity on philosophical grounds; yet, he still recognized both to be the institutional framework for (re)active wills. For centuries, Christianity and the Church had consolidated potentially destructive and particularized (re)active energy and served as a clearly identifiable institutional framework for a collective will to power;[25] in fact, they had prevented the dispersal of (re)active wills into the society at large. As a result, Nietzsche did not wish to eliminate the Church at all;[26] he was interested in maintaining it as an institutional bulwark for (re)active wills.[27] Furthermore, Nietzsche acknowledged the Church to be an opponent of great spiritual worth. Higher types naturally seek to engage powerful rivals on a superior agonistic plane and to affirm their own brand of active will and "immoralism."[28] The eternal return prevents any feelings of *ressentiment*, or eliminationist tendencies, to intrude into the spiritual *agon*. Nietzsche had defined the eternal return as his highest affirmation and his selective standard for the *Übermensch*: the recognition that all wills could never be superseded or eliminated, but that the same wills return in all eternity.

Charles's views, so privately recorded and not intended for publication, would be damaging to himself in their crudity … [I]t is clear that opinions were divided and feelings ran high in this united family, perhaps best explained by a divided loyalty amongst the children between the science of their father and religion of their mother; though the differences of view that existed caused no estrangement between the parents" (Darwin, *Autobiography*, 11–12). This is quoted from the Introduction, published in 1958 by Nora Barlow, the scientist's granddaughter. It was the first to include the suppressed material – seventy-one years after the *Autobiography* appeared as part of Francis Darwin's *Life and Letters of Charles Darwin* (1887)!

[25] Nietzsche had great respect for the fact that Christianity (and Buddhism) had offered the "lowly" in society a niche in a circumscribed metaphysical order and allowed them to find comfort and solace within it: "Perhaps there is nothing more venerable about Christianity and Buddhism than their art of teaching even the lowliest to use piety in order to situate themselves in an illusory higher order of things, and in so doing stay satisfied with the actual order, in which their lives are hard enough" (*BGE* 61).

[26] See the enigmatic "Epilogue of a Free-Thinker" in *GM* I, 9.

[27] "The church has always wanted to destroy its enemies: but we, on the other hand, we immoralists and anti-Christians, think that we benefit from the existence of the church" (*TI* "Morality as Anti-Nature" 3).

[28] "The spiritualization of sensuality is called *love*: it represents a great triumph over Christianity. Another triumph is our spiritualization of *hostility*. It involves a deep appreciation of the value of having enemies: basically, it means acting and reasoning in ways totally at odds with how people used to act and reason" (*TI* "Morality as Anti-Nature" 3).

Darwin's theories first appealed to Nietzsche, because they seemed to signal an "amoral" understanding of nature. Avoiding the traditional "moral" evaluative standards of "good" and "evil," Darwin promoted instead the functional criteria of "fit" and "unfit." Because he had eliminated explicitly "moral" rhetoric from his description of "nature," Darwin no longer operated within the parameters of Christian natural history. He broke with that tradition after refusing to recognize purposeful design or a benevolent Creator (and therefore the retention of absolute "moral" standards) behind evolution.

But despite his effort to work squarely within the confines of "science,"[29] Darwin could not avoid opposition to Christianity. According to his understanding of will to power and *ressentiment*, Nietzsche saw that the Darwinian will to power had to reconfigure the struggle as one between "right" and "wrong," between science and progress versus religion and obscurantism, in order to unleash (re)active energy. The traditional axis of "good" versus "evil" within Christian metaphysics had become transposed into the supporters of "truth" versus the opponents of "truth" within modern science. This transvaluation of evaluative standards meant that the sentiments of *ressentiment* could become directed against a more powerful oppositional force and thereby gain theoretical supremacy.

THE "ANTI-DARWIN(S)," 1888: AN INTERPRETATION

Nietzsche's most important published reference to Darwin appears in *TI* ("Skirmishes" 14), written in 1888. It is significant that the antagonism reflected in the "Anti-Darwin" appears in a collection that was dedicated to "sounding out idols":

This little work is a *great declaration of war*; and as far as sounding out idols is concerned, this time they are not just idols of our age but *eternal* idols, touched here with a hammer as with a tuning fork – these are the oldest, most convinced, puffed-up, and fat-headed idols … And also the most hollow … But that does not stop them from being the *most fervently believed*. (*TI* "Preface")

According to Nietzsche, the idols under review were not only "of the age, but *eternal* idols," for they resonated with particular individual wills at all "historical" times because of the physiological contingency between "idol" and believers. By including him in this collection, Nietzsche

---

[29] See Darwin's letter in footnote 22, above.

signaled that Darwin had become one such "idol," i.e. a world-historical figure that would prove "eternal" – though *not* because of some intrinsic truth-claims, but because he could "embody" and connect with the wills to power of specific, historically recurring types.

Aside from Christ, Darwin was the only other figure of historical prominence in his published work to receive the qualifying prefix "anti-".[30] In the case of *A*, Nietzsche decided to enter into a historically charged debate, which had been raging for centuries and had been defined to a large degree by the forces of ideological opposition. In other words, it had not been the historical figures such as Justinian who had bestowed the title "anti" upon themselves; instead, the "apostates" had been branded as such by Christians, who could point to explicit Bible references upon which to ground their antagonism. By bestowing the title "Antichrist" on himself, Nietzsche made a complex, multi-layered statement intentionally meant to evoke this historic struggle. In the case of Darwin and the "Anti-Darwin," Nietzsche's strategy was slightly, though significantly different. What is important to note, however, is that the title of the passage can refer only to the person of Darwin and not to his followers. Unlike the *Antichrist*, which in German refers to both Christ and his followers (*Christ* can mean "Jesus" and "a Christian"), the "Anti-Darwin" can signify only Darwin.[31]

At this point, I will examine the "Anti-Darwin" passage from *TI* ("Skirmishes" 14), incorporating insights based on the two notebook entries. All three of these passages can be considered a summation of his mature position. The published "Anti-Darwin" can be divided into three parts. In the first part, Nietzsche critiques Darwin for arguing that life reflects a "struggle for existence," when that only represents an exception. Life is not characterized by a state of need, want, or hunger, but rather by superabundance: where there is struggle, it is over power. Malthus should not be confused with nature. Next, Nietzsche states that if struggle does occur, it is not the strong but the weak that prevail. Struggle works out to the

---

[30] There is a smaller, paragraph-sized "Anti-Kant" in the notebooks (*KSA* XI, 445).

[31] In his use of "Anti-", Nietzsche was likely inspired by one of the most famous tracts of antiquity: Caesar's "Anti-Cato," as mentioned in Plutarch (*Plutarch: The Lives of the Noble Grecians and Romans*, vol. II [New York: Random House, 1992], 234). Nietzsche emphasized his rivalry but wished for it to be based on the recognition of the opponent's achievements and stature. He wished to elevate Darwin and engage with him as a serious historical antagonist, but wanted that exchange to be judged as an individual clash of personal wills. In so doing, he underscored what the ancients before the triumph of Christian metaphysics had always understood and affirmed: that personal rivalry was based on the attempt to outshine one's opponent in lived wisdom and virtue, on the ancient notion of *virtù*.

disadvantage of the strong and the privileged. Furthermore, species do not grow in perfection; rather the weak repeatedly gain dominance; they have the numerical advantage and are cleverer. Finally, Nietzsche claims that Darwin had forgotten "spirit." The weak had more spirit than the strong. It was necessary to need spirit in order to acquire it. One let it go once it was no longer necessary. By "spirit," he means "caution, patience, cunning, disguise, great self-control, and everything involved in mimicry."

In the first example, Nietzsche contrasts Darwin's "struggle for existence" with his own theory of will to power. In other words, one should not judge nature from the pessimistic perspective of an individual will ("struggle for *existence*"), but should recognize that wills (and their interpretations) clash in the here and now to maximize power ("struggle for *power*"). Though a Darwinian form of "struggle" can under certain conditions occur, it represents an "exception" – a pocket within nature as a whole. It is at most a subdivision of the larger battle for power. Malthus is not nature but a limited view *onto* nature based on the perspective of a limited type that is in fact *disadvantaged* in the overall clash of wills.

In the second part, Nietzsche takes issue with Darwin's crucial notion of "natural selection": it is not the strong and the "fit" that prevail but indeed the weak. Though this position radically undercuts Darwin's entire theory of evolution, it is entirely consistent with Nietzsche's ideas. In Nietzsche's terms, it is the weak that have the advantage in Darwinian "struggle": when all wills are seen as *equal*, the weak can project their "moral" form of will to power unimpeded. But nature is immoral and, what is more, *if it were allowed to be so*, the strong would project will to power on their own "immoral" terms. Deny the strong an outlet for their brand of "immoral" will, and the will to power of the weak can contain, overrun, and dominate the strong.

In scientific terms, Nietzsche implicates Darwin's "species" with its implied sense of development. Darwin argues that the species evolves from the basis of natural "struggle" and its outcome. "Fitter" forms arise as natural selection "acts on" individual wills. But Nietzsche sees that notion of "struggle" as an exception within the larger scope of life. According to him, there could be no development of the species as such, merely the clash of individual types. In fact, nature "favors" the weak, because they have greater fertility and can outnumber and submerge the strong.[32] An enhancement of the human type does not occur on the level

---

[32] Nietzsche had become increasingly skeptical of Darwin's central notion of "species" (*Gattung*). See my forthcoming entry for "*Gattung*" in the *Nietzsche Wörterbuch* (de Gruyter).

of the "species," but only within the confines of the individual biological will. The strong type achieves a superior instinctual hierarchy and ranking of the instincts and prevails despite obstacles to its will. Still, the achievement of "genius" remains a rarity. Not only are the odds stacked against its emergence – it must prevail against the predominance of lesser wills and their wills to power – but it also embodies a higher level of physiological complexity and instinctual extremity, where the risk of degeneration is so much greater.[33] Such a type can rarely propagate and "hold" itself, whereas the average type is by nature more fecund, more constant, and better suited to its environment.[34] By contrast, the higher type represents a biological dead end, a singular phenomenon.

Finally, Nietzsche refers to the "spirit" of the weak, which Darwin has "forgotten." This final section is somewhat obscure and has led to some interesting, conflicting interpretations. Arthur Danto criticizes Walter Kaufmann's reading, in particular his interpretation of *Geist* ("spirit").[35] Whereas Kaufmann interprets Nietzsche's use of "spirit" as a rejection of Darwin, Danto rightly sees Nietzsche's meaning in a more material, less "spiritual" sense. Nietzsche's subsequent elaboration ("what I mean by spirit") uses Darwin-inspired naturalist rhetoric to characterize "spirit," and his usage clearly undercuts and mocks the more exalted "spiritual" understanding of *Geist* within the German philosophical tradition of the nineteenth century (Hegel).

Yet, Danto believes further that Nietzsche's engagement with Darwin-inspired naturalism indicates overall *agreement* with Darwinian evolution. As a result, he fails to convey Nietzsche's ultimate disagreement with Darwin. According to Danto, Nietzsche makes

the point that "spirit" is something the herd has, but which the strong do not need, although through spirit the herd is able to triumph over the strong. Thus spirit leads to the debasement of the species. Darwin is implicitly criticized for having thought that the "better" – or the "fit" – survive when it is the "unfit" who do instead. If Darwin had not forgotten about spirit, then, he would have seen that there is no progress but a deterioration through evolution. The species gets worse and worse. This, I think is plain, is Nietzsche's point.[36]

---

[33] "The higher type represents a much higher complexity, a greater sum of coordinating elements: for that reason there is also a much greater likelihood of disintegration" ("Anti-Darwin" [*KSA* XIII, 317]).

[34] "The richest and most complex forms – and that is all that the word 'higher type' means – perish more easily: only the lowest hold on to an apparent immutability. The former are seldom achieved and stay on top with difficulty: the latter have a compromising fertility" (ibid.).

[35] Arthur Danto, *Nietzsche as Philosopher* (New York: Columbia University Press, 1965), 187.

[36] Danto, *Nietzsche as Philosopher*, 187–88.

But Nietzsche nowhere makes it plain that he concurs with Darwin's notion of evolution *or* species. On the contrary, his point is that the weak as a collective will to power have triumphed over the strong at this "historical" juncture. For that reason, the weak can no longer recognize that the weapons needed to attain supremacy in their battle against the strong (i.e. all the weapons of "consciousness") are associated with inferiority and weakness ("you have to need spirit in order to get it"). Not surprisingly, the weak can now "discover" all those characteristics exalted in the term *Geist*, because they feel themselves at the pinnacle of "civilization" and have concealed the origins of their own ascendancy. But this is not a question of either scientific progression or debasement of the "species" as such. It signifies a collective will to power that has achieved temporary supremacy through the force of interpretation. The "struggle," then, does not lead to "fitness" or "unfitness," but simply reflects a constant, always occurring, open-ended clash of individual will(s) to power.

DÉCADENCE: CHALLENGE TO THE DEGENERATIONISTS

Nietzsche's notebooks and published works in the late 1880s, as Gregory Moore states, "evince an increasing preoccupation, even obsession, with the phenomenology of 'décadence'."[37] Though he had always focused on individual wills and their physiological constitution, he increasingly incorporated expressions from the medical realm in this last phase, which added an interesting and unexpected rhetorical flourish to the final period.[38] But what were the motives behind his explicit turn to the language of the emerging biological and physiological sciences? And why did he feel the need to resort to such terminology in order to articulate aspects of his mature position?

Nietzsche's concept of decadence was inspired by a passage from a literary essay on Charles Baudelaire by the French critic and novelist Paul Bourget. Nietzsche almost exclusively used the term *décadence* rather than the German *Dekadenz* as he had in earlier texts. Moore is dismissive of

---

[37] Moore, *Nietzsche, Biology, and Metaphor*, 120.

[38] "After 1875 medical terms multiply and become the common coin of Nietzsche's writing. He no longer uses them simply to illustrate his thinking on cultural topics, such as the origin of tragic art or the dangers of an excessive preoccupation with the past; instead, matters of health and sickness become themselves a main object of his reflections, and medical or pseudo-medical categories come to furnish the very framework of his thinking. Indeed by the final stage, by 1888, one can almost say that there *are* no other topics, that the question of health has swallowed up everything else" (Malcolm Pasley, "Nietzsche's Use of Medical Terms," in *Nietzsche: Imagery and Thought*, ed. Malcolm Pasley [Berkeley: University of California Press, 1978], 136–37).

the expression's literary provenance and argues that Bourget's "importance should not be overestimated."[39] Instead, he emphasizes the late-century theorists of decadence and degeneration and their influence on his final writings. Yet, Nietzsche's borrowing of *décadence* from Bourget *is* highly significant, since it highlights his interest in the *cultural*, and far less the "scientific," resonances of the term. Nietzsche adopted the concept because he recognized its value for his project and it allowed him to tap into a discourse that had already been initiated and delineated in the literary and cultural realms. Further, it coalesced well with, and could serve as perfect shorthand for, a historical phenomenon he had been analyzing for well over ten years.[40]

The last point is above all important, because it clarifies some of the ambiguities surrounding his final rhetorical practice. As I have shown, Nietzsche had developed an original variation on Darwin's concept of struggle, whereby individual wills clash in their pursuit of power, not survival. He also premised that morality was not *a priori*, but symptomatic of a particular type of will; it was an interpretation foisted *onto* nature and not expressive *of* nature. In *GM*, he introduced the notion of active and (re)active wills and the related theory of *ressentiment*. He expanded on his earlier ideas of diverse human types and showed how those wills (re)act and interact. No longer abstract "ideal types," they were now embedded within a historical context and exhibited a motive force. Still, Nietzsche's explanation remained highly conceptual and abstract; it was expressed in generic terms such as "active" and "(re)active."

Nietzsche's subsequent incorporation of terminology from the emerging fields of the biological sciences, physiology, and psychology added a further rhetorical accent and depth to his previous analyses. On the one hand, the inclusion of such terms made his theories more "scientific" in that he could now ground them in contemporary medical practices and diagnoses. His previous conjectures about physiological wills seemed to be substantiated by "experts" in the field of physiology and medicine, which vindicated his independent line of inquiry. Even more, he could "flesh out" his earlier theories and make them more vibrant and plastic by

---

[39] Moore, *Nietzsche, Biology, and Metaphor*, 120.

[40] Campioni makes it clear to what extent Nietzsche was informed about, and engaged in, the literary-cultural discussions of Parisian decadence. In their novels, turn-of-the-century "Parisian" writers presented him with the exemplary "types" of decadence that populated modernity (*Der französische Nietzsche*, 293). Through his reading, he "received numerous creative impulses to help him describe the social crisis and the crisis in values, seeing the literary tendencies as symptoms of the more general state of health of an entire society" (*Der französische Nietzsche*, 92).

grounding them in concrete physio-psychological states; these could resonate with the reader on an actual *physical* and *sensory* level.[41] Rather than just speak abstractly about the "weak" will, he could now venture deep into its psyche, tracing its inner symptomatology – its oscillating states of fatigue, depression, resentment. In short, the terminology he gleaned from the "theorists of decadence" rounded out his profile of the weak, (re)active, (and now) *decadent* will.[42]

One crucial distinction must be emphasized. The fin-de-siècle theorists of degeneration and decadence were inspired by the "Darwinian revolution" and interpreted physiological "degeneration" as a symptom of a "natural" scientific evolutionary process; instead of emphasizing species enhancement, however, they focused pessimistically on organic *decay*. Nietzsche, on the other hand, was totally uninterested in (in fact, was radically opposed to) that angle. For him, the "scientific" terms simply added a richer explanatory dimension to his ongoing independent study of the weak, degenerate will as well as the instinctual sources of its "moral" interpretation. It was only that now he had discovered a powerful term with broad cultural resonances – *décadence* – to describe the predominance of such wills and to launch a cultural attack against them.[43]

Furthermore, the degenerationists approached examples of weak, debilitated wills from an implicit moral standpoint. Even though they no longer seemed to ground their evaluations in the traditional standards of good and evil, they continued to work with parallel notions of health, sickness, growth, and decay. They fashioned a metaphysical worldview from *random* samples of sickness, hysteria, and so forth around them. In Nietzschean terms, their instinctual pessimism directed their attention to "decline" and they developed a progressive narrative out of what

---

[41] "Nietzsche's way of writing addresses our affects, feelings, or emotions. It provokes sympathies, antipathies, and ambivalences that lie in the modern psyche below the level of rational decision and impersonal argument. I argue that this is not some gratuitous exercise in 'style' that could be edited out of Nietzsche thought" (Janaway, *Beyond Selflessness*, 4).

[42] There is also a further component of his rhetorical usage of physiological–biological terms. As Bettina Wahrig-Schmidt has shown, decadent writers of the age, particularly the French, used such terms excessively (Bettina Wahrig-Schmidt, "Irgendwie, jedenfalls physiologisch," *Nietzsche Studien* 17 [1988], 436). By incorporating similar rhetorical flourishes, Nietzsche could show that that he could "out-decadent" the decadents, even beating them at their own game. He could prove that he "knew" the decadents, that he was "onto" them, and that he could therefore speak intimately about them as an insider in their own language. See Dirk R. Johnson, "Review of *Nietzsche, Biology, and Metaphor*, by Gregory Moore," *Journal of Nietzsche Studies* 35/36 (2008), 170–73.

[43] "[A] diagnosis of the culture of his time with the goal of responding to the 'types' of decadence and initiating a counter-movement under the sign of Dionysian affirmation" (Campioni, *Der französische Nietzsche*, 331).

was an arbitrary sample of wills. Nietzsche, on the other hand, did not care to promote a master-narrative of degeneration based on "negative" evolution, but to enhance and to deepen his own independent theory of the will. What he critiqued was the weak will's efforts to create a single master-narrative out of what were individual interpretations. Though the moralism of the degenerationists was now implicit, it was inherent in their notion of health, which had become infused with the "good," whereas sickness and disease were regarded as absolute conditions equated with "evil." In short, they continued to evaluate "nature" from an unacknow-ledged *essentialist position*.[44]

THE CASE OF WAGNER: CHALLENGE TO CULTURAL DECADENCE

Nietzsche broadened his attack on cultural expressions of "decadence" in his final year. His former friend and now antagonist Richard Wagner became the centerpiece of two polemical pieces, the *Case of Wagner* and *Nietzsche contra Wagner*. Though much of the material therein came from earlier writings, Nietzsche compiled new editions to make his final polemical thrust against the Wagnerian camp. To this end, he borrowed terminology from the realm of physiology and psychology to make the case that Wagner and his followers were "decadents."

In a clever rhetorical move, Nietzsche employed the language of the "degenerationists" but only to expose them on their own terms. Whereas Wagner and his supporters accepted the "science" of degeneracy, Nietzsche made use of the terms to broaden his understanding of weak wills. For Nietzsche, a "decadent" revealed himself by adopting a "moral" perspective, an absolute perspective, from which to offer an ultimate interpretation of existence. Metaphysics and the "moral" perspective, therefore, became for him symptoms of instinctual decline. The absolutist will to power behind the Wagnerian enterprise reflected a collective instinctual insecurity. By highlighting the instinctual realities behind those wills, Nietzsche was, in effect, building a polemical case

---

[44] The original category of "degeneration" was formulated by "the devout Catholic psychiatrist" Bénédict-Augustin Morel, whose religious views clearly inspired his "scientific" reflections on human degeneration. It is not surprising, then, that (for Morel) "the human being was not the product of a gradual evolution of the species. On the contrary, modern man was, rather, the 'morbid deviation from an original type', a degenerate descendant of the Adamic *Urmensch* of Creation, and the primary cause of his *dégénérescence* – his name for the progressive process of pathological change manifested in visible and gross physical deformity – was original sin itself" (Moore, *Nietzsche, Biology, and Metaphor*, 139).

against the *historical–cultural* ascendancy of specific wills to power via the persona of Wagner.

If one fails, however, to recognize how Nietzsche manipulates language for the purpose of cultural polemics, one can be tempted to judge him on the basis of a discourse which he did not endorse. For Moore, Nietzsche reflects the symptoms of the decadent he tried to project onto Wagner:

> If we adopt a Nietzschean standpoint – that is, one that seeks to reveal the pathophysiology underlying cultural forms – then the extraordinary rhetorical performance in *Ecce Homo* deteriorates into the posturing of the hysteric; the narcissistic and self-mythologizing persona collapses into a pathological vanity and mendacity that seeks to compensate for his chronic lability; and the diversity of his narrative voice is merely the symptom of hysterical capriciousness.[45]

Yet this account fails in two significant ways. For one thing, Nietzsche did not adhere to, but subverted the "science" of degeneration Moore outlines. He also used that terminology for different ends – namely, to deepen his analysis of the "moral," weak, (re)active will, which he had explored in various permutations throughout his mature career. Second, Nietzsche had pre-empted that fairly obvious line of critique – that he was a decadent by his own definition – by unmasking himself as a type of decadent. *EH* famously opens with Nietzsche revealing the constitutional weakness he had inherited from his father and his numerous relapses into decadence.[46]

In contrast to his targets, though, Nietzsche *accepts* his instinctual inheritance and neither tries to conceal it or fight against it, but to affirm and make the best out of it. This position is the opposite of that of the degenerationists. The latter qualify a "degenerate" will in absolutist, i.e. "scientific," terms and from a position of alleged "health," and they then judge that will on the basis of its inheritance, while suggesting the impossibility of escaping one's biological legacy. From their perspective, an absolute notion of sickness or health is (pre)determined from an essentialist point of view. Nietzsche, however, adopts a *relative* standpoint and biological perspectivism.[47] Health and sickness represent parts of a single physiological continuum, or cycle, and are not static or starkly opposed,

---

[45] Moore, *Nietzsche, Biology, and Metaphor*, 191.

[46] "A long, all-too-long succession of years meant recuperation for me, – it also unfortunately meant relapse, decay, the period of a type of decadence" (*EH* "Wise" 1).

[47] Unlike many of the decadents, who tended to evaluate the symptoms of degeneration purely in a negative light and as examples of cultural decline (Campioni, *Der französische Nietzsche*, 317), Nietzsche recognized the great *promise* that resided in instinctual destabilization and confusion (Campioni, *Der französische Nietzsche*, 314).

but reside as potentialities in every human. In such terms, "true" health emerges from a deeper awareness of the cyclicality of health and sickness and the way that diverse perspectives arise from fluctuating individual psychological and physiological states of awareness.[48] The "truly" healthy do not fight against recurrences of decadence, which are inevitable (particularly in the modern era), but accept them as part of the human condition. For that reason, the eternal return becomes the signature of a higher type; with it he acknowledges the (instinctual) cyclicality of life and affirms it in eternity. He also recognizes that attempts to resist one's (physiological) predicament would just be a further extension of decadence.[49]

But Nietzsche's final position here is only recognizable if one accepts his mature anti-Darwinism. The latter has two central components. First, it rejects evolution as a sense of human progression along a single evolutionary continuum: a heightening of the type occurs only within the type, not between or across wills. Correspondingly, a decline of the type ends with the type. This alone undermines the theory of degeneration at its core. Second, there can be no absolute "scientific" standards of degeneration and decadence, i.e. "negative" evolution, only theories from the perspective of an individual will. Instead of wills superseding each other along a single continuum, all wills and their interpretations clash in the eternal here and now. The preponderance of degenerationist theories does not indicate the inherent "truth" of those theories; it merely signifies the preponderance of wills with those interpretations. In the end, Nietzsche did not engage with cultural decadence from a position of theoretical superiority, i.e. from a position of evolutionary "science," but had rather entered into the *agon* as a personal will to power in order to do battle against other wills.

NIHILISM: WILL TO NOTHINGNESS

Like Darwin, Nietzsche focuses on individual wills; but instead of endorsing the vision of an indifferent natural "struggle," he distinguishes between active and (re)active wills. As inextricable parts of organic nature, all wills have to be active to some degree. However, Nietzsche's "active"

---

[48] "[T]he *great health*, a health that one doesn't only have, but acquires continually and must acquire because one gives it up again and again, and must give it up!" (*GS* 382).

[49] "Philosophers and moralists are lying to themselves when they think that they are going to extricate themselves from decadence by waging war on it. Extrication is not in their power: what they choose as a remedy, as an escape, is itself only another expression of decadence" (*TI* "Socrates" 11).

will can project its instincts "immorally" and its will to power is a direct and affirmative expression of its instincts. It is a will at one with nature because it *is* nature; it expends itself beyond "moral" categories and its "natural" rivals are other, like-constituted types.

The dark side of Nietzsche's vision relates to that *other* will – the (re)active will, the one who suffers from the actions of the overpowerful in nature and who cannot compete with them on equal terms. (Re)active types represent the collateral damage of the strong wills' assertive encroachments. In *GM*, Nietzsche shows how the "immoral," though entirely "natural" behavior of the strong had formed a pocket within "nature." This shadow-world emerged as a consequence of the strong's actions in nature, and it was peopled by "lesser" wills who could not assert their will on equal terms (*GM* II, 16). These wills are not truly "active" but (re)active, since their outer-directed energy has been thwarted back against the self through the actions of superior warrior hordes (*GM* II, 17).

Two characteristics define such a weak will. First, it must discharge energy like all wills; however, it can only do so if it first defines an "immoral" target that will allow it to expend its power in "good conscience." At the same time, the weak individual does not feel better after such expenditure of energy but still feels fatalistic and suffers the pain inflicted against the self (*GM* III, 20). The "moralization" of conflict may allow (re)active energy to be temporarily discharged but cannot uproot the core suffering. Second, the metaphysical perspective can give *meaning* to its otherwise absurd-seeming suffering (*GM* III, 17). It allows the weak self both to feel "good" about its fractured will and to release its energy in "good conscience." It can help the weak will to find its place in a "moral" world order and offer it an interpretation from its own point of view, even if that meaning must distort nature at its core to provide consolation. In short, the metaphysical perspective both justifies the (re)active will's existence and gives it a *modus operandi* for its (re)actions.

The phenomenon of nihilism is the corresponding *interpretative product of such instinctually confused and debilitated wills.* The nihilistic interpretations of life born from the perspective of suffering wills challenge all positive and affirmative expressions of existence, because such wills can numerically overrun nature with the projection of their own suffering. Their interpretations "moralize" nature to such a degree that they ideologically negate all "natural" (rarer) expressions of affirmation.[50] The

---

[50] Nietzsche focused increasingly on "nihilism" during his final years, particularly in his notebooks from 1887–88, including his famous discussion on the subject, the "Lenzer Heide" fragment of

preponderance of "moral" wills thus leads to a spread in nihilism – more specifically, interpretations by individuals incapable of expressing will to power affirmatively. As a result, active wills that create their own values based on affirmative power projection become surrounded by the preponderance of nihilistic interpretative wills.[51]

Moreover, (re)active wills are not entirely passive; that would be physiologically impossible, for a self-negating (ascetic) will remains a will – *even if it wills "nothingness"* (*GM* III, 28). Such wills are still "in" nature even while operating from "outside" nature. They can dominate the environment through the force of "moral" interpretation. *Nihilism is the "activity" of "moral" wills via interpretation.* In fact, the interpretation that such suffering types promote is a further means to express their will to power – *without the need even to exert "active" will.*

Nietzsche arrived at this final position by radicalizing Darwin's notion of wills competing in nature. For him, it was impossible to offer a total vision of nature from a position outside of nature, for each will was both a part of it, bound to it, as well as physiologically invested in it. "Nature" "acts" continuously through the instincts. Darwinism offered an explanation for conflict, but its notion of struggle was based on the (re)active energy of weak wills and did not recognize the force of its own will to power via interpretation. Darwin's "science" diminished *active* human energy, rendering anonymous and insignificant the will to power of each individual within the larger scope of "nature." While turning a blind eye to individual actions, Darwin recognized their outcome as a working out of "natural struggle." But in Nietzsche's terms, an active will "consciously" identifies with and affirms its own will. It asserts its power "immorally," "beyond good and evil," and accepts the consequences of its actions; even more, it lives according to the principle of the eternal return of the same.

The phenomenon of modern nihilism defined the historical situation of wills that could not affirmatively identify with their actions and must interpret them "objectively" and beyond their control. A "nihilist" resorts to impersonal (e.g. natural or historical) forces and the "laws of nature" in order to *conceal* its "actions" to itself. He validates his own *inability* to act

---

1887 (*KSA* XII, 211–17). However, for all the times he mentions "nihilism" – eighty-one times in total in the published works and the notebooks (almost exclusively in the final two years) – he refers to it only twelve times in his published works, with the majority of references in *GM* (seven times). The reason this is relevant is that it shows that his "theory" of nihilism was intimately linked to the notion of nihilist *wills*, i.e. to the actual *physiology* of nihilism. The "theory" of nihilism derived from his exploration of weak wills and their turn to nihilist perspectives.

[51] In *GM* III, 26, Nietzsche despairs of modern culture's wide range of nihilist wills *and* the varied permutations of their nihilist worldviews.

by promoting an "objective" view of nature which relativizes and judges human behavior according to outcome (except for "immoral" behavior, which he still condemns). The scientific nihilist both "actively" targets active will via the force of interpretation and sanctions his own brand of (in)"action" by deflecting attention away from the self and towards "natural" processes outside the self. If one were to express it in "moral" terms, the nihilist "absolves" his own brand of will to power by fatalistically accepting the "natural" inevitability of "impersonal" events.

CONCLUSIONS

In his final four years, Nietzsche intensified his opposition to Darwin. While his level of critique became more explicit in *BGE*, it culminated the following year in *GM*. Nietzsche started singling out Darwinian perspectives, though he still subordinated them under a generic "English philosophy." In 1888, however, Nietzsche published one explicit reference, the "Anti-Darwin," and delineated further aspects of his position in the notebook entries from the same year. He had begun to bring to the fore his direct opposition to Darwin himself, not only his followers.

His decision to personalize his opposition was contingent on several factors. First, it was derived from his theory of the master and the collective will, a corollary to the will to power. Throughout the middle period, Nietzsche had focused on individuals who exemplified a collective instinctual reality. Skeptical of the "genius," Nietzsche showed how the "great man" reflected the instinctual reality of his time. The "genius" was the "idol" of his age, through which the collective could realize its will. Second, Nietzsche developed his "practice of war," which is best articulated in his notion of the *agon*. Through singling out the main representative, he could most easily focus attention on the collective will and could engage in an attack without allowing empathy or personal animosity to intrude into the exchange.

In his final year, Nietzsche once more expanded and supplemented his analysis of the weak "moral" will by incorporating terminology drawn from the fields of physiology, psychiatry, biology, and medicine. He became preoccupied by the theories and theorists of decadence and degeneration and the question of the debilitated will. His interest, however, lay not in "degeneration" as such but how the phenomenon reflected the cultural reality of his time. By using the "scientific" tropes of degeneration against its supporters, particularly the followers of Wagner, who were instinctually drawn to them, he rhetorically turned the tables on

them. While the latter adhered to the "scientific" standards of degeneration, which they extracted from the theory of evolution, Nietzsche
approached their theories as symptoms of their own underlying instinctual degeneration.

Finally, Nietzsche spoke increasingly of nihilism, which became his
shorthand for the predominance of "moral"-based interpretations. Here,
nihilism reflected the weak wills' need to believe in master-narratives
of existence in response to internalized cruelty and suffering. Through
such interpretations, they could make sense of, and release, will to power
in "good conscience." In his belief that something "higher," "fitter"
arises from "struggle," Darwin too embraced a variant of nihilism. For
Nietzsche, on the other hand, the projection of will to power was an end
in itself, with nothing higher or superior emerging from struggle. In the
final analysis, the only thing that arises from the conflict of weak wills
was a metaphysical interpretation of existence.

PART II

Nietzsche's Genealogy of Morals

CHAPTER 4

Nietzsche's "nature": or, whose playing field is it anyway?

GM I is steeped in controversy. Fraught with terms such as the "blond beast" and terminology such as Aryan versus Jews, Rome versus Judea, the essay contrasts the Jews, the original race of resentment, with the aristocratic warrior castes, the immoral "beasts of prey." These associations have led some commentators to connect his philosophy with Nazism, and they continue to prevent an adequate assessment of his thinking. But such interpretations overlook a crucial fact: that the central argument of the first essay serves one larger purpose – and, indeed, it is the main purpose behind all three of the essays – and that is to question Darwin's theories of "moral" development and the origins of morality proposed by his many genealogical followers. The historical context of this work must guide our attention to its meanings. Rather than isolate and highlight controversial terms, one must re-embed them into the larger sustained argument of *GM* I as a whole. After all, Nietzsche makes his objective clearer in *GM* than in any other work: subtitled a "polemic," it targets the "English psychologists" and their genealogical methodology in relation to the question of morality.

ENLIGHTENMENT DEBATES ON "NATURE"

The entire argument of *GM* I subverts the unspoken Darwinian assumption that we can agree on a scientific definition for the "state of nature" and that this definition will apply to all organisms. Darwin's attempt to define "nature" according to the principles of "struggle," "competition," and "survival of the fittest" reveals this inherent bias. He does not treat the "state of nature" as an individual perspective on "nature"; instead, random, brutal struggle becomes *the* "objective" assessment of the "natural state." Darwin here continues with a particular strand of Enlightenment thought, which had defined "nature" along similar lines – most influentially, Thomas Malthus's *On the Principle of Population* (1798), the main intellectual inspiration for his theory of "natural selection."[1] Malthus had written his tract in response to the French Utopian Condorcet and the English anarchist William Godwin, who both believed that "nature" exhibited a certain bias towards perfection:

In the late 1790s Thomas Robert Malthus was the Anglican parson of a small country church … At some point he and his father got into a friendly argument over the future course of society. Daniel Malthus followed the French thinkers Condorcet and Rousseau and the English anarchist William Godwin in the conviction that society was on the path toward "perfection". Political, social, and scientific developments were opening new avenues of advancement on all sides, and the further progress of mankind seemed virtually assured. This buoyant prospect, however, the younger Malthus could not bring himself to accept.[2]

Certainly, Malthus's work, too, can be considered a polemic. But its great success resided in its ability to ally with the standards of science and thereby to undermine more effectively the credibility of its opponents:

The language of science and logic permeates the *Essay*, … in the abundance of biological examples that enrich the argument at every turn, and in the repeated invocations of the name, authority, and method of Sir Isaac Newton. Malthus works hard to convince the reader that his conflict with Godwin is one that pits "facts" against "speculation", "science" against "fantasy". If in the process he can ally himself with the revered author of the *Principia Mathematica*, and simultaneously tag the speculations of Godwin as akin to the "wild speculations and eccentric hypotheses of Descartes", so much the better.[3]

Its full title was "An Essay on the Principle of Population, as it Affects the Future Improvement of Society, with Remarks on the Speculations of Mr. Godwin, M. Condorcet, and Other Writers," and it challenged the liberal-progressive "speculations" of French thinkers in particular. The early nineteenth-century "state of nature" debate was divided between Rousseau's Romantic notion of man's fall from a "pure," natural state and a more pessimistic Hobbesian assessment. Ever since the eighteenth century, interpretations had circled around these two hidden axes.

Some commentators have argued that Darwin's depiction of nature conveniently mirrored the conditions of a triumphant capitalism in early

---

[1] "Malthus's law of population in human society legitimized the idea of a *law* of struggle throughout living nature, impressed Darwin with the intensity of the struggle, and provided a convenient mechanism for a *natural* analogue to the changes which he was studying in the selection of domesticated variations" (Young, "Darwin's Metaphor," 452).

[2] T.R. Malthus, *An Essay on the Principle of Population*, ed. Geoffrey Gilbert (Oxford: Oxford University Press, 1993), viii.

[3] Malthus, *Principle of Population*, x.

Victorian England. The similarities between early capitalist society and Darwin's vision are not coincidental, they argue, but reflect society's willingness to equate "natural struggle" with competition in the economic domain. Not surprisingly, Malthus represents the focal point behind this controversy. The question is, in brief: to what extent can Darwin's view of "nature" be considered objective science, if he received his theoretical inspiration from a partisan political tract?[4] The heat of the controversy stems most of all from the implicit challenge to scientific "objectivity" as such. But there is another dimension as well. As Robert Young has implied, Darwin's biology could be taken as a transfigured vision of a clearly political – in this case, capitalist – view of reality. Karl Marx's ambivalent response to the *Origin* is an interesting case in point. Marx praised Darwin's vision as a clear-eyed and "objective" view of man, an important forerunner and scientific corollary to his own brand of "scientific" economic history, while objecting to its association with Malthus's abhorrent capitalist views.[5]

GM is Nietzsche's "contribution" to this already well-established debate. However, it does not follow the traditional trajectory of interpretation. Instead, his text undercuts eighteenth-century assumptions about "man" and "nature" – both the Utopian strand of that thought, exemplified by Rousseau's notion of the "noble savage," and the "pessimistic" legacy of the "English school," represented by Hobbes, Malthus, as well as Darwin himself. Although Enlightenment discussions involved conflicting views, none of the thinkers seriously questioned that one could establish an "objective," "scientific" view of both "man" and "nature," i.e. some universally accepted standard. Even more critical members of the tradition – Marx and Rousseau, for example – believed that it was possible to determine a single, unchallenged standard. If it were not for current institutional and political conditions, one could gain a clear, unprejudiced insight into the "objective" relationships between man, nature, and the state.

Nietzsche broke with the tradition. The insight that drove a wedge between him, his predecessors, as well as his contemporaries was the "will to power." Nietzsche's will to power premised that one could not establish

---

[4] Robert Young and Gavin de Beer represent opposite poles on this issue. According to Young, de Beer "persistently attempted to isolate Darwin's thinking from the ideological context of the period by denying the crucial role of Malthus's theory" (Robert Young, "Evolutionary Biology and Ideology: Then and Now," *Science Studies* 1 [1971], 202).

[5] Robert Young, "Malthus and the Evolutionists: The Common Context of Biological and Social Theory," *Past and Present* 43 (1969), 138.

a single, all-encompassing standard, since interpretations of nature and man were based on the instinctual reality of the individual will. The vision of nature that a particular will promoted could never be an object-ive, exclusive, and exclusionary system, but could only describe the condi-tions allowing for the optimal projection of will. If a single standard *were* at any point to prevail, it would express a *temporary* balance in favor of the historically predominant constellation of wills. It would represent an underlying *physiological correspondence of types.*

TWO "NATURES": THE WARRIOR AND THE PRIESTLY CASTES

In *GM* I, Nietzsche presents a unique perspective on "man's" prehistory, which rests on a distinction he draws between strong and weak wills. Illustrating the distinction historically, he selects two hypothetical "pure" types, or physiological paradigms, which he settles in separate, distinct, and clearly demarcated "natural" arenas. On the one side are the warrior castes, or aristocrats and nobles, "the noble, the mighty, the high-placed and the high-minded, who saw and judged themselves and their actions as good, I mean first-rate, in contrast to everything lowly, low-minded, common and plebian" (*GM* I, 2). Their sole obligation was to themselves, their tribal unit, and to the warrior ethos that distinguished them.

On the other side were the priests of the Old Testament. Belonging to the highest rank in what was originally a priest-dominated social order, these types differentiated themselves from the rest of society on the basis of their priestly rituals and functions and their distinctions between "pure" and "impure" habits. One should not take the latter terms too symbolically, Nietzsche suggests, but should reduce them to their most basic *physiological* constituents: "From the outset the 'pure man' was just a man who washed, avoided certain foods which cause skin complaints, did not sleep with the filthy women from the lower orders and had a hor-ror of blood, – nothing more, not much more" (*GM* I, 6).

His "historical" analysis is intentionally oversimplified – for example, he omits any references to the commercial classes or anything else that might have stood between these two paradigms – because Nietzsche is interested in establishing one central point: namely, that the two extremes existed in entirely different "natural" circumstances and had distinct requirements in early *pre-Christian* history; and that the best terms for their survival depended on diverse, conflicting physiological–biological realities.

The early warrior castes maintained a high state of health and physicality in order to remain in a state of readiness for military conflicts. As a result, they valued hunts and all types of athletic and competitive contests (i.e. the *agon*): "The chivalric-aristocratic value judgments are based on a powerful physicality, a blossoming, rich, even effervescent good health that includes the things needed to maintain it, war, adventure, hunting, dancing, jousting and everything else that contains strong, free, happy action" (*GM* I, 7). But the priestly caste avoided such conflicts, for they undermined their precarious existence and constitutional well-being: "The priestly-aristocratic method of valuation – as we have seen – has different criteria: woe betide it when it comes to war! As we know, priests make the most *evil enemies* – but why? Because they are the most powerless" (*GM* I, 7).

In *GM* I, Nietzsche draws a clearer distinction between strong and weak wills by focusing on two "historical" prototypes – the pre-civilized "Aryan" warriors and the caste of early Jewish priests: "In my *Genealogy of Morality* I introduced a psychology of the opposing concepts of *noble* morality and *ressentiment* morality" (*A* 24). For the first time, he creates a vibrant historical tapestry, which lends motive force to the previously *static* concepts of strong and weak wills, and he illustrates how the interactions between the two forces propelled "history" in a certain direction as a result of their respective instinctual inheritances.

But how does he further distinguish between the two opposing forces? That is, how does the specific "(pre)historical" context deepen his insights into strong and weak wills, and what does that awareness say about his position on Darwin? For it must be re-emphasized that the "historical" analogy in *GM* I does not serve external purposes, i.e. either as a means to romanticize and glorify warriors *per se* or to disparage Jewish priests, but the larger, self-stated internal goal of challenging Darwinist views on nature, man, and evolution.

CHARACTERISTICS OF THE STRONG WILL IN "PREHISTORY"

With the term "strong," Nietzsche signifies the will's successful coordination of the instincts. The strong and active will identifies with its instinctual mastery and affirms it through power projection – though not necessarily against a specific, opposing entity. In *GM* I, Nietzsche excavates the "historical" origins of this strong will – its prehistory.

The original strong types were neither worthy of imitation, nor positive examples. Designated by Nietzsche as "beasts of prey," they inhabited a terrible, cruel, remote, and blood-drenched "age of Bronze." They were archetypes of a bygone era, "cold, cruel, lacking feeling and conscience, crushing everything and coating it with blood" (*GM* I, 11). In that sense, they served a similar function to that of the Homeric heroes for their fifth-century Athenian "descendants." Achilles's warrior exploits, for example, were not meant to incite war and aggression within the parameters of Greek civilization but instead represented certain distilled and aesthetically transposed "warrior virtues" that could instruct later audiences. To prevent false identification with this era and its norms, Nietzsche stresses the lack of correspondence – in a physiological, historical, or political sense – between the pre-civilization "Aryan" warrior class and modern Germans (*GM* I, 11). Between the modern world and the pre-civilized origins of the warrior and priestly castes there existed a decisive, complete, and final rupture. Nietzsche's analysis of the two prototypes serves *an explanatory function*. Like Darwin, he situates his presentation in a paradigmatic, indeterminate pre-civilization. It is his "naturalist" counterpoint to Darwin's conjectures about man's development from prehistorical origins.

The fact that Nietzsche concentrates on the noble warriors' physicality, strength, prowess, and courage has led some to assume that he prizes those "virtues" in themselves – that is, a strong type must exhibit physical strength or reckless courage. But certainly, no form of modern, "civilized" existence could match those ancient warriors in sheer physicality; nor does Nietzsche think it desirable. For him, the archaic "Aryan" warrior hordes were *sui generis*. They were "historical" paradigms – as far removed in time and spirit from any form of modern physiological and spiritual reality as nineteenth-century Christians and Jews were removed from ancient Christian sects and Jewish priests.

In fact, Nietzsche relegates the warriors to the *second* social stratum in his account of the "natural" hierarchy of Manu: "*The ones who are second*: these are the custodians of the law, the guardians of order and security, these are the noble warriors, this is above all the *king*, as the highest formula of the warrior, judge, and preserver of the law" (*A* 57). The "spiritual" leadership he places at the top: "The highest caste – which I call the *few* –, being the perfect caste, also has the privilege of the few: this includes representing happiness, beauty and goodness on earth" (*A* 57). The social hierarchy of Manu had only emerged centuries *after* "pre-civilization" warrior hordes had solidified and codified the foundational superstructure: "[A law book like that of Manu] summarizes the experience, shrewdness, and experiments in morality of many centuries, it draws a conclusion, nothing more" (*A* 57).

NIETZSCHE'S RELATION TO NINETEENTH-CENTURY RACIAL ICONOGRAPHY

Nietzsche's discussion of an "Aryan" type and "blond beast" raises the important question of how some of his ideas might align with the racial iconographies of his time.[6] Certainly, his former association with Wagner and the Bayreuth circle helped him gain insight into the background literature and thinking of the anti-Semitic movement. He also knew of the anti-Semitic activities of his sister, Elisabeth, and her husband, Bernard Förster, who had moved together to Paraguay to found an "Aryan" community based on eugenic principles.[7]

Weaver Santaniello has written extensively on Nietzsche's ongoing battle against late nineteenth-century German anti-Semitism. She argues that scholarly reception tends to downplay or conveniently ignore the lonely position that Nietzsche upheld in the battle *against* the followers of this movement.[8] According to her, Nietzsche knew their literature, but in many decisive points challenged their governing assumptions. Even though he seemed to argue at times on the basis of their positions,

---

[6] Detlef Brennecke challenges the myth that Nietzsche sympathized with the Germanic ideologists, though he shows how the trope of the "blond beast" nevertheless resonated with their racial and nationalistic doctrines. Nietzsche's intentionally provocative and unguarded use of such terms put him at risk of appearing to support theorists whose ideas he decisively opposed (Detlef Brennecke, "Die blonde Bestie: Vom Missverständniss eines Schlagwortes," *Nietzsche Studien* 5 [1976], 123–24).

[7] "The antisemites surrounding Nietzsche include his sister Elisabeth, a vile Christian anti-Semite; her husband Bernhard Förster (the son of a Protestant pastor) who, along with Elisabeth in 1866, cultivated a human breeding colony in Paraguay devoted to Aryan racial purity; Nietzsche's former mentor and ultimate foe, Richard Wagner, with whom Nietzsche broke mainly because of his anti-Jewish racism; Adolf Stöcker, the celebrated pastor and leader of the Lutheran state-church in 19th-century Germany; the (anti-Christian) anti-Semite Eugen Dühring, who was the first to preach Jewish extermination and who is now regarded by historians as the first 'proto-Nazi'; and the Christian theologian Ernst Renan, a leading proponent of the Aryan myth in France who later became an almost-official ideologist of the Third Reich" (Weaver Santaniello, "Nietzsche's *Antichrist*: 19th-Century Christian Jews and the Real 'Big Lie'," *Modern Judaism* 17 [1997], 166).

[8] "Nietzsche's stance has led most commentators to interpret his negative evaluation of Judaism in light of the fact that Judaism gave birth to Christianity, which is his major enemy; others simply to dismiss his views as contradictory; and yet others to grossly distort Nietzsche's texts" (Weaver Santaniello, "A Post-Holocaust Re-Examination of Nietzsche and the Jews: *Vis-à-vis* Christendom and Nazism," in *Nietzsche and Jewish Culture*, ed. Jacob Golomb [London: Routledge, 1997], 24).

his perspectives subtly undermined them from within.[9] The Wagnerians clearly understood these rhetorical maneuvers and were infuriated with his apostasy.[10] But by interpreting *GM* and *A* as, in effect, *anti*-anti-Semitic tracts, she reinserts Nietzsche into the polarized racial debates, which his ideological opponents had themselves spearheaded. This strategy has allowed his works to be discussed on their rhetorical terms. Thus she fails to draw attention to other, farther-reaching philosophical implications of the texts, which challenge the anti-Semitic movement at a far deeper level.

Much more than contemporary expressions of anti-Semitism, *GM* targets the theoretical foundations of Darwinism. Just one of the many implications of this challenge is – *by extension* – Nietzsche's subversion of anti-Semitic doctrines, since the latter received legitimacy and credibility from Darwin's theories. Put bluntly, without Darwinism, racial theorists could never have developed ideologies of Aryan supremacy. It was through creative readings of Darwin that turn-of-the-century anti-Semites could place "traditional" anti-Judaic prejudices, previously founded on religious differences, on scientific *racial* underpinnings.[11] What was before just "intuition" or cultural distinction could now become ideology based on indisputable scientific "fact."

Nineteenth-century "racial science" attempted to establish biological categories of "racial purity," the purest of which was the "Aryan," and to equate "racial purity" with superior "morality" *per se*. Nietzsche rejects both positions. First, he strenuously denies the existence of racial "purity" as such as well as its inherent desirability. Indeed, *GM* I exposes the continuous intermingling of races, castes, and peoples since ancient

[9] Babette Babich also discusses some of *GM* I's controversial passages in her study of Nietzsche's nuanced use of aphorism. She argues that his language seductively draws the anti-Semitic reader into the text, but then makes him complicit in his own anti-Semitism (Babette Babich, "The Genealogy of Morals and Right Reading: On the Nietzschean Aphorism and the Art of the Polemic," in *Nietzsche's On the Genealogy of Morals*, ed. Christa Davis Acampora [Lanham, MD: Rowman & Littlefield, 2006], 183–84).

[10] "The Nazis did not 'like' Nietzsche, they were repulsed and enraged by him precisely *because* he upheld the Jews and dared to defy many intellectual forerunners of the Third Reich" (Santaniello, "A Post-Holocaust Re-Examination," 42).

[11] In *Hitler's Willing Executioners* (New York: Knopf, 1996), Daniel J. Goldhagen stresses the continuity of German anti-Semitic thought, above all in its transition from the anti-Judaic Christianity of the pre-modern period to the racialized anti-Semitism of the post-Darwin era. Though I agree that the former served as the fermenting ground for the latter, it is indisputable that Darwin's evolutionary theories, so widespread in late nineteenth-century Germany, transformed latent anti-Semitic sentiments into eliminationist racial programs based on "respectable" eugenic principles (see above all Weikart, *From Darwin to Hitler* and Stone, *Breeding Superman*).

times – and *at all times*; for Nietzsche, there has never been such a thing as "pure" blood.[12]

Second, he does not equate racial "purity" with higher "morality"; nor is he interested in showing how the "Aryans" embody a superior "morality." He is extremely critical of the Northern (so-called "Aryan") "races," precisely because they could *not* perceive and shake off the "moral" deception impressed upon them by the weak. Consequently, Christianized "Aryans" could become the "moral" vanguards of an expansionist Christianity throughout Europe. Their failure to recognize the deception proves that they were ultimately not "strong" in Nietzsche's deeper understanding of the word:

The fact that the stronger races of northern Europe failed to reject the Christian God does not say very much for their skill in religion, not to mention their taste. They really *should* have been able to cope with this sort of diseased and decrepit monster of decadence. But they were damned for their failure: they brought sickness, age, and contradiction into all of their instincts. (*A* 19)

Nietzsche uses the then *en vogue* term "Aryan" very much *against* its "standard" nineteenth-century racial usage in order to unfold his alternative, contrary typology.[13] For him, "Aryans" represent the *pre*-"historical" warrior castes.[14] They do not embody a superior "morality" based on "racial purity" but, on the contrary, a *non*-"morality" – an outer-directed,

---

[12] Instead, Nietzsche believes a "race" can only *become* "pure," which occurs rarely (*D* 272); this, however, has nothing to do with "blood" and "genetic" properties, but with the ability of a people to fashion themselves into a successful unity and separate identity out of the storehouse of their conflicting instincts and biological traits. It is therefore not a genetic or physiological predisposition but an effective willing – a working on the self on the level of the drives to construct a creative unity. For a fuller discussion of Nietzsche's complex understanding and usage of "race," see Schank, *Rasse und "Züchtung"*.

[13] In some ways, I reject the idea that a "standard" racial iconography existed in the late nineteenth century, which has gained some currency in academic scholarship, e.g. Marc Weiner, *Richard Wagner and the Anti-Semitic Imagination* (Lincoln: University of Nebraska Press, 1995). Nietzsche's acute sensitivity to the undercurrents of his time allowed him to recognize that a potent brew of anti-Semitic prejudices was emerging on the basis of disparate racial theories. Thus, many of the racial theories which he picks up on (and which were reflected in *GM*, particularly *GM* I), were still disconnected, fragmented, and "in the air"; it is only in retrospect that we can appreciate Nietzsche's perspicacity in detecting the formation of what was later to become a coherent ideology.

[14] Of course, Nietzsche's list of "blond beasts" does not even prioritize the Germanic peoples, but equally includes the Roman, Arabian, and Japanese nobility as well as the Homeric heroes, to whom blondness could hardly be attributed (*GM* I, 11). Schank also notes that Nietzsche's etymological approach in *GM* I focuses almost exclusively on Greek words and states of mind (and further, Roman–Latin ones), not those derived from the Germanic peoples. In contrast, for H.S. Chamberlain, the master theoretician of Aryan supremacy and intimate member of the Wagnerian circle, the present-day German peoples were the "exemplary Aryans" (Schank, *Rasse und "Züchtung,"* 273).

affirmative warrior existence "beyond good and evil." In their original "natural" realm, their behavior was not proscribed by any notion of "morality" whatsoever, but reflected an aggressive, outer-directed energy beyond "morality." On the other hand, the Roman under-classes reflected a "moral" outlook on "nature" that was a product of their "natural" surroundings, for they had been subjected into the confines of civilization by more powerful, "immoral," outer-directed wills.[15]

Yet, Nietzsche does seem to agree with and adopt certain racial assumptions and historical perspectives of his time that now seem suspect and spurious – for example, his categorization of the prehistorical warriors as "blond" and the indigenous, eventually conquered peoples as "dark"; or his conviction that the original Celts must have been a blond race (*GM* I, 5).[16] But here again he does not associate light-hued characteristics with superior "morality." Hair color as a "racial" signifier is insignificant and non-consequential for his overall argument. Rather, he employs these fairly common distinctions of the time to indicate the complete historical isolation (perhaps even in a "racial" sense) of two contrasting *types* of existence: a "pure" (blond) warrior existence (beyond "morality") and a "pure" "moral" one – above all, the early Jewish priests.

Of course, by arguing that the eventual intermingling of strong and weak types within civilization did not produce a "fitter" type, but, on the contrary, the predominance of a weakened *Christian* will, Nietzsche not only challenges the myth of Aryan racial supremacy (premised on the intrinsic "racial" purity of the "Aryan" German). At a more fundamental level, he undermines the assurance of a Darwinian genealogical theory based on natural selection: the clash of distinct human types has not yielded a "fitter" human, but the predominance of a debilitated one cut off from "nature" and crippled by the instinctual anarchy introduced and continually imposed by the "moral" perspective.[17]

---

[15] Nietzsche discusses this point further in *GM* II.

[16] Brennecke suggests that Nietzsche might have acquired such racial perspectives from Count Gobineau, the most prominent early theorist of racial inequality, though Gobineau accentuated white skin tone rather than blondness to designate the "Aryan" type (Brennecke, "Die blonde Bestie," 117–18).

[17] Indeed, Nietzsche indicates that the danger to culture resides in the *unsuccessful* "domestication" and assimilation of the "Germanic type" into civilization, so that the former "beast" has not become heightened or ennobled but, on the contrary, instinctually disoriented and debilitated. As a result, his previous "savage" tendencies are only hidden under the veneer of "civilized" values, ready to be unleashed against "moral" enemies in "good conscience." The characteristic of "blondness" might indicate some form of "racial" lineage going back to an earlier Germanic type, but it certainly no longer has intrinsic positive value or any relevance to the present-day instinctual reality of the modern German.

THE STRONG TYPE WITHIN CIVILIZATION

For Nietzsche, the body is the sole source for an active, instinctual, outer-directed, affirmative life. He does not value the contentiousness, the cruelty, the hot-headedness, and the intense physicality of early warriors. He praises the late *spiritual* inheritance of aristocratic forms of existence when the original physicality of the warriors has become refined and "sweetened" within a noble valuation system. The latter respects the instinctual basis of social and personal interactions as well as the boundaries between distinct types and castes (*Pathos der Distanz*). Over time, the spiritual and athletic *agon* replaces the brutal and destructive clash of individual wills, and the strictures of courtly love replace the violent outbursts of the passions.

Nietzsche often emphasizes the brutal sides of the roving warrior hordes; but also the fact that the terrible and violent aspects of their essential nature, so horrible to others in war, were counterbalanced by positive virtues among themselves:

Here there is one point we would be the last to deny: anyone who came to know these "good men" as enemies came to know nothing but *"evil enemies"*, and the same people who are so strongly held in check by custom, respect, habit, gratitude and even more through spying on one another and through peer-group jealousy ... they are not much better than uncaged beasts of prey in the world outside where the strange, the foreign, begin. (*GM* I, 11)

The virtues that nobles exhibit among themselves in later stages of civilization eventually became synonymous with nobility itself: "that everywhere, 'noble' 'aristocratic' in social terms is the basic concept from which, necessarily, 'good' in the sense of 'spiritually noble', 'aristocratic', of 'spiritually highminded', 'spiritually privileged' developed" (*GM* I, 4). They were also the virtues adopted in social and familial exchanges with *like-spirited peers*: "consideration, self-control, delicacy, loyalty, pride and friendship" (*GM* I, 11). Although the historical patrimony of these virtues has long been forgotten or concealed, it is a testimony to their resilience that, despite being uprooted from their historical context and social origins, they continue to serve as *non*-aristocratic imprimaturs of individual character.

Nietzsche's key emphasis throughout is on the passions – both unleashed (violent) and controlled (refined). The warrior existence demanded spontaneity and direct, powerful passions – "a daring charge at danger or at the enemy, or those frenzied sudden fits of anger, love, reverence, gratitude and revenge by which noble souls down the ages have recognized one another" (*GM* I, 10). Ancient warriors required that instinctual reserve, for they had to act with strong, spontaneous instincts to excel in combat against other strong types. Breeding proceeded along those lines: physical qualities were valued that reflected and perpetuated the warrior existence. Later aristocratic cultures eventually built further on the successes of their ancestors and developed more refined versions of those *same* instincts: a higher, keener level of control; superior internal coordination – and *not* suppression or denial – of strong, passionate impulses. While early tribal units had, perhaps, combated and destroyed each other by squandering their outer-directed energy, superior, more successful units had learned to regulate and control their instinctual reserve. Through active contests, agonistic games, and courtly rituals, they learned to maintain and harness outer-directed energy, ennobling it and preventing it from breaking out against other strong types.

NIETZSCHE'S "BLOND BEASTS": THE TRAGIC VERSUS THE PESSIMISTIC REVISITED

What about Nietzsche's infamous "blond beasts?" Once uncaged, "they enjoy freedom from every social constraint, in the wilderness they compensate for the tension which is caused by being closed in and fenced in by the peace of the community for so long, they *return* to the innocent conscience of the wild beast" (*GM* I, 11). Barbarian behavior "in the wilderness" is the instinctual corollary to those virtues nobles exhibit in more codified social relations with one another. The key phrase here is: "they *return* to the innocent conscience of the wild beast." The pre-civilized warrior castes are distinguished, and forever removed from, the modern era through their ability to enter back into the innocence of their warrior-conscience. Within their tribes or aristocratic class, strict norms keep their outer-directed energies in check. In combat, however, the same types have no "conscience" in projecting unharnessed energy against other strong types equally equipped in the active warrior spirit. Their refined interaction among peers in society and their violent aggressive warrior spirit in combat are opposite sides of the *same* coin.

The combative activities of the "blond beasts" in "nature," however, do not reflect a "struggle for existence." By detailing their conquest and carnage in almost exhilarating language, Nietzsche works to counteract the impression of a Darwinian "struggle," for the latter term would be too prosaic, too pessimistic. It suggests *conscious* oppositional energy: one engages in "struggle" in order to survive, to prevail. Nietzsche's more pro-vocative account emphasizes the reverse: not struggle, namely, but rather the entirely "unselfconscious" (*unbedenklich*), i.e. "natural" assertion of will to power. Here, it is irrelevant whether one survives.

Darwin's notion of "struggle" versus the "will to power" reintro-duces Nietzsche's distinction between the tragic versus the pessimistic. Nietzsche identifies with the former (which he variously refers to as the Dionysian or *amor fati*), while he characterizes the Darwinian vision as pessimistic, at times nihilistic. The tragic embodies the awareness that, in conflict with equal forces, the release of strong, active energy ultimately results in death and destruction, the inevitable result of a combative war-rior ethos. The conflict and its consequences do not lead to improvement or progress – either for the individual, the family, or the tribe. On the contrary, they could lead to extermination, enslavement, and the death of loved ones. The tragic reflects insight into the extreme capriciousness of existence and the fact that life and nature do not favor the survival of individual will, but can condone, and seem indifferent to, unjustified annihilation. This recognition does not produce pessimism or resentment against life, though, but tragic affirmation of the same.

Darwin's "nature" also recognizes the dark sides of existence, and he strives to incorporate them into his vision. His "struggle for existence" and "survival of the fittest" acknowledge and try to do justice to the very same realities. Both thinkers return to earliest recorded "history," man's pre-civilization, and attempt to make sense of the same historical evidence, much of which had begun to surface in the nineteenth cen-tury. Darwin, though, comes to different conclusions. His pessimism attempts to reconcile "nature's" brutal realities with a consoling belief in the superior "reason" reflected in evolution: "from the war of nature, from famine and death, the most exalted object which we are capable of con-ceiving, namely, the production of the higher animals, directly follows."[18] Darwin could not explain the horrors of man's prehistory, and its seem-ingly senseless exterminations, unless there was inherent sense; this he develops *within* his notion of the "fittest." Regardless of the conflict and its ("moral") outcome, evolution produces a more "perfect" type: "as nat-ural selection works solely by and for the good of each being, all corporeal and mental endowments will tend to progress toward perfection."[19]

Nietzsche counters Darwinian pessimism with his understanding of the tragic. The Dionysian vision Nietzsche fashions in opposition

---

[18] Darwin, *Origin*, 396.   [19] Darwin, *Origin*, 395.

to nineteenth-century pessimism does not justify or extol violence and bloodshed *per se*, but challenges contemporary efforts to relegate brutality to man's prehistory and to portray current civilization as an improvement or higher "moral" state. For Nietzsche, modern expressions of pessimism were a faint-hearted reconciliation with the tragic and senseless aspects of existence and with the eternal return of the same. By stating that the warrior hordes would, at times, *return* to the "innocent conscience of the wild beast [*die Unschuld des Raubthier-Gewissens*]" and engage in ruthless, bloody combat, he does not encourage a return to that barbaric state[20] (which would be impossible in any case, since there was the intervention of two thousand years of "moral" history and the Christian conscience separating man from his "animal" "ancestors"). He aims to emphasize that in the pre-"moral" phase of man's history, i.e. pre-Christianity, the strong could assert will to power actively and *without* recourse to "moral" justification or need to point to a higher, more perfect, more "moral" outcome to justify their actions. The strong simply sought out the strong: "For he insists on having his enemy to himself, as a mark of distinction, indeed he will tolerate as enemies none other than such as have nothing to be despised and a *great deal* to be honoured" (*GM* I, 10). Conflict did not have a "moral" bias, for strong "immoral" wills do not need to moralize, idealize, or distort conflict in order to project power in *innocent* conscience.

With the subsequent triumph of Christian morality in the interim, man's violent urge has not been suppressed in the least. It has merely been channeled into a moralized good–evil dichotomy, whereby one's aggressions can now *only* be released by targeting *immoral* opponents: "[The man of *ressentiment*] has conceived of the 'evil enemy', '*the evil one*' as a basic idea to which he now thinks up a copy and counterpart, the 'good one' – himself" (*GM* I, 10). To release the *same* violent ruthless nature – for Nietzsche sees *no* physiological progression or evolution, *no* historical "improvement" here, in relation to the past – "moral" man must first determine a metaphysical opponent to assuage his own "*bad* conscience." Pessimism reflects the reconciliation with modern forms of conflict *as well as* the internal justification for them.

---

[20] "The view dies hard that what Nietzsche really wanted was a new barbarism, a return to the nobles of the first essay and that 'disgusting procession of murder, arson, rape, and torture' at which the 'splendid *blond beast*' excels" (Aaron Ridley, *Nietzsche's Conscience* [Ithaca, NY: Cornell University Press, 1998], 128).

THE "MORAL" DEVELOPMENT OF MANKIND

Nietzsche's vision of "nature" undermines any Darwinian outlook for a progression or moral improvement in mankind. For Nietzsche, "strong" is a constant, a physiological essence, and does not represent a stage in man's "historical" development. Quite simply, it is impossible for the strong to be anything but strong: "as though there were an indifferent substratum behind the strong person which had the *freedom* to manifest strength or not" (*GM* I, 13). Like Darwin, Nietzsche places a historical break between those early warrior types and modern man. Both thinkers also acknowledge that many of the early tribal units and the conditions for their existence were exterminated through encroaching civilization. While for Nietzsche, this development occurred with the triumph of Christianity (*A* 22), Darwin implies that internal tribal cohesion, peaceful relations, and cooperation ultimately proved more effective than warfare, thereby producing "fitter" types in relation to changed conditions.

In Nietzsche's view, however, the destruction of the conditions for the outer-directed warrior existence – its so-called "environment," to use a Darwinian term – in no way eradicated the strong will. The strong will is a fundamental, ineradicable essence. Modern civilization merely reduces the "outside," the "wilderness," to which the pre-Christian warriors return in the "innocent conscience of the wild beast." Instead, the strong defines itself in successive generations by retaining its affirmative spirit even through fluctuating unfavorable "environmental" conditions. The strong does not seek a return to some idealized version of the past but remains always in its present.

Darwin, on the other hand, remains puzzled by the seeming incongruity between the decline and demise of warrior values and the emergence of more peaceful, "moral" qualities that had evolved out of prehistorical conflict. It was difficult to explain how the best warriors with the noblest virtues (qualities such as loyalty, courage, manliness) would be the likeliest to perish in battle while arguing that supposedly "fitter" qualities had developed from "natural selection":

He who was ready to sacrifice his life, as many a savage has been, rather than to betray his comrades, would often leave no offspring to inherit his noble nature. The bravest men, who were always willing to come to the front in war, and who freely risked their lives for others, would on average perish in larger number than other men. Therefore it seems scarcely possible (bearing in mind that we are not here speaking of one tribe being victorious over another) that the number of men gifted with such virtues, or that the standard of their excellence, could be increased through natural selection, that is by survival of the fittest.[21]

If those virtues were positive – and Darwin does not in principle deny this – and if they were necessary to preserve the tribe in the "struggle for existence," then how could it be less likely, as a result of high losses in battle, to pass them on? Could it be (in seeming conflict with natural selection) that tribal members who were less courageous, less concerned about the welfare and security of the community, but more likely to survive, had yielded the "fittest"? Darwin explains the contradiction in part by suggesting that the altruistic virtues had proven *more effective* in broader struggle, since they had resulted in superior tribal cohesiveness: "When two tribes of primeval man, living in the same country, came into competition, if the one tribe included (other circumstances being equal) a greater number of courageous, sympathetic, and faithful members, who were always ready to warn each other of danger, to aid and defend each other, this tribe would without doubt succeed best and conquer the other."[22] Darwin argues further that "there is another and more powerful stimulus to the development of the social virtues, namely, the praise and blame of our fellow-men."[23]

The problem was that Darwin had to find a way to reconcile his admiration for the warrior ethos with his awareness that their virtues could not prevail, thus could not be considered "fitter" in accordance with natural selection. He even defends spontaneous behavior against people who only consider deliberate and reasoned actions "moral": "I am aware that some persons maintain that actions performed impulsively ... do not come under the dominion of the moral sense."[24] At the same time, Darwin believes that man can *aspire* to "moral" actions through praise, emulation, experience, repetition, and habit,[25] which he can subsequently pass down through inheritance. He even suggests that "moral" actions so attained might be *superior* to "noble" actions impulsively done: "He who is forced to overcome his fear or want of sympathy before he acts, deserves,

---

[21] Darwin, *Descent*, 163.   [22] Darwin, *Descent*, 162.
[23] Darwin, *Descent*, 164.
[24] Darwin, *Descent*, 87. It seems strange to even argue such a position: it would appear that individuals who do "good" actions spontaneously should have greater reason to be considered "moral" than those who first have to convince themselves. But this just shows how far nineteenth-century "morality" had become a product of "rational" reflection, so that one could only be considered "moral" if one's mind wrestled with "moral" choices.
[25] In the *Autobiography*, Darwin repeatedly emphasizes the importance of approbation and praise in the development of morality, particularly in the development of his own "moral" personality (*Autobiography*, 82).

however, in one way higher credit than the man whose innate disposition leads him to a good act without effort."[26] Thus Darwin reintroduces previously rejected notions of Lamarckian inheritance in order to explain why natural selection might not work so smoothly in the human realm. If one could *become* "fit," then pass that inheritance on to subsequent generations, one could at least explain how one notion of "fitness" (acquired through habit and repetition) could branch off and compete with other standards.

In *GM* I, Nietzsche takes the opposite position. The strong are *the others* – those who perform noble actions spontaneously and without rational calculation, both in the "wilderness" *and* within "civilization." The members of a tribe that achieve morality through deliberation and utilitarian practices are the ones Nietzsche denigrates. For him, the weak assume for themselves the mantle of "morality," because they cannot embody the spontaneity of the strong, cannot compete on their terms, and are too far removed from the higher realm of "nature" and the form of combat that define the strong. Rational deliberation in the Darwinian sense is already an example of physiological degeneration. It describes a biological will unsure of itself, instinctually insecure, torn between reason (deliberation) and instinct (action). Such wills perceive "morality" as a cure and anchor against instinctual decline when it just manifests another form of decadence: "Extrication is not in their power: what they choose as a remedy, as an escape, is itself only another expression of decadence – they *change* the way it is expressed but do not get rid of the thing itself" (*TI* "Socrates" 11).

Nietzsche's theory of strong will circumvents Darwin's dilemma. If the strong is a qualitative essence and always the "fittest" (and *not*, as Darwin suggests, the outcome of an evolutionary process over time), then the *same* virtues admirable in the warrior could be the origin for the "noble" instincts of generosity, gentleness, respect for friends and enemies, loyalty, and pride. These two systems of values were not in conflict with one another or chronologically successive, but existed side by side and originated in distinct physiological realities. Thus, the refined, distilled essence of the strong remains intact *even with* the decline of the warrior existence and his "environment". Furthermore, the "positive" virtues that define the early warriors could remain synonymous with virtue itself *even with* the extermination of the "pre-civilized" warrior conditions and the rise of an oppositional set of Christian "moral" virtues.

[26] Darwin, *Descent*, 88.

ORIGINS OF THE "MORAL" WILL

After he has defined the strong will, both "in the wilderness" and in its
social interactions with like-spirited peers, Nietzsche turns to the weak
"moral" will. He locates its origins among the pre-Christian Jewish
priests. Here, too, Nietzsche is less interested in presenting an objective
picture of the "Jew" in "history" – as little as he is in defining the "aristocrat," "the warrior," "the Aryan" – than he is in contrasting a warrior-
inspired valuation system (strong) and one inspired by the priesthood
(weak).[27] Or, stated in other terms: good and bad (*gut und schlecht*) versus
good and evil (*gut und böse*). His interest in the historical Jews and their
(priestly) values is related to his broader questions in *GM* I and the text as
a whole: what does the introduction of the Jewish-derived "moral" code
do to the interpretation of "nature," more specifically, to the projection of
interpretations into "nature"? And how do Darwinists inherit this specific
legacy?

According to Nietzsche, the early Jewish priests were significant
because they responded to "nature" in a way contradicting all previous
outer-directed forms of *active* existence:

They defined themselves in *opposition* to all the conditions under which peoples
so far had been able to live, had been *allowed* to live, they created for themselves
a counter-concept to *natural* conditions, – they took religion, cults, morality,
history, and psychology, and twisted them around, one after the other, to the
point where they were in irreversible *contradiction to their natural values*. (*A* 24)

An explicitly non-warrior caste, the priests established authority over
their people through the force of social exclusivity and stewardship over
laws, which they interpreted and embodied. Their rule and authority did
not derive, as had been entirely "natural" until then, by projecting power
in direct combat with others, but by focusing attention *away* from physical conflict – an area where they could not compete – and towards an
arena in which they alone could command respect and gain mastery: the

---

[27] In *GM* I, Nietzsche focuses primarily on the Jewish priesthood, because of its significant role in
the subsequent emergence of historical Christianity. In *GM* II and III, however, he goes further
back into human anthropology and discusses the priestly caste in more generic terms; there he
rarely mentions a Jewish connection. His main interest is to define the "priest" as *type*; as he
emphasizes, it can occur in all times, places, and, above all, among all peoples. In these two
essays, he shows how the "priest" as type set the stage for the eventual "slave revolt" in morality
presented in *GM* I. Whereas the Jewish priesthood was crucial for the development of historical
Christianity, the priesthood as an instinctual caste had long before prepared the ground for the
asceticism out of which one dominant strand (namely, Christian values and perspectives, but *also*
modern science) was eventually to grow.

observance of strict habits and ascetic ritual practices. But the priesthood first had to devalue and deprioritize other competitive interpretations of "nature." They had to overturn the standard valuations that *naturally* derived their intrinsic authority and respect from an exposure to, and immersion in, active life.

What is interesting about Nietzsche's analysis is that he reduces priestly authority to just another expression of will to power. Their status does not derive from any higher "moral" authority *per se*; or from the intrinsic superiority of a priestly existence over a warrior one; or from a "moral" one over an "immoral" one. The priests' actions were a self-conscious, entirely "natural" response to a predetermined *physiological* condition; in short, they had no choice: "From the very beginning there has been something *unhealthy* about these priestly aristocracies" (*GM* I, 6). They made their ascetic life-choices in response to their own physiological realities – more precisely, to their states of physical *degeneration*. Though these choices might have seemed logical in themselves – they experimented with ascetic cures to help find a way out of feelings of sickness, inferiority, weakness, resentment, and impotence – their practices only exacerbated their preternaturally weak constitutions: "[B]ut as for the remedy they themselves found for their sickness, – surely one must say that its after-effects have shown it to be a hundred times more dangerous than the disease it was meant to cure? People are still ill from the after-effects of these priestly quack-cures" (*GM* I, 6).

As a consequence of misguided "cures," they intensified the cycle of resentment, hatred, and life-denial; and from these resentment-filled sentiments – that they began to direct against existence itself – "morality" was born. Everything and everyone that reminded them of their own weakness and inferiority – all expressions of health, activity, superabundance, and energy – fomented their hatred and were thus deemed "evil": "one should ask *who* is actually evil in the sense of the morality of *ressentiment*. The stern reply is: *precisely* the 'good' person of the other morality, the noble, powerful, dominating one, but re-touched, re-interpreted and reviewed through the poisonous eye of *ressentiment*" (*GM* I, 11). The priests' acetic way of life and *inability* to act, in turn, was transfigured into the "good."

At this point, Nietzsche treats the ancient Jewish priesthood as a distinct typology and caste and shows how they responded to their instinctual reality and surroundings. For the Jewish priests, the best means of preserving their existence and exerting their intrinsic form of power was to concentrate on their well-being and to keep potentially dangerous intrusions into their life to a minimum. Furthermore, their actions also proved to be an effective will to power over a dispersed "race" that had no other form of political leadership. Even if Nietzsche believes their response to their conditions was misguided and ultimately debilitating, he accepts it as the weak type's "logical" means to gain mastery over instinctual anarchy.

TRIUMPH OF THE "MORAL" WILL THROUGH THE COLLECTIVE WILL OF CHRISTIANITY

Nietzsche's original interest in the physiological roots of the secondary, derivative "moral" perspective shifts, expands, and deepens when he begins to chart the triumph of this shade of will to power via a metaphysical interpretation of all existence in the guise of an expansionist Christianity: "We know *who* became heir to this Jewish revaluation" (*GM* I, 7). Here, Nietzsche's concentration on the historical Jewish priesthood subtly transfers to his much more important argument: the "historical" impact of the weak type through the legacy of a Christian collective will. The weak "actively" step into "world history" and in conflict with the nobles and their valuation system when they convert what was originally a *particular* physiological response to natural and biological conditions by Jewish priests into a *complete* (re)active interpretative force, Christianity, which can then "actively" target and challenge all forms of spontaneous, outer-directed existence: "The instinct of *ressentiment* said no to everything on earth that represented the *ascending* movement of life: success, power, beauty, self-affirmation; but it could only do this by becoming ingenious and inventing *another* world, a world that viewed *affirmation of life* as evil, as intrinsically reprehensible" (*A* 24).

Ressentiment at this point becomes a *creative* (re)active force, expressed through a collective will to power, and not merely a localized resentment or unique response to physiological symptoms: "The 'bad' of noble origin and that 'evil' from the cauldron of unassuaged hatred – the first is an afterthought, an aside, a complementary colour, whilst the other is the original, the beginning, the actual *deed* in the conception of slave morality" (*GM* I, 11). Through the spirit of *ressentiment*, weak wills can establish their own competitive, parallel set of values, enshrined in a "moral" valuation system, which can then assume "active" momentum by "(re)acting" against all forms of active existence, now deemed "immoral."

The key insight here is that interpretations of life and nature are not unchanging and static, i.e. "moral" or "immoral" as such, but are direct, relative extensions of one's physiological inheritance. Christian religion, like ancient Jewish morality and Buddhism, has no spiritual value for Nietzsche other than serving as a window into an underlying instinctual reality. Christianity expanded not because of any higher "moral" legitimacy or inherent superiority, but because a majority confluence of wills in the form of a collective will to power could direct the spirit of *ressentiment* against a more powerful force (the Roman state), branded *in toto* as "immoral": "The Christian movement, being a European movement, was from the very start a whole movement of rejected and dejected elements of every type: – they want to gain power through Christianity. They do *not* express the decline of a race, they are an aggregate of decadent forms from everywhere, who look for each other and huddle together" (*A* 51). Christianity could become, and continue to be, the higher interpretative paradigm, the historical metaphysics, for that confluence of (re)active wills.

Christianity succeeded, Nietzsche is emphatic to point out, because it represented the majority (instinctual) will and the strength of numbers, *not* because of its "moral" message or because of the "moral" corruption of the Roman upper classes. The latter interpretation in particular, he complains, was endemic among historians of antiquity:

[The Christian movement] was *not* (as is commonly believed) the corruption of antiquity itself, of the nobles of antiquity that made Christianity possible: we cannot be harsh enough in opposing the scholarly idiocy that continues to maintain these ideas even today. At the point when Christianity was spreading among the sick, corrupt, Chandala classes throughout the whole *imperium*, the *counter-type*, the nobility, had assumed its most beautiful and mature form. The great numbers gained control; the democratism of the Christian instinct had *won*. (*A* 51)

The latter situation once again reflects will to power. As Nietzsche sees it, this ancient historical conflict was a subtle clash of distinct physiological types whose will to power was articulated via interpretation. Whereas the will to power of the Roman elite was immortalized *within* ancient political institutions, the will to power of the under-classes was directed *against* the foundations of the Roman *imperium* via its "unnatural" bifurcation of the realms of (worldly) "power" and (transcendental) "morality."

Both Nietzsche's "Aryans" and his Jewish priests represent distinct historical typologies. Eventually, the large majority of people living within the Roman empire adopted some form of Christian perspective through the spread of Christianity (particularly among the "barbarian" elements) via Roman civilization and intermarriage. Within a newly Christianized

Europe, there was then little further historical association with either the pre-Christian form of warrior existence or with the ancient Jewish faith of the pre-Christian era. Nietzsche's focus then shifts to the larger question of the weak versus the strong, for Christianity is merely the historical cloak under which this eternal clash of wills occurs: "The two *opposing* values 'good and bad', 'good and evil' have fought a terrible battle for thousands of years on earth; and although the latter has been dominant for a long time, there is still no lack of places where the battle remains undecided" (*GM* I, 16).

Both strong and weak wills have little to do with the original warrior or priestly forms of existences, except for that fact that the strong originally prioritized a physical, active, outer-directed life and tragic outlook, while the weak embodied resentment and a rejection of life expressed through a dichotomized pessimistic interpretation of existence (traditional metaphysics). Yet, Nietzsche adds a further dimension in the present Christianized context. The strong continue to embody active, affirmative will; but they are also physiologically and spiritually strong enough to overcome the "moral" valuation introduced and continuously imposed by the majority of weak wills. They do not oppose or attempt to eliminate the weak, for this would imply an acceptance of conflict on their terms. Rather, the strong continue to assert their power actively without seeking out "moral" opposition. The introduction of the "moral" valuation and the weak type into "history" – "history" itself is a metaphysical construct from the perspective of the weak – has, in effect, changed the nature and quality of the strong. Now it is the ability of the strong to avoid the conflict of weak wills which determines an important aspect of their strength.

A further distinction of the strong within a Christianized context is their ability to see behind metaphysical constructs and their basis in human physiology and to recognize life as the clash of individual wills to power. They recognize in these interpretations the attempt to undermine the strong will, to draw it away from the self and against the self into a fictitious, instinctually debilitating "moral" conflict.[28] "Morality" is one of the means by which weak wills draw the strong into conflict; it

---

[28] Ridley supports the common perception that the strong types are essentially "stupid," which is why the "clever" could triumph over them (Ridley, *Nietzsche's Conscience*, 131–32). (This perspective, it seems, derives from a simplistic projection of current notions of what it signifies to be "strong" – physiological strength, athleticism, perhaps a certain lack of intellectual curiosity and "culture" – into the Nietzschean notion of a strong type, whereas the "intellectual" is seen to be the more "clever" – as though Nietzsche were speaking of "jocks" versus "nerds"! In a

is their own brand of will to power. Instead, the strong assert their will as an expression of their individual form of existence, while they respect other wills as the extension of an alternative instinctual reality (*Pathos der Distanz*). They accept the clashing of wills and interpretations as an inevitable consequence of biologically diverse types, who promote the best conditions for their own form of existence.

The weak will, too, takes on additional characteristics within a Christianized context. Though the resentment of the physiologically compromised Jewish priests was originally directed against life itself, resulting in the transvaluation of "nature" within Jewish religion, this individual resentment only became "active" through the spirit of Christian *ressentiment*. This interpretational will to power could then challenge and undermine all expressions of active will. Just as kindness, openness, candor, generosity became the purified essence of strong wills, so *ressentiment*, originally embodied in Christianity's "good versus evil" distinction, became the signature essence of the weak.

CONTRASTING VIEWS OF "HISTORY"

The "historical" narrative in *GM* I challenges Darwin's worldview in two important ways. For one, it undermines Darwin's genealogical method. At first glance, this claim may appear absurd, since Nietzsche also seems to promote a straightforward genealogical narrative to explain how "morality" had emerged from natural sources. But his account must be linear only because "moral" wills have succeeded in

similar vein, Richard Rorty considers Nietzsche's bellicose masters as "narcissistic and inarticulate hunks of Bronze Age beefcake" [quoted from Mark Migotti, "Slave Morality, Socrates, and the Bushmen: A Reading of the First Essay of *On the Genealogy of Morals*," *Philosophy and Phenomenological Research* 58, no. 4 (1998), 754. First, the primitive strong types were not amoral dimwits in Nietzsche's view, but the more "complete men" (*die ganzeren Menschen*) (*BGE* 257). For them, there was no rupture between strength and spirit: a heightened spirit was matched by a higher level of physicality. Through their original activities in "nature," these types created the foundational infrastructure for all future "historical" development. Second, the reason that strong wills can easily fall victim to the weak is that the strong tend to ignore and disregard the weak and avoid their "moralized" conflict: they are more interested in affirmative power projection and the creation of values. They are not on the same page as the weak and are for this reason often misunderstood and more easily manipulated. Finally, in times of historical decline and decadence (i.e. the periods when the "weak" have the upper hand: they have greater strength in numbers) the strong go "underground": not allowed to project affirmative strength outward, their strength retreats into the depths: "the creative spirit who is pushed out of any position 'outside' or 'beyond' by his surging strength again and again, whose solitude will be misunderstood by the people as though it were flight *from* reality –: whereas it is just his way of being absorbed, buried and immersed in reality" (*GM* II, 24). This intrinsic strength of the strong is then misinterpreted by others as mildness or appears as a certain naïveté.

imposing a "narrative" structure onto what is, for him, an entirely random, open-ended process.[29] In order to break out of the constraints of such an evolutionary account, one must first locate how the original "moral" form of narrative could triumph and come to be considered the only acceptable one.

At a more profound level, Nietzsche's "narrative" of strong versus weak wills denies the linearity of "history" at its core. While the genealogists believe that history exhibits an intrinsic progressive momentum, Nietzsche's will to power challenges that assumption. History does not reflect any form of causal progression; rather, various wills to power clash in the eternal here and now. It is only the success of weak wills which has allowed their reading to dominate. The current numerical advantage of weak wills has effectively destroyed the instinctual (*and* institutional) basis for the strong will, allowing the "moral" interpretation of the weak to succeed.

Nietzsche's "narrative," in effect, operates on two tracks: it unravels the linear development of the "moral" interpretation of "history" imposed by the weak and exposes the type of will that lays concealed behind the triumphant moral perspective. According to Nietzsche, the "moral" will must be, by necessity, an "historical" actor, that is, an individual invested in the struggle he "objectively" narrates. He must, by nature, be a (re)active will, even if that "action" is articulated *through* interpretation, for there can never be a "disinterested" depiction of nature: man *is* nature and continuously expresses "nature" in all his actions.

Darwin and the genealogists, on the other hand, assume that it is possible to place oneself outside of "(natural) history" and to describe the development of "nature" from a scientifically objective standpoint. Even if one can no longer believe that morality has a transcendent, immutable foundation, one must still be able to trace the development of morality within "nature." Nietzsche's will to power implies, in contrast, that there can be no single origin, because morality is a projection of will to power onto nature; there can be only individual clashing wills and interpretations. If there were an attempt to create a single "historical" trajectory of "morality," it is because specific (moral) wills seek to embed (their) "moral" interpretation into nature.

---

[29] This accounts, in part, for the meandering, open-ended "narrative" structure of *GM*, which does not aspire to establish a traditional cause-and-effect schema of historical development.

In the Preface, Nietzsche modestly stresses that his views on morality are only "hypotheses" (*GM* "Preface" 4). With this he suggests that
there can be no single correct hypothesis, because as living beings we are
invested in our positions and articulate our will to power even through
our interpretations. It has only become necessary to explicate the question of the "moral" perspective, i.e. its origins and development, because
the collective will to power of the weak has succeeded in establishing its
parameters of ("moral") interpretation. But the strong will, according
to Nietzsche, stands outside traditional morality and does not even care
about the question – or, at least, only to the extent that it impinges on or
attempts to curtail its own brand of power. For the strong will, "nature"
is essentially "immoral" and must express active, outer-directed will. The
strong does not recognize any (moral) development within "history," only
the clash of individual types.

Nietzsche also claims that the genealogists lack the "historical spirit"
(*GM* I, 2). For Nietzsche, "history" reflects will to power articulated in
the here and now. When a genealogist writes on "history," therefore, he
must by nature "actively" be taking part in the "historical" process he
"dispassionately" narrates; he must, by nature, be taking sides *through*
writing, because he is by necessity a (re)active agent. The "historical" process which the genealogists unfold cannot, according to the will to power,
be a disinterested account of an objective historical process; it must reflect
the will to power of a specific type that imposes its will through interpretation *in* history; that interpretation, in turn, reveals the "nature" of the
instinctual will.

GM represents an alternative form of historical "narrative." It does not
aspire to historical "objectivity," for that is neither possible nor desirable
in Nietzsche's view. Instead, it reflects a *Nietzschean* will to power that
actively seeks to engage with the passions and wills of other historical
agents in the here and now. In other words, *GM* is a highly subjective
polemic that *intends* to confront the triumphant will to power concealed
behind the "moral" interpretation. Thus, Nietzsche's project is less an
attempt to be an objective natural history of morality, a pure genealogy, than a *Tacitean–Sallustian* brand of history, which treats "history"
as an open-ended, ongoing account of competing wills and continuous
struggles. While the actors in the historical pageant constantly change,
the types behind them remain constant, returning in endlessly diverse
"historical" permutations. History here is not a dead text, but the living
embodiment of clashing and personally invested wills.

CONTRASTING PLAYING FIELDS

GM I also undermines Darwin's understanding of "nature." I will use an analogy to illustrate the contrast. While Darwin assumes that "nature" is an interpretational constant, to which all scientists will adhere, Nietzsche argues instead for competing "natures" – that of the weak and that of the strong. Darwin assumes a single playing field, for which "nature" establishes the rules; players are equals; and the one who emerges from "competition" constitutes the "fittest." Though Darwin repeatedly asserts that greater fecundity, i.e. success in leaving behind more progeny ("Growth and Reproduction"), determines the "fittest," he has no illusions that the creation of those conditions – namely, the existential ability to leave behind the most progeny on which selection can "act" – presupposes "fitness": one cannot leave behind progeny if one has been eliminated from competition.

If in each grade of society the members were divided into two equal bodies, the one including the intellectually superior and the other the inferior, there can be little doubt that the former would succeed best in all occupations and rear a greater number of children … Hence in civilized nations there will be some tendency to an increase both in the number and in the standard of the intellectually able.[30]

Nietzsche assumes countless playing fields; players are not equals; and each one asserts its own rules and optimal conditions, and locates the players to compete against. "Nature" is not a single, unified arena, but a multitude of overlapping playing fields, where each party attempts to project will to power according to its own rules and specifications. But the survivor of this "conflict" does not represent the "fittest." "Nature" is oblivious to the outcome of "struggle"; it only "recognizes" competing wills, and it remains neutral to both the outcome on the individual playing fields as well as in their overlap.

In Nietzsche's system, the strong do not engage on the playing field of the weak and vice versa. If the weak were to enter into conflict with the strong on their terms, and play by their rules, they would perish. For this even to occur, however, the weak would first have to understand, accept, and enter onto the type of playing field, which the strong affirm and promote. But this would be impossible, for the weak cannot understand or accept those conditions, that is, they cannot grasp a form of "nature" that

---

[30] Darwin, *Descent*, 171.

lies beyond their own *single* playing field. They can only grasp one playing field, *their own*, where the rules and conditions are set by "nature" itself.

Correspondingly, the strong cannot compete on the playing field of the weak, for the intrinsic character of their affirmative, outer-directed instincts cannot be brought to bear in that form of "nature." However, in attempting to define the rules for all, the weak seek to engage everyone according to their own rules. They do not recognize intrinsic differences (wills to power) in players. Further, they judge victory on their playing field, based on rules that they have imposed, as an indication of "fitness." Yet, this "fitness" only accords to standards that they themselves have defined and enforced. By asserting the best conditions for their own survival, i.e. by setting the rules for a single playing field, it is not surprising that they judge victors in their "struggle" to be "fittest" – they emerge "fittest" from their own brand of "struggle."

The will to power, the *Übermensch*, and the eternal return circumscribe the parameters for the playing field of the strong. Here, there is no "competition," no sense of "fittest," because the domains of the weak and the strong are not in opposition; they are not in competition. They exist side by side; at times, they overlap. The strong seek to project power actively and affirmatively, but according to their own rules and on their own playing field – *as do all individual wills*. With the terms "competition," "struggle," and "survival of the fittest," however, the weak attempt to engage everyone on their own playing field. The latter terms are part of the means to achieve this end. By singling out strong types, forcing them to compete on their terms and not acknowledging the existence of distinct, non-overlapping playing fields, the weak attempt to eliminate distinctions and force everyone to play by their rules. To feel "good" about "competitive" instincts, they must distort and moralize "struggle" to eliminate "competitors" in "good conscience." After all, the single playing field of "nature" determines "survival of the fittest."

In the end, despite his attempts to affirm the eternal return, which demands that one must accept even the return of the "last man" in all eternity, Nietzsche at times despairs of the triumph of the collective will of the weak, for they have succeeded in cutting off strong types from their natural arena and the source of their affirmative energy and have turned them into forlorn figures on the vast, single playing field of the weak:

[G]rant me just one glimpse of something perfect, completely finished, happy, powerful, triumphant, that still leaves something to fear! A glimpse of a man who justifies man *himself*, a stroke of luck, an instance of a man who makes up for and redeems man, and enables us to retain our *faith in mankind*! ... For the matter stands like so: the stunting and levelling of European man conceals *our* greatest danger, because the sight of this makes us tired ... Today we see nothing that wants to expand, we suspect that things will just continue to decline, getting thinner, better-natured, cleverer, more comfortable, more mediocre, more indifferent, more Chinese, more Christian ... The sight of man now makes us tired – what is nihilism today if it is not *that*? (*GM* I, 12)

CONCLUSIONS

Darwin's "nature" presupposes a linear, even progressive momentum. Although the idea that Darwin intended evolution to be understood in the sense of "progression" has been called into question in recent years, he clearly sees evolution as linear in its most basic requirements – that is, with "fitter," "more perfect" variations emerging from conflict. Nietzsche's "struggle" (or more specifically, his random clash of wills) is open-ended, with nothing superior at all emerging. In most cases the strong perish.

For Darwin, "fitness" is relative. Hesitant to assign specific character traits or qualities to the term, Darwin purposely leaves it open, pliant, and functional: "fittest" is simply the variation that leaves the most off-spring on which the selective process can act. Whatever variation survives the ensuing competitive struggle, Darwin deems the "fittest." For Nietzsche, however, "strong" is a physiological constant, regardless of survival or annihilation.

As for their characterizations of "nature," Darwin assumes a pessimistic tone. "Nature" is portrayed as dark, brutal, and competitive. His pessimism is somewhat alleviated by his insight into the evolutionary process as a whole, where "things most wonderful evolve and are being evolved." Thus, "nature's" seeming indifference to struggle is compensated for by natural laws, which select the "fittest." In contrast, Nietzsche's nature is tragic. Nature is supremely indifferent. Strong and weak wills both perish at random, and nature is oblivious to the outcome of any form of "struggle." No value can be assigned to nature; no judgments for or against life can be considered valid as such. Judgments are relevant only as a means to interpret perspectival will to power.

Darwin's "nature" exhibits conflict and competition, necessary preconditions for evolution. Stasis exists nowhere; change, flux, movement, adaptation everywhere. For Nietzsche, nature "reveals" will to power. That will is either outer-directed, affirmative, seeking to maximize power and the conditions for its own existence (strong); or it is oppositional, (re)active, and resentful, directed against all forward-moving, active existence (weak). Conflict occurs at the interstices of these two wills but does not yield superior forms. Instead, various wills strive to project their own power as well as form "nature" according to their personal optimal conditions.

In Darwin's model, "competition" helps "select" the "fittest"; it can thus be considered creative and life-enhancing. In Nietzsche's system, "competition" *per se* does not exist. The latter is merely the means by which (re)active wills assert power against stronger ones, that is, by bringing them onto their playing field and then allowing them to project (re)active force in "good conscience." Strong wills, on the other hand, assert active, outer-directed power in an arena where the weak simply do not "compete."

Finally, Darwin's "nature" presupposes a single playing field. As such, it is a complete, law-bound entity. Within this nature, the "fittest" will emerge. Nietzsche's "nature" exhibits multiple playing fields – at times autonomous, at times overlapping. Individuals determine the rules and conditions according to which the game should be played, and it is the predominant will(s) of the moment that determines the definitional parameters of "nature" as such.

In *GM* I, Nietzsche sets the stage for the critiques of Darwin(ism) in the following essays. By first relativizing Darwin's "nature" and focusing attention on interpretative will, Nietzsche then proceeds to his other two projects: to show how the oppressive will of the strong types in nature produced the breeding ground of "morality"; and to expose the origins of science in the ascetic, "moral" will. All three critiques derive from the important questions he poses in the addendum at the conclusion of *GM* I:

Indeed, every table of values, every "thou shalt" known to history or the study of ethnology, needs first and foremost a *physiological* elucidation and interpretation, rather than a psychological one; and all of them await critical study from medical science. The question: what is this or that table of values and "morals" *worth*? needs to be asked from different angles; in particular, the question "value for *what*?" cannot be examined too finely. (*GM* I, *Note*)

There could hardly be a more radical challenge to the foundations of Darwinism. It is a perspective Nietzsche pursues from various angles throughout all three essays.

CHAPTER 5

The birth of morality out of the spirit of the "bad conscience"

In my previous analysis, I focused on Nietzsche's and Darwin's contrasting views of nature. While he discussed alternative moral valuation systems in *GM* I, Nietzsche's larger concern was to characterize the will to power of distinct physiological types. The implications of Nietzsche's theory of the will to power challenged Darwin's mechanistic conception of nature. In *GM* II, Nietzsche's interests extend beyond an examination of guilt and (bad) conscience, as its title ("'Guilt,' 'bad conscience,' and related matters") suggests. It also explores more than the origins of morality and its relationship to the bad conscience. *GM* II concentrates on man's early socialization process and the emergence of the "state." It thus continues with his line of argumentation, which undercuts Enlightenment assumptions about man, nature, and the state.

But whereas *GM* I shifts between two dominant typologies, the aristocratic and priestly valuation systems, *GM* II concentrates primarily on the origins of a *third* will – the derivative "moral" will, or the man of "bad conscience." Nietzsche argues that the rudiments of the "moral" will were located in earliest civilization, but that the future spread of morality first required a warrior unit of superior organization suppressing nomadic tribes, thus laying the psychic groundwork for the "bad conscience." Although morality *did* arise from the instincts of individual wills (and here Nietzsche and Darwin agree), it flourished only among a specific *sub*-group – namely, wills enslaved by warrior castes. It was born from their instinctual anarchy. This view was diametrically opposed to that of Darwin and his followers, who sought for the origins of morality in man's (social) instinct, arguing that it had then spread as a result of (moral) man's relative *success* in the struggle for existence.

INTERPRETATIVE DIFFICULTIES WITH *GM* II, 1–2

The sections *GM* II, 1–2 – and *GM* II as a whole, for that matter – have generated scholarly confusion, since the relationship of the (positive) example of Nietzsche's "man who can make promises" appears to contrast starkly with the negative foil of the man of guilt and bad conscience, who becomes the focal point behind the remainder of the essay. Who is this so-called "sovereign man," the one who can make promises? How does he relate to the man of "bad conscience"? And above all, what is the difference between the two?

Christopher Janaway[1] and Mathias Risse[2] barely engage with the first two sections and proceed directly to the essay's central discussion of the "bad conscience." On the other hand, Christa Davis Acampora takes issue with the prevalent interpretation that treats the autonomous man of the first two sections as Nietzsche's ideal, virtuously synonymous with his "higher man,"[3] though she too avoids discussion of how this type might relate to the man of "bad conscience." None of them therefore manages to resolve the apparent discrepancy between the essentially positive description of a "sovereign individual" in the first two sections and the subsequent analysis of "that other 'dismal thing,' the consciousness of guilt, the whole 'bad conscience'" (*GM* II, 4).[4]

Nietzsche's meandering expository style in *GM* II, which weaves in and out of random historical periods over vast stretches of indeterminate time, certainly does not make it any easier. For many, *GM* II is the most complex essay of the entire work.[5] But for that reason it becomes imperative to

---

[1] Janaway, *Beyond Selflessness*, 124–42. In a recent article, Christopher Janaway devotes a little more space to the "sovereign individual," but still seems quite unsure of what to make of him: "Views differ on the mysterious 'sovereign individual' who seems so important for a few pages but never reappears in Nietzsche's work. The passage leaves us uncertain about who this individual is, was, or might be. We can question whether such a type of human being is supposed to have existed after the age of the morality of custom was over or during its later stages, whether sovereign individuals are supposed to have existed once and then faded away into history, or indeed whether there are sovereign individuals around today or whether they have ever existed at all" (Christopher Janaway, "Beyond Selflessness in Ethics and Inquiry," *Journal of Nietzsche Studies* 35/36 [2008], 129).

[2] "I hardly touch on exegetical problems raised by the initial three sections" (Mathias Risse, "The Second Treatise in *On the Genealogy of Morality*: Nietzsche on the Origin of the Bad Conscience," *European Journal of Philosophy* 9 [2001], 56).

[3] Christa Davis Acampora, "On Sovereignty and Overhumanity: Why It Matters How We Read Nietzsche's *Genealogy* II:2," in Acampora, ed., *Nietzsche's On the Genealogy of Morals*, 156.

[4] David Owen argues that Nietzsche uses the positive ideal of the "sovereign individual" in the first sections of the essay as a rhetorical device only so that he can then contrast it with the negative image of the man of bad conscience which we have become (Owen, *Nietzsche's Genealogy of Morality* [Montreal: McGill-Queen's University Press, 2007], 102).

[5] Perhaps because of its inherent complexities, scholars have focused less on *GM* II than on the other two essays. Janaway writes that *GM* II "has been comparatively poorly served by extended commentary" and "[i]t is perhaps symptomatic of the slight attention *GM* II has generally received that the introduction of the excellent edition of Clark and Swensen (1998) includes only a single paragraph of commentary on the essay, contrasted with a whole section devoted to each

decipher the connection between the first two sections and the subsequent sections on the "bad conscience" or else the interpretation of the essay as a whole remains incomplete, implausible, and ultimately contradictory. The problem, in my view, is that readers simply assume that Nietzsche adheres to an evolutionary narrative exposition. This explains why they have difficulty in analyzing the rest of the essay in relation to the first two sections. But the entire argument of *GM* II subverts the linear narrative certainties of naturalist genealogy, for Nietzsche does not track a *single* (moral) development for "mankind" but pursues strands of *simultaneous* historical development according to his principle of the "two-fold history of morality."[6]

THE SOVEREIGN INDIVIDUAL AS PRODUCT OF SUCCESSFUL SOCIALIZATION

Once again, it helps to focus our attention on the role of the instincts and drives and their relationship to one other. First, one must keep in mind that Nietzsche always deals with distinct instinctual realities, not just abstract conceptions. His unfolding of human history and the complex relationship of the various strands of development should never obscure the fact that Nietzsche operates with individual interrelating human types, or wills to power. Even though *GM* II often focuses on various stages of human "history," the wills to power it evokes always characterize the intrinsic nature of distinct physiological types at a particular moment in time. The latter do not merely "act out" history or represent historical abstractions, but project their instinctual will to power *into* "history." Nietzsche's perspective, in turn, expresses his own will as he impresses *his* interpretation onto the "historical" record.

Nietzsche's premise in *GM* II, 1–2, which must be set off to a large degree from the exposition that follows, is that the man "who can make promises" is the result of a socialization process extending far back into earliest anthropological time. Nietzsche had developed some of these ideas in previous works, and he even refers readers back to specific passages in *D* (*GM* II, 2). There, he had argued that the earliest humans were

---

of *GM* I and *GM* III" (Janaway, *Beyond Selflessness*, 124). Risse concurs, writing that "[t]he first treatise has attracted most scholarly attention, but much less work has been done on the second treatise" (Risse, "The Second Treatise," 55).

[6] In the Preface (*GM* "Preface" 4), Nietzsche refers back to *HH* I, 45, for his first intimations of the "two-fold prehistory of good and evil." But he deepened and expanded on these insights by the time of *GM*, including a lengthier exposition of the subject one year earlier in *BGE* 260.

socialized by a strict "morality of custom," to which they had to painfully adhere. Even though many of these rituals and practices may now seem absurd – "for example those [customs] among the Kamshadales forbidding the scraping of snow from the shoes with a knife, the impaling of a coal on a knife, the placing of an iron in the fire – and he who contravenes them meets death" (*D* I, 16) – they had the important function of keeping custom alive. The practices had etched into man a memory rendering him "predictable" within nature. For only by being a predictable "human animal" could he become part of a functioning community greater than his individual "animal" self.

Perhaps the most relevant development in his thought between *D* and *GM* was how he further elaborated on his idea of a twofold history of humanity. Whereas he had previously approached the question of early morality as a straightforward genealogical question applying to *all* mankind, Nietzsche now presents a bifurcation in early human history leading to two separate historical "developments" – the eventual emergence of a master morality and a slave morality. Both had their origins in the anthropological beginnings of civilization; however, they had different "historical" trajectories that eventually led to different human typologies. *GM* was written to fill in the gaps and to explain the historical context behind the emergence of different human types and their respective valuations.

In *GM* II, 1–2, Nietzsche emphasizes that the earliest form of "socialization," barbaric by our standards, required cruelty as well as punishments in order to realize a human type who could become part of a successful, flourishing tribal unit. Despite the coercive measures employed, this process was ultimately successful, for the end result was a truly predictable human who could make promises:

> The immense amount of labour involved in what I have called the "morality of custom," the actual labour of man on himself during the longest epoch of the human race, his whole *prehistoric* labour, is explained and justified on a grand scale, in spite of the hardness, tyranny, stupidity and idiocy it also contained, by this fact: with the help of the morality of custom and the social straightjacket, man was *made* truly predictable. (*GM* II, 2)

GM II, 1–2, focuses on the "positive" consequences of these procedures. Through the latter, man was truly made predictable, meaning he formed a "memory" – but only when it was necessary *for him*, that is, in moments that he needed to make promises. Nietzsche emphasizes throughout, however, that the state of *forgetfulness* is the primary and "natural" one, while memory is secondary, or derivative. He makes this point, since he wishes to emphasize that the strong type only "remembers" when he needs to relate to other equal, like-spirited wills. Only to those other superior types does promise-keeping extend. Otherwise, this higher type simply "forgets," eliminating unnecessary "lesser" stimuli that distract from his higher power-functions.[7]

The way in which he characterizes this autonomous "maker of promises" is consistent with other passages where Nietzsche qualifies the instinctual nature of the higher will. In *GM* I, he mentions Mirabeau as a superior person, who could not form *ressentiment*, since he forgot slights and offenses that would gnaw away at lesser types: "[Mirabeau] had no recall for the insults and slights directed at him and who could not forgive, simply because he – forgot" (*GM* I, 10). In *EH*, he characterizes the man "who has turned out well" as someone who *instinctively* lets many things slip through and selects only what is good *for himself*: "He instinctively gathers *his* totality from everything he sees, hears, experiences: he is a principle of selection, he lets many things fall by the wayside" (*EH* "Wise" 2).

Nietzsche now applies this notion back into early human history in order to locate its origins. Man was made pliant and predictable with the harshest procedures based on the ancient "*technique of mnemonics*": "'only something that continues *to hurt* stays in the memory' – that is a proposition from the oldest (and unfortunately the longest-lived) psychology on earth" (*GM* II, 3). In other words, memory had to be made, so ancient man "thought," by etching *pain* into the organism. This inscribed pain not only helped to make him predictable; more significantly, the painful process was eventually *forgotten* at the end of the long chain when the "ripe fruit" of the autonomous individual appeared. At this point, the latter released himself from custom, sloughing it off, because he had become the "perfect" embodiment of previous procedures. His higher instinctual health was reflected in the fact that he had internalized the "right" habits (namely, the ones demanded by earlier custom), but had no "memory" of, and no longer required, the cruel customs first needed to create

---

[7] Lawrence J. Hatab speaks of an "active forgetting," one which "opens up an alternative to slavish resentment because it is the letting go of *moral offense*" (Lawrence J. Hatab, *Nietzsche's "On the Genealogy of Morality": An Introduction* [Cambridge: Cambridge University Press, 2008], 70). Hatab seems to suggest volition, a *process* of forgetting, whereas Nietzsche suggests forgetting is the primary instinctual default mode for the strong: they remain oblivious to most stimuli unless they relate to promise-keeping among peers bred into them as a counterforce to natural forgetting.

predictability. He had become both hardened and softened – inured to the pain that would crush lesser wills, but softened in that his instinctual self-mastery – and *not* instinctual repression – had produced a will that was "simultaneously hard, gentle, and fragrant" (*EH* "Wise" 2).[8]

IMPLICATIONS FOR DARWINISM

Three points bear mentioning in Nietzsche's analysis in relation to Darwin. The first relates to the question of Nietzsche's perspective on cruelty as an alleged *instinctual* feature of man. For Nietzsche, man is cruel insofar as "nature" itself can be considered "cruel"; and man cannot possibly extract himself from the nature that he embodies.[9] Nevertheless, even though he describes by analogy some of the painful procedures that primitive tribes must have inflicted to make early man "predictable," Nietzsche does not suggest that pain is the best (or the only) method of creating a fully accountable human type.[10] Rather, pain was simply the first thing that primitive man "naturally" grabbed hold of in order to instill human predictability, and it was almost fortuitous that it resulted in the "ripe fruit" of the sovereign individual.[11]

At the same time, Nietzsche suggests that it is possible to "spiritualize" and channel human cruelty into "higher" endeavors (e.g. the *agon*):

[A]lmost everything we call "higher culture" is based on the spiritualization and deepening of *cruelty*. The "wild animal" has not been killed off at all; it is alive

---

[8] One must contrast this becoming autonomous as a result of a successful and "natural" fulfill-ment of the mores with the individual, who feels he can never fulfill his people's customs. The latter type feels the horrible chasm that separates his personal inclinations from the expectations of the community's duties and customs, and he realizes that he will forever remain torn between the two. See Nietzsche's discussion of St. Paul (*D* 68) as well as *GS* 117.

[9] In contrast, Janaway emphasizes that *cruelty* is *GM* II's "central train of thought" (Janaway, *Beyond Selflessness*, 124).

[10] Nietzsche, in one of the subtle ways he typically qualifies his statements, regards the primitive infliction of pain as "a proposition from the oldest (and *unfortunately* the longest-lived) psych-ology on earth" (italics mine) (*GM* II, 3). Though he does not agree with the methods ("unfortu-nately"), he nonetheless recognizes their historical validity.

[11] One of the common errors of Nietzsche scholarship is to believe that his seemingly dispassion-ate presentation of certain "historical" strands of development indicates his implicit agreement with them. But Nietzsche very much takes issue with the standards of nineteenth-century "real-ist" historiography, which worshipped "success" and embraced a "historical" development sim-ply because it was a "fact" and had proved determinant. He believes that a historical strand or procedure could be entirely misguided, wrong, or foolish, and actually be disadvantageous for humanity – and still have been historically influential. The objective of his critical genealogical approach is to make us aware of the primitive origins of some of our most cherished practices – for example, the impact of cruelty – so that we can learn to "correct" our behavior and not blindly act out ingrained patterns as a result of millennia of misguided practices.

and well, it has just – become divine. Cruelty is what constitutes the painful sensuality of tragedy. And what pleases us in so-called tragic pity as well as in everything sublime, up to the highest and most delicate of metaphysical tremblings, derives its sweetness exclusively from the intervening component of cruelty. (*GM* II, 6, quoted from *BGE* 229)

In short, Nietzsche recognizes cruelty as an essential feature of the will to power but distinguishes between different levels and shades of cruelty – in particular, the cruelty of the priestly types and the men of "bad conscience."[12] Whereas the "nature" of the "ripe fruit" of successful socialization might appear cruel and "evil" to those not bred to make promises – in fact, *must* appear "cruel" to them, since they act supremely indifferent to those "others" – Nietzsche suggests that the former are far less cruel than ascetic wills (who enjoy inflicting pain on themselves and others) and the men of "bad conscience" (who must "tame" their inner nature by inflicting terrible cruelty on the anarchy of their instincts). For Nietzsche, cruelty resides in the nature of interpersonal relationships. If the strong project their active will, they *must* inflict pain on wills not accustomed to their higher form of self-mastery.[13] They do not *seek* to inflict pain and cruelty on others but lesser wills must *feel it as such* if their wills are tangentially affected.[14]

Moreover, Nietzsche indicates that the creation of an autonomous will was not the "reason" behind the use of customs and punitive practices, but rather that earliest men had used these methods with different immediate goals and motivations; it was only pure chance that something

[12] Janaway acknowledges the relationship between cruelty and the will to power (Janaway, *Beyond Selflessness*, 127), but he tends to lay his greatest emphasis on cruelty as an independent instinctual feature differentiated from the will to power.

[13] This is also the insight behind the controversial anecdote of the eagle ("bird of prey") and the lamb in *GM* I, 13, which has become the focus of much recent interpretation. It is in the nature of the eagle to appear cruel to the lamb, even if it just acts out its intrinsic predatory nature. It would be ridiculous, however, to speak of the eagle being "cruel" as such, just as it would be to say that the lamb is "good," because it cannot be predatory and falls prey to the eagle. It is in the predatory relationship of the eagle to the lamb that the (human) *interpretation* of "cruelty" gets transposed onto what is a natural act.

[14] A good example of a "sublimation" of this expression of cruelty in the realm of culture can be found in Bizet's *Carmen*, the opera which Nietzsche discovered in November 1881 and which he highly prized. Carmen is a type of "higher" woman, whom one cannot tame or master ("Love is a rebellious bird"). In her final rejection of Don José, Carmen must appear "cruel" to him. However, she merely responds to her indomitable nature, which by consequence must crush her ties to José. She does not *intend* to be cruel, but her actions must impinge on his servile nature. José's murder of Carmen, in turn, reflects the cruelty of a less powerful type, who cannot bear *not* to dominate the will of the woman who spurns him. Both wills just act out their intrinsic natures. "I do not know any other place where the tragic wit that is the essence of love expresses itself so strongly, is formulated with so much horror as in Don José's last cry, which brings the work to an end: Yes, I have killed her, / I – my beloved Carmen!" (*CW* 2).

"higher" arose; it certainly could not have been predicted. But even if the process was fortuitous and used unnecessary, bizarre methods, Nietzsche does not quibble with the procedure since the end product proved successful. At the same time, he will show that other developments from the same period were not as positive and led down darker avenues – such as to the "bad conscience," for example. Thus, the creation of a superior individual is no way programmed into the process; nor was there a linear development out of it. It was entirely haphazard – one strand almost miraculously ending in a superior will, but the other strands leading to cruelty expressed in different ways and for different ends. Nietzsche thus challenges the genealogists' efforts to project purpose and meaning into primitive procedures to locate a goal, "morality," that they have already predetermined. He also undercuts their efforts to chart a *single* genealogical strand for "morality" as such.

Finally, Nietzsche breaks here from Darwin's understanding of the emergence of mind and consciousness. At the end of *GM* II, 1, Nietzsche clarifies how the autonomous product of successful socialization "thinks": "In order to have that degree of control over the future, man must first have learnt to distinguish between what happens by accident and what by design, to think causally, to view the future as the present and anticipate it, to grasp with certainty what is end and what is means, in all, to be able to calculate, compute" (*GM* II, 1). Though the process of early socialization may have been entirely haphazard, its product is not: the man who appears as a "ripe fruit" has achieved instinctual self-mastery and can prioritize his instinctual life. He can separate out within himself the necessary from the unnecessary and project that self-assurance outward. He is thus able to make *himself* a "future" – *his* future. This process of power projection for the purpose of creating a personal "future" is not intrinsic to nature but the result of the *successful* coordination of the autonomous will's instinctual life. Nowhere does Nietzsche mention the evolution of "reason" or the power of the "mind" in this equation, because he wishes to stress the *instinctive* nature of this so-called "thinking."

Contrast this description with Nietzsche's later depiction (*GM* II, 16) of those other unfortunate wills – those overpowered by the "beasts of prey," who needed to direct their energy against themselves rather than outward: "They felt they were clumsy at performing the simplest task, they did not have their familiar guide any more for this new, unknown world, those regulating impulses that unconsciously led them to safety – the poor things were reduced to relying on thinking, inference, calculation, and the connecting of cause with effect, that is, to relying on their 'consciousness', that most impoverished and error-prone organ" (*GM* II, 16). Nietzsche compares these forcefully subjugated wills with sea animals "forced to either become land animals or perish." The wills subjugated by more powerful wills, therefore, could not act according to what was "natural" to them, for the energy of their will (which should have been naturally oriented outwards) was forced inward. This was the birth of "(bad) consciousness," according to Nietzsche – a "mind" not attuned to nature as such, but to a realm actually cut off from nature, where man was "reduced to ... thinking, inference, calculation, and the connecting of cause with effect."

From the basis of his twofold history of morality, he therefore posits two "consciences": first, the "conscience" of the "autonomous man," the product of successful socialization, whose "conscience" reflects truly "higher" instinct and results from a strict morality of custom.[15] Second, the "consciousness" of wills forced into the folds of civilization by stronger autonomous wills that now had to "get by" by inference, calculation, and "intellect," since their instincts could not freely unfold and adapt to natural circumstances "in the wild". Though one realm was entirely created by the other within nature – the stronger, autonomous wills had "created" the realm of the "slaves" – the two worlds represent two distinct, non-contingent "natural" arenas.

---

[15] Nietzsche almost hesitates to use the word "conscience" for this sovereign individual's "rare freedom and power over himself and destiny": if he needed a word for this awareness, he would call it his "conscience" (*GM* II, 2). Nietzsche is required to find an inadequate word – namely, one tinged by the Christian perspective – for a state of being, for which his higher type does not even have a concept. In fact, one can clarify much of the interpretive confusion surrounding the first sections if one recognizes how he uses the inflated language of moral idealism as a foil for his own brand of "naturalism," which purports to better embody the "historical sense" (*GM* I, 2). Precisely by not buying into the genealogists' "scientific" account of human prehistory, which he feels has already been imbued with the "moral" perspective, Nietzsche offers a "truer" "natural" account of the "historical" record (part of what had been laid out in earlier works such as *D*), in which "morality" becomes the incidental side-effect of non-moral, strong wills. But by then co-opting the terminology of "moral idealism" to characterize his *non*-moral types, Nietzsche slyly inserts his own non-moral model of the "autonomous individual," one that has no point of contact with the idealist project, into the language of the idealists in order to undercut the categories they use to describe their "ideal": Nietzsche's "ripe fruit" in the modern clothes of the "sovereign individual" is, indeed, the polar opposite of *their* vision of a morally autonomous individual. At the same time, he drives this point even further home by showing in the remainder of *GM* II that their *actual* ideal is *his* man of "bad conscience" – a type hardly at all autonomous, but a derivative form of the higher will, full of festering resentment. Finally, once again Nietzsche is forced to work within the dictates of the genealogical discourse of his time in order to engage this "system" from within; in order to challenge the genealogists' perspectives, he has to operate within their theoretical framework, i.e. their project of naturalizing "morality." This means, in turns, adopting, co-opting, parodying, mocking, and undercutting their suppositions.

THE EMERGENCE OF "GUILT" IN A NON-MORAL SENSE

Nietzsche then begins, in *GM* II, 4, to discuss how that "other 'dismal thing', the consciousness of guilt, the whole 'bad conscience', come[s] into the world." Here he does not refer back to the "promise-keeper" introduced in *GM* II, 1–3, rather he now shifts his attention to an entirely different phenomenon ("that *other* 'dismal thing'"): the so-called "bad conscience." The latter will remain the focus of *GM* II and will merge with the above discussion of how the earliest tribes were enslaved by superior wills (first introduced in *GM* II, 16).

Nietzsche maintains that the earliest forms of punishment were not "meted out *because* the miscreant was held [morally] responsible for his act," but out of a spontaneous sense of "anger over some wrong that had been suffered, directed at the perpetrator," much in the same way that "parents still punish their children" (*GM* II, 4). In Nietzschean terms, this "punishment" is expressive of an active will to power spontaneously released on an "offender" – someone who has encroached on and violated his (more powerful) will. Based on Nietzsche's description of anger release in response to an infringement of personal power, this behavior is less "punishment" than the acting out of will on will. (It is also indicative of higher types; weak wills do not release anger directly, which allows it to fester into *ressentiment*.) At this stage, there is no "moral" culpability: both parties act spontaneously according to their instinctual needs.

The "stepping out" of this "natural" expression of active power projection occurs when the perpetrator is not immediately "punished"; instead, the act of anger is held in check and the "injured party" seeks to arrange an equivalency with the perpetrator instead of inflicting pain through immediate power release. The injured party seeks redress for withheld "punishment" and creates an equivalence of injury and pain, whereby the perpetrator must pay back in some form of "pain installments" to satisfy his injured will. Nietzsche speculates that this equivalence of injury and pain most likely originated in the practices of trade and commerce: "[W]here did this primeval, deeply-rooted and perhaps now ineradicable idea gain its power, this idea of an equivalence between injury and pain? … [I]n the contractual relationship between *creditor* and *debtor*, which is as old as the very conception of a 'legal subject' and itself refers back to the basic forms of buying, selling, bartering, trade and traffic" (*GM* II, 4).

In *GM* II, 5, Nietzsche pursues further this newly introduced "developmental" strand. He suggests that the notion of punishment as deferred pain infliction developed in the beginnings of human commerce. Instead of immediately acting on injured will, the "injured" party holds back on direct "punishment" in order to seek gratification through mediated pain. Pain was no longer a "natural," tangential effect of will acting upon will (i.e. inflicted pain resulting out of anger as a result of an injury against one's will), but became the consequence of an entire *mechanism of cruelty*, whereby "satisfaction" was derived by seeing another party suffer personal loss and injury. Though originally economic – some form of "money, land or possessions of any kind" had to be offered in compensation – this process of forfeiture eventually took on the form of the pleasure that one derived in inflicting pain for pain's sake: "the pleasure of having the right to exercise power over the powerless without a thought, the pleasure '*de faire le mal pour le plaisir de le faire*', the enjoyment of violating: an enjoyment that is prized all the higher, the lower and baser the position of the creditor in the social scale" (*GM* II, 5).

As Nietzsche makes clear in *GM* II, 5, this process is not comparable to the process sketched out in *GM* II, 1–2, where the rigid morality of custom had fortuitously led to the autonomous individual. There are three subtle indications to argue for this reading. First, Nietzsche states in the beginning of *GM* II, 5, that the "person making the promise has to have a *memory made* for him" (italics mine): precisely not being autonomous, and having landed in a subservient position of "debt" (guilt) with another will, the "guilty party" (better here: the party "in debt") is forced into a position where he must have a memory *made* for him by another will, i.e. the promise of debt repayment. In order to relieve himself of guilt/debt (*Schuld*), he must first pay back his creditor – in pain. Whereas the original process of arbitrary pain and punishment inflicted by the morality of custom had led *by accident* to an autonomous will, this derivative mechanism is *purposeful*, allowing an *inferior* will to inscribe cruelty onto a will that has fallen into his hands. Rather than eventually liberating himself from the morality of custom, this will has a sense of "guilt" indelibly etched into his consciousness.

Second, Nietzsche indicates that this procedure ran rampant in the *subservient* strata of earlier civilization, specifically, he suggests, in the commercial, administrative, and priestly realms. The cruel processes were itemized and even found their way into ancient legal documents: "[I]n particular, the creditor could inflict all kinds of dishonour and torture on the body of the debtor, for example, cutting as much flesh off as seemed appropriate for the debt: – from this standpoint there were everywhere, early on, estimates which went into horrifyingly minute and fastidious detail, *legally* drawn up estimates for individual limbs and parts of the body" (*GM* II, 5). Nietzsche suggests, however, that this behavior did not reflect the superior valuation of a master race, but the will to power of inferior castes. For example, he considers it "*a more Roman* pricing of justice, when Rome's code of the Twelve Tables decreed that it did not matter how much or how little a creditor cut off in such a circumstance, '*si plus minusve secuerunt, ne fraude esto*'" (*GM* II, 5).

As a warrior nation, Rome had imposed its "master" valuation on its subject peoples in the Mediterranean world.[16] But Rome could never completely eradicate, though it tried to curtail, the wider populace's more openly cruel customary practices. These examples of mediated, vicarious cruelty must have appeared barbaric to the Romans' sense of active, spontaneous "justice." "Justice" properly understood *must*, in fact, reflect the power of higher, active wills, who at times intervene against the cruel excesses found among the socially inferior forces of *ressentiment*: "Historically speaking, justice on earth represents … the battle, then, *against* reactive sentiment, the war waged against the same on the part of active and aggressive forces, which have partly expended their strength in trying to put a stop to the spread of reactive pathos, to keep it in check and within bounds, and to force a compromise with it" (*GM* II, 11).

Finally, Nietzsche emphasizes that the pleasure gained by inflicting pain on a "guilty" party (i.e. the one who must repay his "debt" to a "creditor") is a *vicarious* act: it is the pleasure someone receives who can (at least indirectly) partake in a process of "punishment" exclusively reserved for masters. This "action" has become a channeled, sadistic pleasure that allows a socially inferior will to feel momentarily superior to a will temporarily in its power and to enforce "punishment" – particularly if the right to punish has already been transferred to a higher authority: "Through punishment of the debtor, the creditor takes part in the *rights of the masters*: at last he, too, shares the elevated feeling of being in a position to despise and maltreat someone as an 'inferior' – or at least, when the actual power of punishment, of exacting punishment, is already transferred to the 'authorities', of *seeing* the debtor despised and maltreated" (*GM* II, 5). "So, then," Nietzsche concludes, "compensation is made up of a warrant for and entitlement to cruelty."

---

[16] Nietzsche contrasts the cruel practices of ancient Egypt with the noble legal code of Rome, which had incorporated Egypt as a client nation into its empire: "as in Egypt, where the corpse of a debtor found no peace from the creditor even in the grave – and this peace meant a lot precisely to the Egyptians" (*GM* II, 5). Nietzsche always contrasted Egypt negatively with the aristocratic Greco-Roman legacy, particularly because of the all-pervasive influence of its priesthood.

THE CONNECTION BETWEEN PUNISHMENT
AND "GUILT"

In *GM* II, 4–5, Nietzsche traces the notion of "guilt" back to the creditor–debtor relationship, where an equivalency between injury and pain was created and where the creditor could punish by demanding some form of (originally monetary) compensation from the debtor. Though this process gave the creditor the right to inflict pain on the debtor not able to fulfill his obligation, it did *not*, Nietzsche insists, awaken a feeling of guilt in the delinquent debtor; nor was that even considered its "intention." But he then proceeds to show how a transactional process grounded in ancient economic practices *could* develop into an elaborate mechanism for inflicting pain.

Nietzsche subsequently engages in a lengthy excursus about the phenomenon of punishment and its relationship to "guilt" (*GM* II, 12–15). He argues, in brief, that the earliest forms of punishment did not have the "purpose" of instilling guilt or even creating a "guilty party." In the case of the creditor–debtor relationship, for example, he shows that punishment was not even meant to coerce "guilt," but simply to gratify the cruelty of the creditor by allowing him to partake in the master's right to punish. He then challenges the notion that punishment as such had any broader purpose at all and instead might have had multiple "purposes" depending on its *immediate* aim, which (in the short run) was to instill some form of memory through pain. To drive home this interpretation, he itemizes in a lengthy passage in *GM* II, 13, the numerous ways in which punishment was implemented in order to achieve different localized results, none of which necessitated arousing a feeling of guilt in the "victim."

There are three reasons why the analysis of punishment becomes important for him at this point, and they all reflect an aspect of his implicit critique of Darwin. First, Nietzsche wishes to decouple our almost intuitive association between punishment and the question of (moral) guilt. Because of our subsequent moralization of the punishment question, we have erroneously come to believe that a person punished must be (morally) "guilty" of an offense. But Nietzsche's analysis of early means of punishment shows, indeed, that punishment did *not* have any set purpose or single strand of development, but rather a multiplicity of purposes for discrete "offenses" that only later became entangled in a single master-narrative:

With regard to the other element in punishment, the fluid one, its "meaning", the concept "punishment" presents, at a very late stage of culture (for example, in Europe today), not just one meaning but a whole synthesis of "meanings" [*Sinnen*]: the history of punishment up to now in general, the history of its use for a variety of purposes, finally crystallizes in a kind of unity which is difficult to dissolve back into its elements, difficult to analyse and, this has be stressed, is absolutely *undefinable*. (*GM* II, 13)

Believing in the perpetrator's inherent "guilt" was far from the minds of primitive executors, and it did not even enter into the consciousness of these executors that the people with whom they were dealing were to be considered "guilty." The plant of the "bad conscience," Nietzsche argues, did not grow out of such a "soil." Rather, to such primitive punishment enforcers, "it was a question of someone who caused harm, an irresponsible piece of fate" (*GM* II, 14). Even less did it penetrate the consciousness of those consigned to punishment for their actions; they merely endured their punishment:

> For millennia, wrong-doers overtaken by punishment have felt *no different than Spinoza* with regard to their "offence": "something has gone unexpectedly wrong here", *not* "I ought not to have done that" –, they submitted to punishment as you submit to illness or misfortunate or death, with that brave, unrebellious fatalism that still gives the Russians, for example, an advantage over us Westerners in the way they handle life. (*GM* II, 15)

Nietzsche even suggests that punishment in earliest times actually *prevented* the sensation of guilt from arising within the "guilty" party: "If we just think about those centuries *before* the history of mankind, we can safely conclude that the evolution of a feeling of guilt was most strongly *impeded* through punishment, – at any rate, with regard to the victims on whom the primitive measures were carried out" (*GM* II, 14).

These explanations serve Nietzsche's larger purpose of decoupling the connection between punishment and guilt in "popular perception" – i.e. that punishment supposedly has the "value of arousing the *feeling of guilt* in the guilty party" (*GM* II, 14). With this line of critique, he targeted the theories of a Darwinist whose work he understood best – that of his former friend Rée. Rée had argued that punishment was the naturalist origins for the emergence of morality. Inspired by Darwin's theories, Rée sought a genealogical explication along Darwinian lines that could offer a non-metaphysical grounding for morality, which he located in punishment.[17] But in his elaborate deconstruction of punitive practices, Nietzsche tried to prove that the practice of punishment and the question

---

[17] Small, *Nietzsche and Rée*, provides the definitive account of their relationship as well as Rée's body of thought.

of guilt remained entirely distinct entities in the minds of early humans; and that punishment was, indeed, *ineffective* in eliciting a feeling of guilt in the perpetrator. Though Rée's was just one single Darwinian hypothesis at the time, Nietzsche effectively challenged one of the first and most cogent of the evolutionary explanations for the emergence of morality.

Second, Nietzsche frustrates the genealogists' efforts to pursue an essentially linear trajectory for the development of morality at a more fundamental level. In the case of punishment, he separates out the much older act and procedure (of punishment) from its alleged "purpose." By itemizing the various "objectives" of punitive procedures, all dictated by the immediate circumstances, he argues that "punishment" has no intrinsic meaning but only a score of arbitrary meanings subsequently (and erroneously) projected into it. The procedures of punishment are neutral and fixed; the meanings, however, are fluid; and rather than a single line of "meaning," there are multiplicities of simultaneous meanings, each of which has a unique narrative strand in its own right: "[T]he procedure itself will be something older, predating its use as punishment, that the latter was only *inserted* and interpreted into the procedure" (*GM* II, 13).

Specifically, Nietzsche questions the standard methodology of the genealogists, who resort to the categories of usefulness and utility in order to explain how something might have been used for a specific purpose. When they approach a particular historical phenomenon, Nietzsche argues, they ground a sense of causation into the object, thereby giving it a particular purpose or thrust towards a specific goal. The supposed utility of a practice is then used to chart its later "evolution" in a certain direction (teleological principles): "the matter [of punishment] is *not* to be understood in the way our naïve moral and legal genealogists assumed up till now, who all thought the procedure had been *invented* for the purpose of punishment, just as people used to think that the hand had been invented for the purpose of grasping" (*GM* II, 13).

One can interpret Nietzsche's position as a challenge to teleological explanations, and one can claim that he targets only one *form* of Darwinian interpretation, not evolution itself. But I suggest that he challenges more than the standard teleological perspective, primarily the utilitarian one. For Nietzsche's emphasis here is not on the evolution of the practice as such, i.e. on the way that punishment was fundamental and then eventually evolved into a mechanism for punishing a "guilty" party. Rather, Nietzsche's focus is on the process of *interpretation* – specifically, how various strands of interpretation from individual wills have been projected into what was an entirely *neutral* phenomenon – or, rather, a series of unrelated, distinct processes. In other words, no evolution in any single direction is going on at all here; there are only competitive perspectives and meanings projected into events. According to Nietzsche, the will to power reflected in individual interpretations gives meaning to what are essentially random and disconnected processes.

But Nietzsche *does* care to disentangle one specific strand – the one leading to "morality," or more precisely, to the dominance of the moral *interpretation*. However, he pursues this objective not because this strand of "development" had been "selected," but because (the predominance of) "moral" wills had prioritized *their* interpretation and had come to monopolize and "moralize" the "historical" record. He must thus disentangle the simultaneity of interpretative strands and conjecture how one particular strand could have triumphed and diminished other narrative threads.

Finally, Nietzsche separates punishment from the issue of "guilt" in order to argue that earliest man did not even forge a connection between guilt and punishment. At that time, punishment had not yet been "moralized" but was simply treated as a natural fact of life to be endured. Among the strongest in ancient times, punishment could not even yield the slightest pang of conscience. By looking for a semblance of guilty conscience among the condemned in earliest history, Nietzsche argues, "people are violating reality and psychology even as it is today: and much more so for the longest period in the history of mankind, its prehistory! The real pang of conscience, precisely amongst criminals and convicts, is something extremely rare, prisons and gaols are *not* nurseries where this type of gnawing pang chooses to thrive" (*GM* II, 14).

In effect, Nietzsche creates a typological distinction in earliest man. Whereas in one group a feeling of guilt *never* arose, even after being punished, in another group there emerged a type in which "guilt" became equated with punishment and which felt itself "guilty" in its very core – and therefore *worthy* of punishment. Nietzsche then locates the instinctual will that could serve as the breeding ground for such a sensation of "guilt" among the enslaved masses of ancient times. It was there that an *existential* feeling of "guilt" hatched, festered, and contributed to the idea that one was *in essence* "guilty."

Having argued that punishment *per se* did not need to lead to a sense of guilt or bad conscience, Nietzsche returns to the earlier narrative strand that he had dropped during his lengthy digression on punishment – namely, the one locating the rudiments of a moralization of "guilt" in the creditor–debtor relationship. There, the *notion* of "guilt" as deferred retribution had started – though it alone did not produce an intrinsic *feeling* of guilt in the "victim": it had merely created the interpretational framework in which the subsequent moralization of "guilt" could occur. In order for the moralization of "guilt" to materialize, that one strand of development would first have to coalesce with another independent "development" – the "bad conscience" created among wills enslaved by superior warrior hordes.

THE BIRTH OF THE "BAD CONSCIENCE" FROM "STATE"-FORMATION

In *GM* II, 16–18, Nietzsche introduces the historical "events" that produced the "bad conscience" and eventually allowed it to merge with the feeling of guilt. Nietzsche argues that the bad conscience arose within the confines of the "state" and civilization. But what does he mean by "state," a word he puts in quotation marks and does not use in its traditional sense? There are two important requirements that he lays out: first, the "state" was created from the top down by more powerful warrior units that subjugated poorly organized nomadic peoples; and second, the earliest "state"-formation signified an expansion of civilization and an increasing stratification based, in part, on the forced suppression of a slave population. A primitive human collective becomes a "state" when it goes beyond the parameters of its original tribal unit and imposes a top-down infrastructure on other wills. Their enslavement is the precondition for a "higher" civilization with ever-increasing complexity and stratification. With this understanding, Nietzsche not only challenges modern state theories, which see the state emerging from below on the basis of a (social) contract,[18] but he also establishes for the first time the historical reservoir for the bad conscience: the instincts of the slaves forced against their wills into the confines of an *imposed* civilization.

Nietzsche here continues with his theory of the twofold history of mankind. In *GM* I he had presented the concept of two dominant typologies with their respective "natures" – that of the master and that of the slave. But in *GM* II he conjectures how these two groupings might have arisen "historically." While he showed how the morality of custom, through a painful work on man, had created tribal units that were affirmative and outer-directed (the strand leading to the "masters"), Nietzsche had to explain where the opposite of this outer-directed will might have

---

[18] "In this way, the 'state' began on earth: I think I have dispensed with the fantasy which has it begin with a 'contract'" (*GM* II, 17).

emerged, that is, where will to power could *not* be freely and affirmatively expressed but, instead, could become linked with *existential* "guilt" and "bad conscience."

Nietzsche explains this phenomenon by showing how the peoples enslaved by the roving warrior hordes became the "objects" worked upon by superior wills. Instead of a rigid morality of custom working among equals and *by chance* creating predictability, stronger wills here brutally subjugated "lesser" wills so that they could fulfill *their* higher function. Even if this process might mirror the original "senseless" and *entirely random* cruelty of the morality of custom, it represented something essentially different – a sudden, dramatic break from the instincts' direct rapport with nature, creating, in effect, a *second* nature:

> The first assumption in my theory on the origin of bad conscience is that the alteration was not gradual and voluntary and did not represent an organic assimilation into new circumstances, was but a breach, a leap, a compulsion, an inescapable fate that nothing could ward off, which occasioned no struggle, not even any *ressentiment*. A second assumption, however, is that the shaping of a population, which had up till now been unrestrained and shapeless, into a fixed form, as happened at the beginning with an act of violence, could only be concluded with acts of violence, – that consequently the oldest "state" emerged as a terrible tyranny, as a repressive and ruthless machinery, and continued working until the raw material of people and semi-animals had been finally not just kneaded and made compliant, but *shaped*. (*GM* II, 17)

The "bad conscience," then, was not the so-called "conscience" as it had emerged out of the strict morality of custom (*GM* I, 1–2) – even though it too had been formed by harsh measures; it was a lesser, derivative form. In other words, it "was not gradual and voluntary and did not represent an organic assimilation into new circumstances," but reflected a forceful, purposeful, and immediate crushing and grinding down of will by a successful conquering race.[19] For the "objective" of this conquering tribe was to create, *intuitively*, a higher political structure based on a clear demarcation of social functions, where the slaves were to act as broad foundation and the conqueror "race" were to represent its operational crown: "What they do is to create and imprint forms instinctively, they are the most

[19] Nietzsche emphasizes the *suddenness* of these warrior hordes' brutal arrival on the scene amidst the more docile nomadic peoples in contrast to the long, gradual work of the morality of custom over time (*GM* II, 1–2). This effect is reinforced stylistically through his rhetorical practice: "He observes that the aggressor type appeared on the scene much as it appears in the thick of his narrative: suddenly, unpredictably, and without adequate explanation" (Daniel Conway, "How We Became What We Are: Tracking the 'Beasts of Prey'," in Acampora, ed., *Nietzsche's On the Genealogy of Morals*, 308).

involuntary, unconscious artists there are: – where they appear, soon something new arises, a structure of domination [*Herrschafts-Gebilde*] that *lives*, in which parts and functions are differentiated and related to one another, in which there is absolutely no room for anything that does not first acquire 'meaning' with regard to the whole" (*GM* II, 17).

ASPECTS OF THE "BAD CONSCIENCE"

Four components of Nietzsche's position need here to be highlighted. First, the process of violence and cruelty inflicted on the suddenly enslaved nomadic peoples is not the same as the cruelty man inflicted on himself via the morality of custom in earliest prehistory but rather a parallel, derivative form of this. The main difference is that the morality of custom first arose among a primitive people in order to create predictability and responsibility and, therefore, the possibility of communal living. Yet, this process, once again, did not create "memory" or "consciousness" as such, but only localized memory, namely, *when it was required* – i.e. when the individual *needed* to make promises to other like-willed peers. Otherwise, the default mode among individuals worked upon by the "morality of custom" was essential *forgetfulness*: "[T]his necessarily forgetful animal, in whom forgetting is a strength, representing a form of *robust* health, has bred for himself a counter-device, memory, with the help of which forgetfulness can be suspended in certain cases, – namely in those cases where a promise is to be made" (*GM* II, 1).

The violence inflicted on subjugated wills *also* made them predictable; however, it was a predictability achieved by the slave's violent working on his own inner nature in order to achieve some form of "acceptable" (i.e. from the masters' point of view) outer instinctual totality. Not permitted to express its instincts "naturally" – namely, outwardly – the enslaved will must somehow tame and suppress the *same* demands of its instincts in order to achieve "predictability" – more specifically, the outward docility and obedience demanded by its masters:

Lacking external enemies and obstacles, and forced into the oppressive narrowness and conformity of custom, man impatiently ripped himself apart, persecuted himself, gnawed at himself, gave himself no peace and abused himself, this animal who battered himself raw on the bars of his cage and who is supposed to be "tamed"; man, full of emptiness and torn apart with homesickness for the desert, has had to create from within himself an adventure, a torture-chamber, an unsafe and hazardous wilderness – this fool, this prisoner consumed with longing and despair, became the inventor of "bad conscience". (*GM* II, 16)

The slave becomes a perfect function of his master's will; and it is only as function of the master's superior will that his outward behavior is condoned.

But whereas the forgetting and sloughing-off of painful experiences and offenses come "naturally" to the "autonomous individual," it is the opposite with the subjugated slave. For such a will's natural healing powers have been violently undermined and its natural instincts have been internally thwarted and confused. As a result, the pains and offenses it suffers become indelibly etched into its "consciousness" and any release of that pain can only be aired in the spirit of *ressentiment*. Here, too, man has been given a "memory" – but a *permanent one*, i.e. one that leads to a "passive inability to be rid of an impression once it has made its impact" (*GM* II, 1); he becomes an instinctual will that *can never forget its injuries*.

Second, Nietzsche emphasizes that the *same* will to power – or, as he alternatively refers to it here, the same "instinct of freedom" – is at work in both the aggressive wills' subjugation of others in nature and in the subjugated wills' violent rechanneling of natural outer-directed energy back into themselves and against themselves – *even if* the two processes differ in their outcome:

We must be wary of thinking disparagingly about this whole phenomenon because it is inherently ugly and painful. Fundamentally, it is the same active force as the one that is at work on a grand scale in those artists of violence and organizers, and that builds states, which here, internally, and on a smaller, pettier scale, turned backwards, in the "labyrinth of the breast", as Goethe would say, creates bad conscience for itself, and builds negative ideals, it is that very *instinct for freedom* (put into my language: the will to power): except that the material on which the formative and rapacious nature of this force vents itself is precisely man himself, his whole animal old self – and *not*, as in that greater and more eye-catching phenomenon, the *other* man, the *other* men. (*GM* II, 18)

Third, as Nietzsche indicates above, the process of *internalizing* will to power is almost synonymous – though on a much "smaller, pettier scale" – with the outer-directed "state-building" resulting from the more powerful conquerors ("those great artists of violence and organizers"), except that the "political" organization that the subjugated wills create is *in themselves*, in the "labyrinth of their breast". Yet, instead of a clear hierarchization based on a "natural" ranking of the instincts, these wills must make sense of, organize, and form an identity out of instinctual chaos and give meaning to competing, self-contradictory demands. Not being able to identify with the "natural" power projection that had led to the aggressive wills' "state" organization in the first place, these wills must invert the "natural" order of power projection in order to be able to project their wills outward in the only acceptable form (i.e. for their masters).

The "political" institutions that such types of "bad conscience" will ultimately create will therefore be fraught with internal dissension and contradiction, and they will always tend toward dissolution and chaos (*décadence*). Once such wills subvert the "natural" political hierarchy of the ancient world (more precisely, numerically overrun it) and thereby succeed with their "slave revolt," these wills of "bad conscience" can only succeed in creating a political order reflective of their own tortured instinctual worlds and based on a subversion of all "natural," affirmative values (nihilism). While they regarded the strong wills of the ancient world as essentially "evil," they fashioned themselves as the "good," which allowed them to marginalize expressions of active, outer-directed energy and to cut them off from their natural arena. This process led to the hollowing out of the ancient state-formation at its core.

Finally, the "bad conscience" creates a parallel "ideal" world of the imagination that has no point of contact with the "natural" world, i.e. the actual world of aggressive, outer-directed instincts of the strong. Nietzsche conjectures that the new "soul" created by such men of "bad conscience" might even have been the fermenting ground for the concept of "beauty" as such. For such broken wills, "beauty" merely expresses the opposite values of everything that the enslaved will instinctually represents and despises in itself:

[T]his whole *active* "bad conscience" has finally – we have already guessed – as true womb of ideal and imaginative events, brought a wealth of novel, disconcerting beauty and affirmation to light, and perhaps for the first time, beauty *itself* ... What would be "beautiful", if the contrary to it had not first come to awareness of itself, if ugliness had not first said to itself: "I am ugly"? (*GM* II, 18)

This process of imaginative projection from the perspective of a tortured will can explain why the opposite "values" of what the "self" (i.e. the "bad conscience") embodies – the "ideals" of "selflessness, self-denial, self-sacrifice," and altruism[20] – could assume an even higher, positive valuation than actual natural values; and how those values could then take on a life of their own, standing permanently in competition with

---

[20] "So much, for the time being, on the descent of the 'unegoistic' as a *moral* value and on the delineation of the ground on which this value has grown: only bad conscience, only the will to self-violation provides the precondition for the *value* of the unegoistic" (*GM* II, 18).

that "other" world – the "natural" world of the strong. However, the construction of such an "ideal" world, Nietzsche concludes, arises from instinctual cruelty. It is the product of the shunted instincts' cruel work on the interior world in order to shape some sort of personal identity and totality out of instinctual chaos: "This secret self-violation, this artist's cruelty, this desire to give form to oneself as a piece of difficult, resisting, suffering matter, to brand it with a will, a critique, a contradiction, a contempt, a 'no', this uncanny, terrible but joyous labor of a soul voluntarily split within itself, which makes itself suffer out of the pleasure of making suffer" (*GM* II, 18).

THE CONFLATION OF "GUILT" WITH THE "BAD CONSCIENCE"

After his discussion of the "bad conscience" and its emergence among forcefully enslaved wills, Nietzsche again picks up his earlier narrative strand: the origins of guilt in primitive economic exchange practices (*GM* II, 4). Returning to a point *before* the "bad conscience," he argues that later generations eventually transferred the economically derived concept of "debt" – once it had found entry into the legal sphere (*GM* II, 6) – over to the religious domain.[21] Here, it was understood as the sense of "debt" that the community owed its successful ancestors: "The relationship of a debtor to his creditor in civil law, about which I have written at length already, was for a second time transformed through interpretation, in a historically extremely strange and curious manner, into a relationship ... of the *present generation* to their *forebears*" (*GM* II, 19).

Over time, the "indebtedness" that descendants felt toward their ancestors grew stronger and stronger – even more so, if the tribe proved successful – and this sense of guilt soon mingled with a sense of fear and dread once the ancestors had receded into distant memory:[22] "Following this

---

[21] This is where the semantic connection between "guilt" and "debt" (German "Schuld" happens to express both, a nuance of meaning which cannot be rendered in English) becomes relevant for Nietzsche's overall argument.

[22] Risse writes that "[i]t is only through the impact of Christianity that the bad conscience as a feeling of guilt arises" (Risse, "The Second Treatise," 56). Yet the feeling of guilt/debt, which far precedes the bad conscience, is rooted in a general feeling of owing back to one's ancestors (and exists even among masters). The "impact of Christianity," therefore, had nothing to do with the phenomenon of "guilt" as such. Rather, Christian metaphysics offered an explanatory paradigm that could make sense of the internalized cruelty that the man of "bad conscience" inflicted on himself; further, it made that *sensation* of guilt *essential*, since it anchored the psychological self-perception of "bad conscience" in an "eternal" metaphysics, rendering it ineradicable. Christianity also allowed for a "politics" of *ressentiment*: if I felt myself subservient to a "God"

line of thought, the *dread* of the ancestor and his power, the consciousness of debts towards him, increases inevitably, in direct proportion to the
increase in power of the tribe itself, that is, in proportion as the tribe itself
becomes ever more victorious, independent, honoured and feared" (*GM*
II, 19). Nietzsche recognizes in this process the possible origins of man's
belief in the gods – the original ancestors having become transposed into
almighty beings, towards whom one felt a potent mixture of awe, reverence, guilt, and dread:

> If you think this sort of crude logic through to the end: it follows that through
> the hallucination of the growing dread itself, the ancestors of the *most powerful*
> tribes must have grown to an immense stature and must have been pushed into
> the obscurity of divine mystery and transcendence: – inevitably the ancestor
> himself is finally transfigured into a *god*. Perhaps we have here the actual origin
> of gods, an origin, then, in *fear*! (*GM* II, 19)

The feeling of guilt and indebtedness towards their ancestors subsequently grew with the expansion of civilization and their descendants'
adoption of their divinities. The sense of "guilt" and fear towards one's
ancestors also trickled downward and outward, and it was eventually
assimilated into the "lower" ranks of civilization, i.e. by the vast subjugated populations, which instinctively mimic the behavior patterns of
their masters: "(Those large populations of slaves and serfs who adapted
themselves to the divinity cults of their masters, whether through com-
pulsion, submission or mimicry, form the transitional stage: from them,
the inheritance overflows in every direction.)" (*GM* II, 20). "The feeling
of indebtedness towards a deity," Nietzsche concludes, "continued to
grow for several millennia, and indeed always in the same proportion as
the concept of and feeling for God grew in the world and was carried

---

and "guilty" before Him, allowing me to "act out" punishment on my instinctual life, then the
"others" (i.e. the masters) were "evil" if *they* did not defer to *my* God; their intrinsic "immorality"
(from my perspective) would allow me to mete out "His" punishment to them. The problem with
Risse's explanation is that it follows the standard "cause-and-effect" historical pattern, which
Nietzsche undercuts. Christianity is not a one-time historical "event" that suddenly appears; it
is a complete interpretational system that makes sense of a "material" condition already firmly
established, i.e. the bad conscience. As a form of metaphysics, it appeals only to such weakened wills – the strong, in contrast, remain immune to the mechanism of metaphysics – and
it will always "speak" to those wills as long as they remain in the state of "bad conscience."
Finally, the "bad conscience," predating Christianity, can also exist *without* Christianity (and
with modern science): i.e. even if one overcomes Christianity as a belief system (for example, by
espousing modern forms of atheism), the instinctual reality and the entire awareness of the "bad
conscience" have already been ingrained into the physiology of the will. This process – whereby
"guilt" has been indelibly etched into the will, even while "God" has lost its hold on the popular
imagination – is constitutive of contemporary nihilism (see *GM* II, 21) – *a much more significant
historical phenomenon* than traditional Christianity (and one that now exists alongside it).

aloft" (*GM* II, 20). Eventually, "[t]he advent of the Christian God as the maximal god yet achieved, thus also brought about the appearance of the greatest feeling of indebtedness on earth."

At this point, Nietzsche has argued for the origins of the God belief (out of the creditor–debtor relationship); the means by which the belief in god(s) spread through subsequent generations (successive conquests and the adoption of customs and beliefs by servile populations); and the connection of the feeling of guilt with the belief in the divinity (through the sense of indebtedness towards one's ancestors). His next and last step in this long, gradual process is to connect guilt with the bad conscience in order to explain how man could feel a sense of indissoluble guilt as an overriding *existential* condition. For, while earliest man had felt indebtedness and a burden towards his ancestry, he could always "pay off" that debt by observing piety and customs.[23]

The feeling of existential guilt arose among the violently subjugated peoples of "bad conscience." Though they inherited the notion of the gods and the attendant feeling of guilt from the masters, they eventually transfigured that awareness into a permanent sense of "guilt" that could never be "paid off." Furthermore, they (mis)interpreted their tortured inner life, which arose from inner-directed cruelty, as signs of an "original guilt," as a manifestation of a hopeless inadequacy toward God; and they punished their natural inclinations, their old "animal self," based on a particular reading of "God" in which the divinity was the opposite of any affirmative instinctual expression. Never being able to fulfill the lofty conceptions demanded by their "God," the men of "bad conscience" had to fall impossibly short of His expectations, which just increased their sense of guilt and inadequacy:

In "God" he seizes upon the ultimate antithesis he can find to his real and irredeemable animal instincts, he reinterprets these self-same animal instincts as debt/guilt before God (as animosity, insurrection, rebellion against the "master", the "father", the primeval ancestor and beginning of the world), he pitches himself into the contradiction of "God" and "Devil", he emits every "no" which he says to himself, nature, naturalness and the reality of his being as a "yes", as existing, living, real, as God, as the holiness of God, as God-the-Judge, as

---

23 The identification of guilt/debt with "God" as, in effect, the ultimate creditor, to whom one's debt can never be paid off, has resulted in a deepening internalization of the guilt complex instead of its reversal and disappearance, which should have been the more natural development: "With the moralization of the concepts debt/guilt and duty and their relegation to *bad* conscience, we have, in reality, an attempt to *reverse* the direction of the development I have described, or at least halt its movement: now the prospect for a once-and-for-all payment *is to be* foreclosed, out of pessimism, now our glance *is to* bounce and recoil disconsolately off an iron impossibility, now those concepts 'debt' and 'duty' *are to be* reversed" (*GM* II, 21).

God-the-Hangman, as the beyond, as eternity, as torture without end, as hell, as immeasurable punishment and guilt. (*GM* II, 22)

Nietzsche exposes this mechanism of self-inflicted pain and "guilt" as the redirected will to power of a broken-down type that cannot find "natural" expression in outer-released energy against other wills and so must redirect the same energy against the self: "that will to torment oneself, that suppressed cruelty of animal man who has been frightened back into himself and given an inner life, incarcerated in the 'state' to be tamed, and has discovered bad conscience so that he can hurt himself, after the *more natural* outlet of this wish to hurt had been blocked" (*GM* II, 22). The mechanism of "guilt" is *his* means, his original means, to inflict pain on a permitted "object": *himself*. "Debt towards *God*: this thought becomes an instrument of torture" (*GM* II, 22).

It is important to re-emphasize that this behavior too reflects "active" will, "except that the material on which the formative and rapacious nature of this force vents itself is precisely man himself, his whole animal old self – and *not*, as in that greater and more eye-catching phenomenon, the *other* man, the *other* men" (*GM* II, 18). In other words, despite the hidden efforts of the individual's internal work on its instincts, it is a form of individual will *even if* that action takes place "driven from sight" and within the "soul" and cannot be spontaneously directed outward or recognized from without. For it is still an "action" *against* the self; and this "split-off" will assumes the role of, simultaneously, judge, interpreter, and condemner of its own instinctual life. In that process, it finds *itself* "guilty," thereby giving itself license to "punish" its "other" "animal" self:

We have a here a sort of madness of the will showing itself in mental cruelty which is absolutely unparalleled: man's *will* to find himself guilty and condemned without hope of reprieve, his *will* to think of himself as punished, without the punishment ever being equivalent to the level of guilt, his *will* to infect and poison the fundamentals of things with the problem of punishment and guilt in order to cut himself off, once and for all, from the way out of this labyrinth of "fixed ideas", this *will* to set up an ideal – that of a "holy God" –, in order to be palpably convinced of his own absolute worthlessness in the face of this ideal. (*GM* II, 22)

NIETZSCHE'S "NATURALISM" VERSUS DARWINIAN NATURALISM

I will now contrast Nietzsche's and Darwin's descriptions of morality's origins based on two common constituents of their thought: their belief that morality revealed naturalist origins[24] and had emerged from a dynamic process of wills competing within nature; and morality had expanded through state formation, that is, within the parameters of a successful socialization process. To summarize *GM* II briefly, Nietzsche first argued that morality of custom had rendered man predictable. Antecedent to this process, primitive man exhibited forgetfulness and an obliviousness to community. Pain was instrumental in the process of "memory"-formation, though it did not have a specific "meaning" or purpose; it was randomly employed. Whatever methods succeeded in "reminding" the will of commitments were used, no matter how senseless and brutal the mechanism now appears to us. However, this random process did not make the person more "moral," only "predictable" to others. He could make promises and commitments when necessary, and his allegiance was to other like-willed individuals. Eventually, he no longer needed rigid strictures and customs after the powerful bonds of earlier communities had loosened, since he had internalized the behavior required by the original custom.

On the other hand, a will so full of respect and gratitude towards its kind is a wild, "innocent" beast of prey when it comes to other less organized, less aggressive nomadic tribes. The active will to power unleashed in the wild makes the latter subservient to its will. The "bad conscience" emerges from the instinctual reservoir of such subjugated wills. While this "morality" is a product of natural conflict, it is a derivative, lesser form of will to power that cannot project itself in "innocent" conscience. Thus, "morality" may be an entirely "natural" phenomenon, in that it originates in the will, but it expresses a specific instinctual reality. It is not a historical phenomenon *per se*, nor a stage in the evolution of mankind, but an interpretation projected into nature based on the instinctual requirements of specific wills.

The tension in Nietzsche's naturalistic account resides in the following dichotomy: while forced to present this "development" as a series of successive stages in history, he actually conceives of it as a series of simultaneous, interlocking, but not necessarily interrelated events. For him, it is always a question of wills "acting" in the here and now. But he must explain how a specific interpretation was able to suppress other

[24] On this point, I agree with Clark, who writes that Nietzsche's "naturalistic" perspective in *GM* "treats morality as a phenomenon of life, as a purely natural phenomenon, one whose existence is to be explained without any reference to a world beyond nature, a supernatural or metaphysical world" (Clark, "Introduction," xxii). But once again, concordance with Darwin on this one question does not signify an agreement with his "naturalism."

competing narratives, and he must do this while working within the parameters of the historically ascendant paradigm – contemporary (evolutionary) naturalism. Though he seems to indicate that the inception of the "bad conscience" (or, in his understanding, "morality") is a singular, sudden, one-time occurrence – i.e. when "superior" aggressive warriors forced nomadic tribes into submission – that represents only one strand of "development" resulting from wills clashing in nature. It is, indeed, an unintended, though inevitable, side-effect of clashing wills.

Darwin, too, denies a transcendent basis for morality and instead approaches it as an entirely this-worldly, human-based phenomenon. Its emergence and development had to be made consistent with the requirements of natural selection. But while Nietzsche sees morality as just one single strand of interpretation, Darwin accepts "morality" as a historical given – namely, as a code of conduct that had evolved from primitive origins into an uncontestable natural "fact." Furthermore, the way in which Darwin explains how the "moral sense" had evolved through natural selection, though flawed, is still tenable; it does not necessarily contradict the spirit of the theory itself. Tribes that had proven more social, cohesive, and cooperative were more successful in the struggle for existence than less organized competitors, and their variation was favored: "Such social qualities, the paramount importance of which to the lower animals is disputed by no one, were no doubt acquired by the progenitors of man in a similar manner, namely, through natural selection, aided by inherited habit."[25] The difficulties arise when Darwin must explain how individuals might come to *surrender* their "active" will to a higher collective authority, for he could not envision superior active wills projecting power downward, only the authority of a state that had evolved out of the community itself.

To resolve the dilemma between the individual and the collective will, Darwin presupposes an "instinctive sympathy" in man, a sentiment he shares with other animals. Darwin cannot say when this instinct evolved in humans, but he does recognize it as the source for man's "moral sense": "In order that primeval men, or the ape-like progenitors of man, should have become social, they must have acquired the same instinctive feelings which impel other animals to live in a body; and they no doubt exhibited the same general disposition."[26] Thus, "morality" – or, more specifically, the ability to cooperate within the community – evolved from original "instinctual sympathy." The latter became more deeply ingrained through communal approbation, the force of habit, and inheritance.

---

[25] Darwin, *Descent*, 162.   [26] Darwin, *Descent*, 161–62.

Punishment for transgressions also contributed to the reinforcement of social tendencies, though Darwin emphasizes other factors such as positive example, repetition (habit), and possible inheritance:[27] "Ultimately a highly complex sentiment, having its first origin in the social instincts, largely guided by the approbation of our fellow-men, ruled by reason, self-interest, and in later times by deep religious feelings, confirmed by instruction and habit, all combined, constitute our moral sense or conscience."[28]

In this fashion, Darwin could avoid presenting the state as a creation by particular wills. The state did not reflect specific interests or factions, i.e. the will to power, but had evolved out of the social, sympathetic side of man's nature. Though Darwin does not deny that egotistical motivations continue to exist within this structure, he believes that evolution would eliminate "selfish" traits and would promote altruistic virtues over time: "Looking to future generations, there is no cause to fear that the social instincts will grow weaker, and we may expect that virtuous habits will grow stronger, becoming perhaps fixed by inheritance. In this case the struggle between our higher and lower impulses will be less severe, and virtue will be triumphant."[29]

For both Nietzsche and Darwin, then, state-formation was crucially involved in the development of morality – but for diametrically opposed reasons. While for Darwin the communal bonds that emerged from man's instinctual sympathy allowed for a greater cohesiveness and solidarity among members of a community, it was the robust, unbroken egotism of warriors, for Nietzsche, which had formed the "state" structure. However, it was a hierarchically structured "state," with an aristocracy as its crown and a large mass of subjugated wills as its foundation. The slaves were made pliant to their masters' wills and served as the lowest, servile functions in a steep, broad-based social pyramid. According to Nietzsche's model, then, "morality" had emerged from *below* – specifically, from the spirit of "bad conscience" that arose from the thwarted will to power of social inferiors. "Morality" did not represent the terminological *opposite* of "egotism," that is, the gradual

---

[27] In the *Autobiography*, Darwin repeatedly refers to the importance of *approbation* for moral development and how it served as a crucial motivating factor in his own life: "If [man] acts for the good of others, he will receive the approbation of his fellow men and gain the love of those with whom he lives; and this latter gain undoubtedly is the highest pleasure on this earth" (94). "All this shows how ambitious I was; but I think that I can say with truth that in after years, though I cared in the highest degree for the approbation of such men as Lyell and Hooker, who were my friends, I did not care much about the general public" (82).

[28] Darwin, *Descent*, 165–66.   [29] Darwin, *Descent*, 104.

overcoming of egotism through a refinement of the "moral sense," but *just another expression of egotism* from the optic of the tortured man of "bad conscience."

CONCLUSIONS

GM II presents Nietzsche's alternative theory for the origins of morality. His explanation appears to be entirely naturalistic. Like Darwin, he accepts that morality has no transcendental foundation and originates in human "prehistory." Nietzsche agrees also that morality emerged from socialization. Darwin locates a single instinctual source for "morality": man's "instinctual sympathy." Since he accepts this as the origin of communal life and the "moral sense," he prioritizes positive reinforcement, since that alone could fortify the inherent "sympathetic sense." A more fully developed communal spirit could counteract over time the "natural" tendency among humans to particularize and act on private interests, thus undermining the community.

According to Nietzsche, however, historical "developments" need to be explained on the basis of active, outer-directed will to power. Man's default position is amoral power projection, or "innocent" egoism. Since Nietzsche does not believe that morality can possibly deny egoism, he must explain how that particular understanding of morality had arisen and could achieve predominance. This he achieves through his concept of the "two-fold history of morality," where "morality" becomes the "historical" by-product, the unintended side-effect, of power projection on the part of strong, active wills.

Nietzsche presents two dominant trajectories, or historical narrative threads. The one led to the creation of a "sovereign individual." Here, Nietzsche focuses exclusively on the "negative" components of pain and cruelty. Since he does not recognize an intrinsic "moral" sentiment in man, as does Darwin, he must explain how outer-directed power works on others to create a sense of predictability among an entirely egotistical, self-oriented "man-animal." This sense was achieved via a harsh morality of custom, which had the fortuitous effect of producing an autonomous individual – one with a *higher, healthier* sense of egoism. Able to make promises to like-spirited types, the sovereign individual eventually liberated himself from the earlier forms of cruel, arbitrary customs that had set the stage for his arrival. But such "free" wills were the descendants of others who had directed their will to power against less aggressive tribes

in the wild.[30] Subjugated, these tribes became the functions and extensions of their masters' will. Here, among such types, the "bad conscience"
arose and from this instinctual reservoir an alternative valuation system
was born: the complete metaphysics of "morality."

This simplified summation of Nietzsche's highly complex, interwoven,
and multi-layered argument in *GM* II subverts Darwin's evolutionary
premises on three significant levels. For one, the "bad conscience" of
the slaves was the contingent product of active will on the part of warrior tribes with superior organization. But the "morality" born out of
the "bad conscience" is *also* an expression of (re)active egoism – it *must*
be, since altruism is only a chimera from the perspective of "bad conscience" – even if that egoism does not accord with the understanding
of "nature" from the perspective of the strong. Though Nietzsche focuses
on interpretation – more precisely, on the *act* of interpretation from the
perspective of "bad conscience" and *ressentiment* – he recognizes that the
individual wills of "bad conscience" are flesh-and-blood *actors* in "history." The "moral" perspective is not merely an abstract conceptual reality; it is first and foremost an instinctual one;[31] by their very existence as
natural beings, "moral" wills *must* project will to power through interpretation. For this reason, the sheer number of subjugated wills in the
ancient world, expressing their wills via Christian "institutions," could
subvert the Roman state without even directly confronting or overthrow-
ing its political structures.

Second, Nietzsche presents this process as only marginally causal –
one process (the random exploits of conquering warrior hordes) leading contingently to the creation of a second (the emergence of the "bad
conscience" among enslaved wills). But *GM* II is so complex to decipher
because Nietzsche neither believes in, nor adheres to, a causal, "evolutionary" account, but instead emphasizes the simultaneity of wills acting in
history as well as the psychological processes that occurred as a result of
certain "active" events. These are not one-time events *per se*; they are a

---

[30] "*They* [the conqueror and master race] are not the ones in whom 'bad conscience' grew; that is
obvious – but it would not have grown *without* them, this ugly growth would not be there if a
huge amount of freedom had not been driven from the world, or at least driven from sight and,
at the same time, made *latent* by the pressure of their hammer blows and artists' violence" (*GM*
II, 17).

[31] My main disagreement with Deleuze's model in *Nietzsche and Philosophy* (despite its brilliance)
is that its analysis of active and (re)active wills and *ressentiment* remains too conceptual and historically abstract, too Hegelian; and Deleuze does not show active and (re)active wills as living
actors whose will to power is articulated through interpretation.

series of interrelated, contingent episodes that emerge spontaneously from active projection of will to power.

As a result, Nietzsche can never pursue one narrative strand alone, but shows rather how various strands temporarily merge and create new permutations based on the preexistence of specific instinctual realities.[32] For example, the development of the conceptual strand of "guilt" out of the very material beginnings in the creditor–debtor relationship could later develop into the definitional basis for "guilt" in an existential sense once it could coalesce with the separate, unrelated psychological phenomenon of the "bad conscience" (which, in turn, was the product of the very real material suppression of individual wills). What was originally an "amoral" and unrelated experience – the state of indebtedness based on deferred punishment and the attendant license to inflict cruelty – could be transposed into an existential understanding of "guilt" from the perspective of wills not able to shake off the feelings of "bad conscience" in relation to their disoriented instincts. Christian metaphysics could then make sense of a confused instinctual reality arising from inward-directed cruelty, and "moral" wills could enact a "slave revolt" simply by embodying a majority confluence of (Christian) wills.

Finally, Nietzsche's "genealogical" method does not recognize historical "facts" *per se* or intrinsic meaning in certain events, only *interpretations*. In other words, strands of meaning that coalesce around events only receive motive force as a result of the momentary constellation of instincts that "enliven" them.[33] For example, punishment might have been one of the main mechanisms to render man predictable, but there was no intrinsic meaning to punishment other than the specific requirement demanded at the moment. With this form of explanation, Nietzsche undercuts the entire methodology behind the explanations of the genealogists, who first locate a procedure, then project into it an all-encompassing and overarching metaphysical "meaning" for man's moral development.

GM II, therefore, not only posits a possible alternative hypothesis for Darwin's theory of "morality" based on natural selection; even more, its arguments pull the rug out from underneath his and his followers'

---

[32] Clark also talks about strands of interpretation and the need to disentangle the strands "so that we can see what is actually involved in" a term's use (Clark, "Introduction," xxv). But Nietzsche recognizes the continuous simultaneity of different strands of interpretation; it is only through the dominant collective will to power of the moment that a particular strand of interpretation is "enlivened" and given precedence and exclusivity over others.

[33] In this, Nietzsche reveals his anti-Hegelian approach to history. Hegel's philosophy of history conceptualizes historical trends and separates them off from actual human agents. Nietzsche recognizes how Darwin adopts this Hegelian strategy when he says "without Hegel no Darwin."

genealogical methods *per se* as well as the "logic" of their evolutionary narrative. In this manner, Nietzsche reveals Darwinian "naturalism" to be an *alternative* metaphysics to the Christian one, with its "morality" merely requiring an alternative theoretical framework and grounding. But by showing that "morality" is not a given, but rather a psychological construct arising from instinctual wills to power clashing in the eternal here and now, Nietzsche took Darwin's ideas to their ultimate, radical conclusion, thereby subverting the evolutionary narrative at its very core.

CHAPTER 6

Darwin's "science": or, how to beat
the shell game

GM III finalizes and radicalizes Nietzsche's anti-Darwinian critique by undermining the entire belief in the possibility, even desirability, of scientific truth. The essay does not center exclusively on science. It focuses roughly equal attention on other aspects of the "ascetic ideal" – specifically, its connections to art, philosophy, and religion. But its final exposure of the ascetic imperative behind nineteenth-century science represents the resounding climax of both the essay *as well as* the text as a whole.[1] *GM* is a single and sustained polemic against the extension of Darwinian premises to the important study of man. Further, it argues against the inviolability of those premises as a result of their transfiguration into scientific "truth." Nietzsche's decision to dedicate an entire work to the question of Darwinian genealogy reveals his prescience in understanding that Darwinism would represent a credible and historically influential contemporary interpretation, a "*scientific*" paradigm, of man and nature.

At the same time, Darwin's resounding success at the late century and beyond has obscured the historical context of Nietzsche's critique. Having occurred at the inception of the "Darwinian revolution," his analysis suggests alternative philosophical vantage points *before* Darwin's biological perspective had solidified into "objective," canonical science. By reinserting *GM* into its historical context, we will regain an interpretative stance easily overlooked thanks to our facile focus on Darwinian versus anti-Darwinian (i.e. Christian) forces – that is, the seductive historical narrative of a now triumphant Darwinism. By resituating *GM* into its historical and cultural setting, we can learn to comprehend, as Nietzsche

---

[1] Most recent commentaries on *GM* have recognized the importance of *GM* III for the text as a whole and many seem to sense that the last sections of *GM* III, in particular, play a crucial role in Nietzsche's overall project (see the articles by Conway, Hatab, and Janaway in *Journal of Nietzsche Studies* 35/36 [2008]). But while some sense that the last sections *might* implicate the truth imperative of modern science, none goes so far as to argue that Nietzsche's *attack against scientific truth* represents the culmination of the entire text.

himself did, how the debates that fed into Darwinism were still open, fluid, and undecided.

ASCETICISM AS A FORM OF WILL TO POWER

Nietzsche's theory of the will to power suggests that all physiological entities seek to maximize the conditions of their personal power: "Every animal ... instinctively strives for an optimum of favourable conditions in which to fully release his power and achieve his maximum of power-sensation" (*GM* III, 7). Rather than treating the human species as a stage in the larger process of organic evolution, Nietzsche holds individuals to be self-contained physiological examples of unique and unhistorical wills to power, constantly clashing in the here and now. From this perspective, it would become impossible to establish a single grand narrative for "man" as such. Instead, the notion of "man" was itself a psycho-physiological construct from the perspective of a specific biological will. That entity evaluates from the basis of its own biological reality and cannot inhabit contending interpretations existing outside its instinctual parameters.

GM III continues with this mode of thinking. It treats the various interpretations as expressions of particular instinctual realities or types. Not concerned with the inherent truthfulness or historical accuracy of various interpretations as such, Nietzsche posits that all interpretations are reducible to a particular instinctual constellation. In this essay, he breaks down his analysis from the rubric of the "ascetic ideal" – that is, whether a particular perspective on life reflects *ascetic principles*. Asceticism itself, in turn, reflects Nietzsche's broader claim that all human existence must either affirm life in all things or, alternatively, be directed against life at its core. For Nietzsche, the latter reflects a perversion of the (affirmative) life-principle in the sense that it pits life against life: "A self-contradiction such as that which seems to occur in the ascetic, 'life *against* life', is – so much is obvious – seen from the physiological, not just the psychological standpoint, simply nonsense. It can only be *apparent*" (*GM* III, 13).

But Nietzsche not only considers the ascetic perspective a *relative* interpretation and he not only interprets it as an expression of a particular internal coordination of the instincts. Far more, he considers it a form of biological (*re*)action – namely, the only means by which degenerating life can sustain itself in highly unfavorable conditions: "*the ascetic ideal springs from the protective and healing instincts of a degenerating life*, which uses every means to maintain itself and struggles for its existence; it indicates a partial physiological inhibition and exhaustion against which the deepest instincts of life, which have remained intact, continually struggle with new methods and inventions" (*GM* II, 13). Thus, he both relativizes all perspectives through the theory of the will to power and evaluates them under the rubric of whether they reflect outer-directed, affirmative will to power or emerge, rather, from the defensive reaction of a weak, degenerating will, one which can only preserve itself through ascetic means.

THE QUESTION OF DARWINIAN "SURVIVAL"

The above distinction again suggests the notion of Darwinian "survival." Some Darwinists argue that Darwin never explicitly equates "survival" with "deserving to survive." Danto maintains that Nietzsche had misunderstood this component of Darwin's thought. Along with many other thinkers in the nineteenth century, Nietzsche had inserted a "normative component into the notion of fitness or unfitness. Blond beasts would drop like flies were the oxygen to disappear for ten minutes from the earth's atmosphere. But clams might survive that nicely."[2] It is, indeed, doubtful that any serious thinker would disagree with this. But the implications of Nietzsche's critique target the "objective" notion of survival, not only that of fitness. The fact that clams would survive such environmental change does not mean that they were "fitter" than blond beasts just because they had survived. It simply means that this type of organism would survive, period. To imply, however, that these organisms had an intrinsic quality that allowed them to survive – and therefore suggest they were "fitter" – meant taking a neutral biological characteristic, and one for which the organism could claim no credit, and turning it into a "virtue." In short, it meant projecting a *meaning* or higher significance into the "fact" of survival.

Nietzsche, in fact, argues the reverse. For him, it is Darwin and his followers who insert a normative component into the fact of survival; it becomes a "virtue" in itself. Nietzsche, on the other hand, does not wish to eliminate normative standards at all; nor does he demand an "objective" criterion by which to measure natural selection (such as the preservation of the species for the Darwinists); rather, he argues that such "normative" valuations are unavoidable and should, indeed, be made explicit and openly acknowledged (see the addendum to *GM* I, 17).

Contemporary Darwinists now argue that Darwin never projected a normative element into survival. A particular organism could survive in

---

[2] Danto, *Nietzsche as Philosopher*, 188fn.

specific environmental conditions even if it were repugnant to our moral sensibilities. Darwinism only evaluated species preservation and the fitness for survival, not how that survival affected our value judgments.[3] If one were to eliminate, for a moment, the question of whether Darwin had suspended moral judgment on this issue, which is in itself doubtful, it is interesting to note that on this particular point Nietzsche could almost be said to agree with Darwin. For Nietzsche does not interest himself with the question of whether certain wills survive better under particular conditions and could increase their chances for survival or whether such a process can be viewed objectively. He merely goes further in that he implies that Darwinism itself is a specific perspective on that process by claiming that such survivors are fitter, even relatively speaking. Nietzsche instead postulates that Darwin's theory is an interpretation that can always be said to exist alongside other possible interpretations and that its theoretical dominance and evaluative standards are contingent on the momentary constellation of instinctual wills.

Based on this assumption, Nietzsche's "higher" type would not "survive" in a Darwinian world, because the standard of "survival of the fittest" in itself reflects the will to power of a particular will or constellation of wills. For example, the momentary success and survival of a specific social group – let us say, the industrial and technocratic classes of the nineteenth and twentieth centuries – does not prove their intrinsic "fitness" or superiority over any other classes at the time or in "history." Rather, it represents the momentary success of a common constellation of biological wills in asserting their existential conditions in relation to other competing "historical" wills.[4]

Correspondingly, the relative success and propagation of a particular class along with its interpretation does not eliminate competing wills. It just signifies the temporary prioritization, and marginalization, of one specific strand of interpretation vis-à-vis others. Since Nietzsche's higher

---

[3] Darwin equivocates on this issue: "Even Darwin himself admitted that survival does not result in 'perfect' forms of life, that 'contrivances of nature' preserve beings that are sometimes 'abhorrent to our ideas of fitness'. On the other hand, this is not a typical expression of his position. More typical is the belief that those individuals and species that avoid extinction are 'new and improved' forms of life and that success in nature is measured by the preservation of those who are the 'fittest'" (Stack, *Nietzsche and Lange*, 159–60).

[4] All three major political movements (liberalism, communism, and fascism) in the past 150 years since the publication of the *Origin* (as well as the scientific communities within those political cultures) have been able to accommodate Darwinism into their ideological systems. Every one of the political elites in these respective systems, that is, has not recognized a conflict between the social implications of theoretical Darwinism and its own political legitimacy. Even the Catholic Church has made its peace with Darwinism and has acknowledged key aspects of its tenets.

type is characterized by the spirit of the *agon* – active energy asserted in a forum outside the parameters of "nature" – he cannot "survive" within a prevailing interpretative climate which privileges (re)active, eliminationist energy. Moreover, the fact that Darwin works with a functionalist paradigm (survival/the fittest), yet fails to challenge morality as such, means that he still conceives of competition within the framework of a "moral universe." But the latter interpretation and reading of nature most powerfully reflect a specific type's marginalizing, (re)active will to power.

The division in *GM* III into the categories artist, philosopher, priest, and scientist further underscores this distinction. Nietzsche does not treat these types as progressive stages in human history, but as simultaneous, competitively clashing typologies. Each of these identities serves as an interpretative shell that allows a specific biological type to assume an easily identifiable social form. Though outer shells shift according to the historical conditions (or "environment," to use a Darwinian term) – for example, the decline of the status of priest does not indicate a decline, or supersession, of the type as such, but rather a decline in the value, stature, or prioritization of that specific shell as an expression of will to power within the social hierarchy – the biological types behind the mask change only marginally.[5]

For example, the type "priest" does not decline in significance because religion ceases to exert authority in the society or because the doctrines of religion have been discredited or exposed as "superstition" by science. Instead, the shell of priest continues to remain at all times an attractive, viable option, despite (or even because of) opposition to its beliefs. Alternatively, the same instinctual type will locate other shells which might offer it a similar, conducive interpretative fit under changed social conditions, one which will present it with an appropriate social scope for its will to power.[6]

PRIESTLY WILL TO POWER

Nietzsche's "priest" offers other interesting points of contrast. As I have argued, Darwin reached an uneasy accord with the forces of established

---

[5] In one of the "Anti-Darwin" passages in the notebooks, Nietzsche writes: "The type remains constant; one cannot 'dénaturer la nature' ... Everything competes in order to maintain the type" (*KSA* XIV, 133).

[6] Nietzsche's repeated characterization of Kant as a clandestine priest (*verkappter Priester*) reflects this awareness: Kant as a "priestly type" had slipped into the shell of "philosopher" while his will to power still reflected its latent theological origins and aspirations.

religion. Though careful to distance himself from radical expressions of atheism so as not to offend the status quo, he had nothing but contempt for the doctrines of established Christianity, as controversial excised passages from his *Autobiography* reveal.[7] In fact, Darwin exhibited many of the intellectual characteristics of the Enlightenment, including scorn for established religion and faith in the ideals of science.

According to Nietzsche's understanding, the priestly shell never disappears. It continues to attract the same type of instinctual will or takes on new, slightly altered external forms. In that sense, the industrial modern era is not inherently "superior" to the Middle Ages, for example, but is only a period where competitive "moral" wills have succeeded in establishing the interpretative framework for *their* optimal form of existence while successfully marginalizing other existence-threatening wills. The temporary success of Darwinism as the predominant interpretative perspective represents only a provisional truce between two competitive constellations of wills.

Nietzsche also in some ways admires the priest as such, for the very reason that he can acknowledge the existence of the instinctual type, while recognizing that the priestly interpretation reflects just an embellishment of the type. Since he has no illusion about the priestly perspective as such, that is, as an ultimate truth-claim about God, he is free to approach the perspective as a particular manifestation of the will to power, one which can emerge at all times and places: "Let us consider how regularly and universally the ascetic priest makes his appearance in almost any age; he does not belong to any race in particular; he thrives everywhere; he comes from every social class" (*GM* III, 11). Furthermore, the priest represents a formidable intellectual adversary, a true *challenge* to the "higher type." Rather than treating the priest as an opponent to "truth" who needs to be suppressed, Nietzsche respects the formidable strength, durability, and psychological acuity of the type as well as the persuasive power of its metaphysical perspective. The priestly will represents both the extremes of decadence as well as its antithesis – the will to power over degenerating life, both its own and others'. The strength of the priestly type resides

---

[7] Darwin's wife excised the following statement from his *Autobiography*: "[I] have never since doubted even for a single second that my conclusion was correct. I can indeed hardly see how anyone ought to wish Christianity to be true; for if so the plain language of the text seems to show that the men who do not believe, and this would include my Father, Brother and almost all my best friends, will be everlastingly punished. And this is a damnable doctrine" (Darwin, *Autobiography*, 87). Mrs. Darwin said that she would dislike the passage to be published – "it seems to me raw."

in its ability to master the anarchy of its instincts and to focus them as a form of (re)active (interpretative) will against a more powerful opposSitional force.

The instinctual decadence of the priest also permits him psychoSlogical insight into the herd he directs and controls as well as into the rivals that stand in his way. The latter he approaches – if in the form of the "beasts of prey" – with all the weapons of the "spirit": "He will not be spared from waging war with predators, a war of cunning (of the 'spirit') rather than of force, it goes without saying" (*GM* III, 15). Through cleverness, patience, and guile, the priest thrusts himself into the higher realm of active and affirmative wills, sowing discord and instinctual conSfusion among them while attempting to create dependence on his form of authority and "cure": "If forced by necessity, he would probably even step among the other kind of beast of prey themselves, in all likelihood with bearish solemnity, venerable, clever, cold, deceptively superior, as the herald and mouthpiece of more mysterious powers, determined to sow suffering, division and self-contradiction on this ground wherever he can, and only too certain of his skill at being master of the *suffering* at any time" (*GM* III, 15).

In respect to his modern rivals, namely, contemporary natural scienStists and free-thinkers, the priest responds with the inherent superiorSity and caution that his "spiritual" form of existence has allowed him to cultivate through centuries of covert warfare against higher forms of existence. Superior "logic" and "intelligence" or a systematic challenge to his metaphysics cannot defeat or derail him, for he has proven to be the more durable, psychologically acute type in his historical resilience. Nietzsche ultimately does greater justice to the psychological depth and acuity of the priestly type, because he eliminates the immaterial question of "truth" from his psychological profile of the priest. The nineteenth-century natural scientists' commitment to the ideal of scientific truth, on the other hand, has prevented them from recognizing how Christian metaphysics represents merely the extension of the priest as an instinctSual type. Christian superstitions, dogmas, and miracles are not historical obstacles in the path towards "truth," as Darwin and his followers believe, but the necessary and intrinsic accouterments of priestly will to power. Superstitions are not counterfactual, that is, but are "logically" embedded within a complete metaphysical system that even allows for superstitions as legitimate "proofs" of a Christian "moral universe."

Finally, Nietzsche's "priest" is a highly self-conscious and cynical manipulator of truths which for him are simply provisional means to exert will to power. Rather than subscribing to the truth and morality of his public utterances, the priest uses his keen psychological insight to uncover the ambiguity and relativity of those terms and then instrumentalizes that awareness so that he can manipulate and tyrannize the herd under his "moral" stewardship. The priest can thus be considered the first decisive step in the direction of a transvaluation of values, except that he opts for the power and the authority that accrue from the control of his charges by maintaining and manipulating "moral" categories.

Priestly will to power could also explain why the Darwinists could underestimate the tenacity and resilience of institutional Christianity even when confronted with the "evidence" of Darwin's theories. The Darwinists' faith in evolution and in "truth" as such led them to frame their struggle as one between "enlightenment" and "superstition," where the superior "logic" of evolution would ultimately convert skeptics to their cause. But in Nietzsche's view, Christianity's longevity resides least of all in the inherent veracity of Christian metaphysics, but in the priestly caste's psychological acuity and finesse, and its astute manipulation of its and others' instinctual decadence. The priest's actual *superiority* over the modern scientist in Nietzsche's eyes resides in his lack of naïveté about "truth" and in the fact that he *knows* the metaphysical constructs to be instruments in his larger, long-term objective of total will to power.

ASCETICISM AND THE ARTIST

Nietzsche's critical assessment of the ascetic phenomenon does not lead him to reject asceticism outright. Rather, the crucial question becomes whether (1) ascetic practices are temporarily introduced in order to enhance life and project the force of affirmation; or (2) whether asceticism gives birth to an elaborate interpretative apparatus, developed from the perspective of a specific will, which it then directs against all life via (re)active energy. *If* the latter, a metaphysical interpretation of life is positioned in the spirit of *ressentiment* against all individual manifestations of will to power as active, creative, life-affirming force.

"Good and evil" as the dominant poles within a "moral universe" arise from the second brand of asceticism. The latter asceticism erects interpretative polarities rather than recognize how evaluations only express physiological–biological realities. It is not a willed, temporary, and self-imposed constraint on active energy in order to enhance life-affirmative individual will (i.e. a "positive" brand of asceticism), but a physiologically contingent, (re)active impulse focused against *all* expressions of active life affirmation as such. The latter asceticism is achieved by embedding ascetic values and interpretations into the foundations of life itself and then by metaphysically interpreting existence as a reflection of ascetic principles.

The first question Nietzsche poses in *GM* III is: What do ascetic ideals mean for the artist as instinctual type (*GM* III, 2–4)? Using his former friend Wagner as his prime example of the artist, Nietzsche argues that the great artist can only create a world based on his own physiological reality; he does not have access to a "higher" reality as such.[8] All other considerations (e.g. political, social, or personal) are either subordinated to his ultimate purpose (creation of the artwork) or become experiential fodder for aesthetic production. It is therefore impossible for the artist to interpret or analyze his inspirational moments, for he would need to delve into the instinctual reserves behind his creative drives and, what is more, to be truthful about such an understanding.[9] As a result, "the artist" can never claim unique insight into a greater metaphysical truth or "morality" ("a sort of mouthpiece of the 'in itself' of things, a telephone to the beyond [*ein Telefon des Jenseits*]" [*GM* III, 5]); he can only express certain inner biological realities, his *own* realities, through the medium of the artwork; these are later transposed – via a supposedly "disinterested," "objective" interpretation of those drives – into "moral" categories. In short, the artist can recognize *his* truths in things; he (and his interpreters) only later projects *their* "moral" meanings into his creations.

The problem arises, Nietzsche continues, when a great and complete artist such as Wagner attempts to go beyond his natural instinctual limitations and to inhabit a type of existence which he cannot embody or when he gets tired or bored of his existence and wants to enter into a different reality from his own, for once becoming an active agent, rather than just a passive medium for his instinctual drives: "A perfect and complete artist is cut off from what is 'real' and actual for all eternity; on the other hand, we can understand how he can occasionally be so tired of the eternal 'unreality' and falsity of his inner existence that he is driven to despair, – and that he will then probably try to reach into that area strictly forbidden to him, into reality, into real *being*" (*GM* III, 4).

---

[8] This is just a reiteration of a position Nietzsche had already held in *HH* (see Chapter 1).
[9] Nietzsche claims that most people, on account of their "moral" naïveté, are not ready to understand and appreciate the *true* well-springs of great artists' creative energy, which are "beyond good and evil": "These 'good people', – all of them now moralized root and branch and disgraced as far as honesty is concerned and ruined for all eternity: which of them could stand a single *truth* 'about man'! ... Or, to ask more pertinently: which of them could bear a *true* biography" (*GM* III, 19).

When such an artist then attempts to "leap into his opposite," he ends by promoting values that run counter to his own instincts – even to the principles that allow him to be creative in the first place. In the case of Wagner, the non-ironic effort to embody the chastity, purity, and "virtue" of a "Parsifal" undermined the upright, healthy sensuality he had previously championed, a sensuality that had been the libidinal well-spring of his creative energy. *Parsifal* taken as a *serious* work can only provoke laughter – the pathetic spectacle of a sensualist turning against himself and his passions and suddenly promoting a life-negating asceticism. The problem that Nietzsche has with Wagner, in the end, is not that he presents the role of Parsifal at all – every great artist enters into numerous, at times opposing roles and guises – but that he sacrifices and loses sight of artistic goals, integrity, and mastery for the sake of *becoming* a projection of his aesthetic fabrications – even his physiological antithesis.[10]

The artist, then, represents the opposite of ascetic principles,[11] forever removed from the real world and the sphere of action by the virtue of his aesthetic sensibility and creative temperament. But the artist need not be directed with the spirit of resentment against forms of life beyond his reach. His vision can still represent an apotheosis of affirmative instincts. The artist can permit himself, and indulge in, the freest expression of instinctual, spiritualized energy. In fact, it is only through a lack of ascetic control and through a non-judgmental acceptance of all his instincts and passions that the great artist can imagine the richest and broadest spectrum of human life, thought, and possibilities.

Nietzsche, in short, criticizes the artist for his submissive role toward life but not for his artistic temperament *per se*. Though necessary for aesthetic production, artistic self-absorption prevents the artist from developing a principled position in relation to the problems of life and the political powers of the moment. He is too busy seeking patronage and privileges and riding the waves of public opinion to take a principled stand on the great issues of existence:

[10] For Nietzsche, the decadence of his age resided, in part, in modern artists' pathetic attempts to slip into the heroic poses and garbs of past ages and to project their overripe aesthetic sensibilities into types far removed from their own instinctual realities: "Would you believe that as soon as you strip them of her heroic skin, every single Wagnerian heroine becomes pretty much indistinguishable from Madame Bovary! – which lets you see that Flaubert *could* have translated his heroine into Scandinavian or Carthaginian and, properly mythologized, offered her to Wagner as a libretto" (*CW* 9).

[11] Except in cases such as the aged Wagner, who used aesthetic means to promote an ascetic program.

Let us put aside artists for the time being: their position in the world and *against* the world is far from sufficiently independent for their changing valuations *as such* to merit our attention! Down the ages, they have been the valets of a morality or philosophy or religion: quite apart from the fact that they were, unfortunately, often the all-too-glib courtiers of their hangers-on and patrons and sycophants with a nose for old or indeed up-and-coming forces. (*GM* III, 5)

Nietzsche concludes, then, that in the case of the "artist," ascetic ideals mean "*nothing at all*".

PHILOSOPHICAL ASCETICISM AS LIFE-PRACTICE

Nietzsche's subsequent focus is on the philosophical type (*GM* III, 5–10). The "philosopher" compares more favorably to "the artist," for at least he takes a principled stance towards the very same worldly temptations beckoning the artist: "And with that we come to the more serious question: what does it mean if a genuine *philosopher* pays homage to the ascetic ideal, a genuine, independent mind like Schopenhauer, a man and a knight with a brazen countenance who has the courage to be himself, knows how to stand alone and does not wait for the men in front and a nod from on high?" (*GM* III, 5).

The philosopher avoids those worldly temptations, Nietzsche argues; however, he does so not from an inherent sense of "virtue," but rather because they would inhibit him from expressing his instinctive brand of active will. The philosopher's dominating will, the one which subordinates all auxiliary drives and passions, is expressed in a heightened form of contemplative existence. Through it, the philosopher can distance himself from everyday pressures, demands, and temptations. In certain cases, this philosophical stance can be interpreted as a *positive* expression of asceticism: like a jockey or athlete, the philosopher temporarily imposes on himself an ascetic regimen for the purpose of enhancing his performance (*GM* III, 8).

The problem is not that the philosopher attempts to achieve a contemplative distance from life or assume an ascetic position towards beauty, for example. Nietzsche even finds a certain amount of asceticism necessary for the active projection of will in other domains – e.g. in the competitive *agon* – as well as for the philosopher's form of contemplation: "a certain asceticism, a hard and hearty renunciation with a good will, belongs among the most favourable conditions for the highest spirituality, as well as being part of the most natural result of it" (*GM* III, 9).[12] The problem arises when asceticism becomes isolated; when its origin as a *temporary* self-imposed mode of existence gets obfuscated; and when it gets interpreted as the essence of life through philosophical interpretation. It then no longer reflects a physiologically contingent mode of personal self-control for the goal of even greater, heightened active will. It becomes a foundational principle of life mediated through the philosopher's lens. Thus, what began as the optimal conditions for a *particular* type of existence – an essentially philosophical–contemplative type seeking to maximize the conditions for *its* will to power – eventually developed into the "philosopher's attitude par excellence."

How did this transference occur? That is, how did asceticism as *life-practice* get transformed into asceticism as *life-principle*? The philosopher was originally conceived by himself and others as a curious, brooding, community-threatening, life-undermining organism. Instinctually attracted to a contemplative, non-warlike brand of existence, the philosopher was forced to justify his life-practice to others, for he had the dominant customs and traditions of the community at large against him. If he wished to engage in isolated contemplation against communal norms, he first had to create an aura of fear and authority around his "unusual" life-practice: "All that was inactive, brooding and unwarlike in the instincts of contemplative men surrounded them with a deep mistrust for a long time: against which they had no other remedy than to conceive a pronounced *fear* of themselves ... Because they found in themselves all their value judgments turned *against* themselves, they had to fight off every kind of suspicion and resistance to the 'philosopher in themselves'" (*GM* III, 10). The problem was: the only interpretative shell available to the fledgling "philosopher" was that of the *previously conceived* priestly type:[13]

---

[12] When dealing with the artist as type, Nietzsche also gives examples of positive forms of asceticism; those also included Wagner. In Wagner's early works, Nietzsche states, he had incorporated the ideal of chastity, i.e. an "ascetic ideal," into his music; but that was only to gain the position and freedom from which to praise the virtues of sensuality: "For there is not, necessarily, an antithesis between chastity and sensuality" (*GM* III, 2). This unique perspective on sensuality could even be considered "Wagnerian." Furthermore, in the example of Goethe, sensuality could serve as a form of stimulus toward enhanced life from the position of a self-imposed asceticism. In the opposition between chastity and sensuality, "the best and the brightest amongst them, like Goethe, like Hafiz, actually found in it one *more* of life's charms" (*GM* III, 2).

[13] In his discussion of the priestly type, Nietzsche several times uses the interesting signifier *Raupe* and *Raupenform*. Nietzsche argues that the philosopher has always had to slip into the pre-established "caterpillar-form" (*Raupenform*) of the priest (*GM* III, 10). The *Raupe*, or caterpillar, is also the pre-stage, or larva, of the butterfly before metamorphosis. In the *Wahrig* German dictionary, *Raupe* is succinctly defined as "the larva of the butterfly." Nietzsche probably knew

The peculiarly withdrawn attitude of the philosophers, denying the world, hating life, doubting the senses, desensualized, which has been maintained until quite recently to the point where it almost counted for the *philosophical attitude as such*, – this is primarily a result of the desperate conditions under which philosophy evolved and exists at all: that is, philosophy would have been *absolutely impossible* for most of the time on earth without an ascetic mask and suit of clothes, without an ascetic misconception of itself. To put it vividly and clearly: the *ascetic priest* has until the most recent times displayed the vile and dismal form of a caterpillar, which was the only one philosophers were allowed to adopt and creep around in. (*GM* III, 10)

Despite the fact that the philosopher first had to conceal himself behind the mask of priest in order to be able to actualize his brand of existence, Nietzsche argues for one crucial distinction between them. Whereas the priest embodies ascetic principles and claims metaphysical justification for them, the philosopher only pays lip-service to ascetic ideals, for he sees in the latter the freedom to express his own brand of will: "Consequently, what does the ascetic ideal mean for a philosopher? My answer is – you will have guessed ages ago: on seeing an ascetic ideal, the philosopher smiles because he sees an optimum condition of the highest and boldest intellectuality [*Geistigkeit*], – he does *not* deny 'existence' by doing so, but rather affirms *his* existence and *only* his existence" (*GM* III, 7). The philosopher, in short, recognizes too many self-serving advantages for his active understanding of will to power as well as too many "bridges to independence" to offer significant opposition to asceticism – even though he never confuses his specific life-practice with ascetic principles.

On the other hand, asceticism's appeal as a life-practice often places the philosopher dangerously close to asceticism as life-principle. It even allows him to misrepresent the original nature of the ascetic ideal in relation to his own objectives. Emerging from the cultural shadow of the priest, but retaining his mask, the philosopher "had to *play* that part [*darstellen*] in order to be a philosopher, he had to *believe* in it in order to be able to play it [*um es darstellen zu können*]" (*GM* III, 10). As a consequence, the philosopher did not necessarily recognize the interpretational discrepancies between his form of asceticism (as a means to create personal autonomy and cultivate active will) and asceticism as originating in the priestly interpretative paradigm (*ressentiment*-driven will).

the etymological roots of the Latin word "larva," which had negative connotations. Its meanings included "evil spirit, demon, devil" and it "also was used for a terrifying mask ... In Medieval Latin 'larva' could mean 'mask or visor.' 'Larva' is therefore an appropriate term for that stage of an insect's life during which its final form was still hidden or masked" (*American Heritage Dictionary of the English Language*).

Furthermore, the contingent overlap of philosophical asceticism and the original priestly perspective has often induced philosophers to sympathize with priestly-derived metaphysics. It has also led subsequent "moralizers" to confuse the philosopher's ascetic life-practice, i.e. his means to personal power enhancement, with higher "morality" as such, i.e. asceticism at the root of existence.[14] As a result, the philosopher, like the artist (though for different reasons), has not been in a strong enough position historically to challenge the ascetic ideal. He has been physiologically too close to its "positive" forms to offer resistance to its negative manifestation in the form of metaphysics.

PRIESTLY ASCETICISM AS LIFE-PRINCIPLE

According to Nietzsche, the priest is the original embodiment of asceticism as life-principle, and the distinction between active and (re)active wills first came into existence through him. While the philosopher seeks to enter into the *agon* (partially via a restricted application of asceticism) by channeling active will to power in a forum outside nature, the priest seeks to turn nature itself into a competitive *agon*. He targets all higher forms of existence on the basis of *ressentiment*, for its spirit is the powerful catalyzing force that enables instinctually weak wills to bundle and direct (re)active energy against a more powerful rival.

The ascetic interpretation is the key ingredient in the priest's struggle. Promoting an alternative, denatured existence, one where all active, life-affirming forms of life are either marginalized or discredited, the priestly interpretation creates a dichotomized model. Instead of embracing an active, affirmative understanding of nature, priestly types establish a separate, self-contained ascetic realm, where ascetic principles represent a commanding interpretative bulwark against active expressions of life. The priests then become mediators and interpreters of this "higher" realm. But before metaphysics can be directed against higher forms of active existence, asceticism first has to exist as a pre-established life-practice rooted

---

[14] Nietzsche's assessment of Plato as the "bridge to Christianity" stems, in part, from the misperception surrounding Plato's "innocent" ascetic stance (see *TI* "Skirmishes" 23). According to Nietzsche, asceticism as life-practice allowed Plato to cultivate greater will to power via his philosophical project. Although aspects of Plato's philosophy clearly reflected ascetic principles, this does not mean that he had to have projected asceticism into the origins of life. However, Plato's inflated regard for the world of forms and his belief in their higher "truth" made it easier for one later to abstract Plato's philosophy from the "real world" and to juxtapose that "world" with the "ideal world." Isolated from its context, in the Middle Ages this perceived duality could become the philosophical bridge to the self-contained "moral" realm of Christianity.

in specific instinctual conditions. Nietzsche's biological–physiological analysis of the priest as instinctual type locates the roots of metaphysics in the degeneration of the priestly type and in the misguided regimen priests practice to combat instinctual degeneration.[15]

While Darwin posits that the "unfit" are weeded out in the larger "struggle for existence," Nietzsche counters that weak wills do *not* die out, but in fact continue to cling to existence through a rigid ascetic regimen. Not able to enter into the superabundant, active existence in which the warrior type thrives and excels or to participate in an open-ended understanding of nature, weak wills cultivate an isolated niche within nature and engage in ascetic practices that sustain them there. These misguided practices, which prove how sick they are at their very physiological core, only further remove them from the natural realm.

Nietzsche directs two major critiques against such practices. For one, he criticizes the practice *as* practice. Rather than helping the priest to become healthier, stronger, and more vigorous, ascetic practices result in the reverse: they serve to make the type more irritable, rancorous, and debilitated. Asceticism severs the priest's relationship to nature further and makes him more resentful. It promotes in him a sense of impotence and a thirst for (compensated) self-mastery, power, control, and revenge. In short, the ascetic "cures" are ineffective as cures; they should not even be considered a "cure." These curative (mis)choices reveal a profound instinctual insecurity and root degeneracy on the part of the priestly type, for it *chooses* a practice that further undermines its body's instinctual reserves. Nietzsche's concept of *ressentiment* as (re)active energy is directly expressive of the actual resentment that the individual feels and directs against life on account of dangerously misguided ascetic regimens in the physiological realm.[16]

---

[15] Ridley highlights the fact that the priest derives from the nobles; this shared genealogy explains his arrogant confidence that he, too, can be a creator of values and compete with the noble: "the priest is a noble, that is one who understands himself as entitled to coin values, to identify his own character traits as exemplifying the good" (*Nietzsche's Conscience*, 115). However, the earliest priests had fallen away from the heightened physicality of their social caste thanks to traces of instinctual degeneration; later, the priestly genealogy no longer even needed to share aristocratic origins. What then comes to define the priest is his ascetic regimen and his resentment against the noble valuation (to which he can no longer aspire).

[16] By highlighting at length his own dietary and recreational habits, and by stressing their importance (*EH* "Clever" 1–3), Nietzsche wished to prove that he had intuitively chosen the "correct" forms of life-practice. By not making the ascetic (mis)choices of the priest, he implies that he was "at root" healthy and could therefore avoid, or at least diminish, the risk that physical ailments and personal resentments could become transferred into the philosophical project itself.

But the much more dangerous repercussion of such misguided ascetic practices – and this is the basis for Nietzsche's more fundamental second critique – is that the spirit of resentment and revenge caused by misguided ascetic regimens becomes hardened within a complete metaphysical system, which then becomes directed against all active, affirmative, bountiful existence – that is, against all instinctually active wills to power. Since the ascetic regimen removes them from those areas in which the active will feels most instinctually secure and "in this world" – areas requiring superabundant vigor and heightened physicality – the priestly castes develop a deep-seated hatred and resentment for that natural realm and for that form of active existence. The "world" that lies beyond their physiological reach thus becomes transposed into the shorthand for "evil."

Here resides the birth of the metaphysical perspective. Through existential hatred arising from fundamental instinctual degeneration, the priestly caste establishes an opposition between nature and a denatured alternative realm, in which the roots of active existence (i.e. all outer-directed activity and combativeness, healthy sensuality, full, vigorous appetites) are devalued and targeted by asceticism. Within that alternative realm, the very forms of life-practice most conducive, stimulating, enjoyable, and natural for active, affirmative modes of existence are the ones degenerating priestly types target as threatening and dangerous.

For Nietzsche, all organic existence must reflect will to power. Since the priestly type cannot engage a form of active will within Nietzsche's "nature," he still must discharge some form of energy; for life is in essence will to power. That form is not the same as that expressed by the active and outer-directed strong type within nature, however – the ascetic type has chosen to remove itself from that natural realm – but instead becomes (re)active energy directed against all active existence – more specifically, against the physiological roots of active existence – via the ascetic life-principle embedded at the "origins" of life. In order to become "active," the weak will must first locate a form of existence that will allow it to discharge its energy. Specifically, it must seek out an "immoral" opponent, one against which it can appear "moral," and that type is the strong type that resides within nature. Action in this case is essentially *re*action, for a weak will only projects energy if it can create a metaphysical duality, an interpretational goad, allowing it to discharge power in "good" conscience.

Thus, Nietzsche rejects the notion that religious life, or philosophy, is a passive, contemplative form of existence that seeks to attain a higher spiritual awareness outside nature. This interpretation itself is the consequence of the "moral" perspective from sympathetic observers who believe that such a non-active, contemplative existence can be achieved within life and, further, that this life represents superior "morality" as such (a perspective first introduced and promoted by the priest). The will to interpret life as a reflection of ascetic ideals – not just as a place for (however misguided and limited) ascetic practices – points to a (re)active interpretative will that needs hostile forms of nature to justify and promote its denatured interpretation. Indeed, the priestly will to power represents the most arrogant, all-consuming, fanatical, and commanding will that has ever existed:

The ascetic ideal has a *goal*, – this being so general that all the interests of human existence appear petty and narrow when measured against it; it inexorably interprets epochs, peoples, man, all with reference to this one goal, it permits of no other interpretation, no other goal, and rejects, denies, affirms, confirms only with reference to *its* interpretation (– and was there ever a system of interpretation more fully thought through?); it does not subject itself to any power, in fact, it believes in its superiority over any power, in its unconditional *superiority of rank* over any other power, – it believes there is nothing on earth of any power that does not first have to receive a meaning, a right to existence, a value from it, as a tool to *its* work, as a way and means to *its* goal, to *one* goal. (*GM* III, 23)

The ascetic priest does not just seek out a single identifiable rival within nature ("[a] something in life"), against whom he can engage personal will to power; that would express the spirit of the *agon*. He singles out *all* of nature ("life itself") as an opponent; and he targets all representatives of that active, affirmative nature through the cumulative force of his ascetic interpretation. The latter is ultimately even more powerful than active energy, for it is directed against the very well-springs of active existence – the supreme physicality and overpowerful instinctual reserve of the strong will:

[A]n ascetic life is a self-contradiction: here an unparalleled *ressentiment* rules, that of an unfulfilled instinct and power-will that wants to be master, not over something in life, but over life itself and its deepest, strongest, most profound conditions; here, an attempt is made to use power to block the sources of the power; here, the green eye of spite turns on physiological growth itself, in particular the manifestation of this in beauty and joy. (*GM* III, 11)

Once again in imitation of the active nobles, the *primary* form of life, the priest develops his unique form of competitive *agon* – the metaphysical *agon*.[17] Through the force of his metaphysical interpretation – and not

---

[17] Nietzsche also argues the same for Socrates as a philosopher: the style of dialectics he "invented" was a creative variation of the *primary* form rooted in the ancient athletic *agon*: "[Socrates]

through direct contact with the strong, in which he could not prevail – he thrusts himself into the world of the strong and undermines the latter's instinctual reserve through the force of his subversive ascetic interpretation. Expressed in the terms of a Nietzschean contradiction: ([re]active) will to power is used to undermine the basis for (active) will to power.

"BAD CONSCIENCE": FERMENTING GROUND OF THE ASCETIC INTERPRETATION

Surprisingly, though, the real danger derives not from priestly (mis)interpretation. In an instinctually secure and flourishing society, the peculiar life-denying message of the priest would be suspect and fall on deaf ears. But the priest as decadent is a physiological necessity, and he will emerge from all classes, races, and peoples. Moreover, the priest controls and manipulates the ascetic interpretation. He has himself under ascetic control while he seeks to extend his domination through the ongoing clandestine struggle against higher forms of existence.

The real danger resides elsewhere. The true contagion comes from the (re)actions of essentially strong types, who have been instinctually confused and debilitated through the ascetic interpretation. These are individuals, perhaps physiologically predetermined for an active existence, but whose outer-directed energy has been instinctually thwarted and directed against the self, against nature: "The *sickly* are the greatest danger to man: *not* the wicked, *not* the 'beasts of prey'" (*GM* III, 14). These wills are not meant for a life of ascetic practices or principles, but through historical circumstances (originally, through the enslavement of client nations) have become suffering, hateful, resentful, active–reactive organisms that seek both an explanation for their suffering and an outlet and release from suffering. These masses of "caged-in animals," these *broken* "beasts of prey," form the foundation and forward thrust of all active–reactive movements. Thus, it is not the priest in particular who succeeds in furthering the ascetic ideal in history, but those whom the priestly interpretation has infected, weakened, and debilitated.[18]

discovered a new type of *agon* ... he was its first fencing master in the noble circles of Athens ... He fascinated by appealing to the agonistic drive of the Greeks" (*TI* "Socrates" 8).

[18] Once again, Nietzsche critiques the Germanic peoples, because they were not strong enough to recognize the degeneration of the priestly message and then absorbed its inner contradictions and expanded it "naïvely" as their own form of Christianity: "The fact that the stronger races of northern Europe failed to reject the Christian God does not say very much for their skill in religion, not to mention their taste" (*A* 19).

Priestly metaphysics is the elaborative interpretative system over which the priest resides and which he manipulates in order to actualize his dominating, overarching will. As a complete system, however, this metaphysics is only interesting for what it reveals about the suffering inflicted by successive generations of priestly asceticism. In itself, i.e. as an expression of a supposedly higher realm of "truth," metaphysics for Nietzsche has no meaning, no relevance, no higher access.

Furthermore, the keywords of (Christian) metaphysics, though they might have a physiological reality and objectivity for those who have been confused and debilitated by (Christian) morality, do not make the system any more real or descriptive of nature: "that 'sinfulness' in man is not a fact, but rather the interpretation of a fact, namely a physiological upset, – the latter seen from a perspective of morals and religion which is no longer binding on us" (*GM* III, 16). Concepts such as "sin," "guilt," "repentance" are only religious interpolations of physio-psychological inner states that have arisen as a result of the pain and suffering of weakened types subjugated by more powerful wills and then kept under surveillance by the priestly caste. Unable to release active will within nature, weak wills need to make sense of strange, new, inner states of consciousness that emerge from energy directed against the self. These concepts give a meaning and coherence and a sense of interpretative totality to an entirely new breed of (internal) "nature," which has arisen thanks to will to power directed against the self in the form of internalized cruelty:

Man, suffering from himself in some way, at all events physiologically, rather like an animal imprisoned in a cage, unclear as to why? what for? and yearning for reasons – reasons bring relief –, yearning for cures and narcotics as well, finally consults someone who knows hidden things too – and lo and behold! from this magician, the ascetic priest, he receives the *first* tip as to the "cause" of his suffering: he should look for it within *himself*, in *guilt*, in a piece of the past, he should understand his suffering itself as a *condition of punishment*. (*GM* III, 20)

The priest then steps in and offers an interpretation and some sense of solace and consolation; he proffers his "narcotic" for the suffering – Christian metaphysics. Most of all, and that is part of the "cure," the priest can change the direction of the potentially self-destructive and debilitating active energy directed against the self; he sanctions its release and prevents it from corroding the self: "the priest is the *direction-changer* of *ressentiment*" (*GM* III, 15). But he not only offers the sufferer of "bad conscience" a reason for his suffering; what is more, he also finds him a ("moral") culprit, a "guilty" party, one against which he can vent his pent-up energy outwardly instead of against the self:

For every sufferer instinctively looks for a cause of his distress; more exactly, for a culprit, even more precisely for a *guilty* culprit who is receptive to distress, – in short, for a living being upon whom he can release his emotions, actually or in effigy, on some pretext or other: because the release of emotions is the greatest attempt at relief, or should I say, at *anaesthetizing* on the part of the sufferer, his involuntarily longed-for narcotic against pain of any kind. In my judgment, we find here the actual physiological causation of *ressentiment*, revenge and their ilk, in a yearning, then, to *anaesthetize pain through emotion*. (*GM* III, 15)

Presenting the suffering and weakened individual with an "immoral," i.e. "guilty" target ("the nobles are to blame for your suffering"), the priest enables him to channel outward dangerously bottled-up energy. Simultaneously, he can anaesthetize his psychic pain through a compensatory emotional rush, allowing him (at least temporarily) to deflect psychic suffering. Outbursts of religious epidemics throughout history, Nietzsche suggests, can be explained according to this "curative" principle, i.e. the need to deaden internal pain, induced by inner-directed cruelty, via priestly-sanctioned "moral" euphoria. The ascetic ideal serves as the means to permit emotional release and emotional excess: "*The ascetic ideal utilized to produce excess of feelings*" (*GM* III, 20). Both components, in unison, can momentarily overcome and compensate for the suffering of internalized cruelty among the sufferers of "bad conscience."

THE SCIENTIST AND THE ASCETIC IDEAL

At this point, it becomes possible to pursue the following questions: What does Nietzsche's analysis in *GM* III have to do with Darwin and his science? How is this essay as a whole directed against Darwinism? Is it not primarily a critique of (priestly) asceticism? Is not the priest the true focal point? Nietzsche's entire argument until this juncture has undermined the Darwinian worldview from various angles. Now he can present his summation: nineteenth-century science represents the last and most significant outpost of the ascetic ideal. The priest as type is not his prime target; after all, many nineteenth-century scientists and free-thinkers leveled far more hostile indictments at Christianity. It is the scientist. For the scientist promotes the illusion of fighting against ascetic ideals while paving the way for their ultimate triumph. In fact, science has allowed the ascetic imperative to become even more entrenched as the genealogical pendant to priestly asceticism: "Both of them, science and the ascetic ideal, are still on the same foundation – I have already explained –; that is to say, both overestimate truth (more correctly: they share the same faith that truth can*not* be assessed or criticized, and this makes them both *necessarily* allies" (*GM* III, 25).

The structure of *GM* III is built around the following questions:[19] Who promotes the ascetic ideal? Who opposes it? Nietzsche's conclusions are: (1) the artist is too opportunistic and self-absorbed to care enough about asceticism; he rarely practices is, he rarely challenges it; (2) the philosopher hides behind the ascetic ideal, and he benefits too much from its outward manifestations as life-practice to offer serious opposition to it as life-principle; (3) the priest is the originator of asceticism, which expresses his instinctual degeneration. He will fight against any opponents to the ideal. Nietzsche now poses his culminating question: And the scientist? Does not modern science present the most definitive opposition to the religious–ascetic interpretation? The final essay is set up to debunk that myth.

There are two interrelated components to his argument. The first deals with the self-image of modern science; the second with the asceticism of the scientist. His first critique counters the illusion that scientific method and progress undermine the basis for religious superstition. According to the Enlightenment, the proliferation of scientific knowledge will eventually dislodge faith in traditional forms of (Christian) religion. If one were to express it in Darwin's own words: "freedom of thought is best promoted by the gradual illumination of men's minds, which follows from the advance of science. It has, therefore, been always my object to avoid writing on religion, & I have confined myself to science." Based on this assumption, religion as an acceptable metaphysical totality will lose its hold on the imagination of humanity, and religious speculation will lose credibility as scientific knowledge is further disseminated. To express it in Darwinian terms: evidence and knowledge in the field of evolutionary biology – for example, scientific facts about the survival and extinction of species – will render the Christian-based narrative of man's origins obsolete.

Nietzsche counters this optimistic prognosis in two ways. Since the Copernican revolution ushered in the modern era, scientific advances have diminished man's self-worth, dignity, and centrality, giving him a "*piercing* sensation of his nothingness":

[M]an seems to have been on a downward path, – now he seems to be rolling faster and faster away from the centre ... *All* science (and not just astronomy

---

[19] Nietzsche offers his own form of summary in the first section of *GM* III.

alone, the humiliating and degrading effects of which Kant singled out for the remarkable confession that "it destroys my importance" ...), all science, natural as well as *unnatural* – this is the name I would give to the self-critique of knowledge – is nowadays seeking to talk man out of his former self-respect as though this were nothing but a bizarre piece of self-conceit. (*GM* III, 25)

Ironically, however, scientific discoveries have *not* erased the demand for pseudo-sciences and speculative metaphysics. Instead, by furthering an awareness of man's insignificance and unworthiness, modern science has actually opened the doors wider to alternative modes of metaphysical speculation. Metaphysicians and transcendentalists now have a "winning hand." Liberated from the binding constraints of medieval Christian theology, they can now pursue (and with the best "scientific conscience") what their "hearts desire" – namely, "secret passageways" back to the old ideal, the ascetic ideal. Thus, discoveries in science have not diminished the proliferation of alternative accesses to the truth; they have inspired metaphysicians to recapture "higher" hidden realms: "who would blame the agnostics if, as worshippers of the unknown and the secret, they worship *the question mark* itself as God" (*GM* III, 25).

If man's significance no longer derives from his centrality within the cosmos or his "moral" distinction from the animals, it must reside in some other criterion: free will; speculative thought; belief in the divine, the cosmos; sublimity in nature. The pressures and recognition of his insignificance – even more – his awareness, thanks to the explosion in scientific knowledge, that he can never know everything, leads man to embrace the ascetic ideal with even greater fervor: "'There is no knowing: *consequently* – there is a God'" (*GM* III, 25).

Nietzsche also argues that the dominant thrust of modern science since Copernicus has *not*, as people assume, been directed against God, religious sentiment, or faith as such, but primarily against the superficial accretions of religion – the baroque embellishments and interpretative excesses of traditional Christian theology:

[The] relationship [of science] to the ascetic ideal is certainly not yet inherently antagonistic; indeed, it is much more the case, in general, that it still represents the driving force in the inner evolution of that ideal. Its repugnance and pugnacity are, on closer inspection, directed not at the ideal itself but at its outworks, its apparel and disguise, at the way the ideal temporarily hardens, solidifies, becomes dogmatic – science liberates what life is in it by denying what is exoteric in this ideal. (*GM* III, 25)

The agenda behind modern science has been to purify man's access to "truth" by peeling away the outer crust of superstitions and miracles and the outgrowths of dogmatic religiosity that have sprung up around it ("the exoteric"). Yet, this process of purification has not undermined the demand for faith. It actually helps pave the way for a higher, more sublime (i.e. ascetic) appreciation of the "divine" at work in "nature." To use the example of Darwinism, the "facts" of evolution will render meaningless Christianity's competitive set of "interpretations" based on faith and superstitions. But Darwinists then proceed from the *same* assumption – namely, that a "scientific" understanding of a *contrary* set of "facts" will increase our reverence for nature's hidden intentions. To paraphrase Darwin: the beauty that resides in the manifold display of natural selection will point to the true grandeur of nature's workings.

Nietzsche's will to power underlies the second component of this critique. For Nietzsche, metaphysical explanations are projections of the internal coordination of the instincts. Interpretations are both reflections of, and means to, individual power. But as avenues to a higher truth or morality, they have no intrinsic significance. In Nietzsche's understanding, wills and their interpretations are forever clashing in the here and now. Therefore, it is not a question of "truth" (and certainly not one of "progress"), but of projecting will to power against other wills or constellations of wills, while the dominant interpretation of the moment reflects the prevalent collective of wills.

For example, in the period before Darwin, the Christian naturalists' paradigm of nature represented the dominant constellation. For Nietzsche, however, the relevant question did not concern the "truth" of the respective interpretation as such – that is, Darwin's version of nature as opposed to the Christian naturalists' – but what type of will (active or [re]active) lay concealed behind the interpretation and sought power through it: "I do not want to bring to light what the ideal *did*; rather simply what it *means*, what it indicates, what lies hidden behind, beneath and within it and what it expresses in a provisional, indistinct way, laden with question marks and misunderstandings" (*GM* III, 23). If the will, in any way, claims ultimate "truth" for its position, it must represent the ascetic imperative: "that unconditional will to truth, is *faith in the ascetic ideal itself*, even if, as an unconscious imperative, make no mistake about it, – it is the faith in a *metaphysical* value, a *value as such of truth*" (*GM* III, 24).

Nietzsche, to recall, distinguishes between two brands of asceticism: one which seeks a degree of distance from life and its pressures, but only as a means to maximize active will; and one which assumes a fundamental antagonism to life from a denatured perspective outside nature. The latter represents the original priestly asceticism. Though both the philosopher and the scientist derive genealogically from priestly asceticism, the philosopher only conceals himself behind the previously established ascetic mask of the priest to accommodate his own contemplative mode of (active) will (asceticism as life-practice). He does not necessarily promote an ascetic interpretation of existence, but merely uses temporary asceticism in order to project *his* form of will to power.

The scientist, unlike the original philosopher, however, does not temporarily slip into the ascetic shell. He is drawn to science as the very manifestation of ascetic life-principles. The scientist assumes a "neutral" position from which to gain a higher access to "truth." The difference is that the scientist, unlike the priest, remains unaware of priestly asceticism's original reinterpretation of nature. Instead, the scientist unwittingly adopts the ascetic fallacy, bequeathed by the priestly type, that a secure position from outside existence, i.e. a denatured "objective" realm, can be located and inhabited and, further, that this ascetic realm can serve as point of entry for an ultimate insight into life, existence, and nature: "'the truthful man, in that daring and final sense which faith in science presupposes, *thus affirms another world* from the one of life, nature and history; and inasmuch as he affirms this "other world", must he not therefore deny its opposite, this world, *our* world, in doing so? ... Our faith in science is still based on a *metaphysical faith*'" (*GM* III, 24).

The "scientific" perspective, therefore, does not perceive itself to be one possible interpretation from a particular vantage point and, *by necessity*, biologically contingent. It believes itself to be an "objective," *ultimate* assessment – removed from nature so as to better contemplate the "truth." But the central question for Nietzsche is: does scientific asceticism in the end allow for an affirmative, active projection of will to power in Nietzschean terms; or does it, too, in the end reflect a (re)active will directed against all outer-directed creative energy through an ascetic interpretation of existence?

SCIENTIFIC RATIONALISM: NATURAL ALLY OF THE ASCETIC IDEAL

Scientific asceticism reflects the latter in two significant respects. For one, despite the fact (or better: *because of* the fact) that the scientific interpretation derives from the genealogy of the priest, it must be directed against the other rival brand of asceticism – namely, the one originally introduced by the priest. Priestly metaphysics must emerge as science's direct competitor and most bitter rival because both claim to offer an ultimate vantage point from outside "nature" in order to better contemplate nature. Though scientific "truth" might appear to refute God, the struggle between the two competitive systems actually resides in the interpretational (and mutual) exclusivity of each ascetic paradigm.

The scientific will to power is not an attempt to project active power in a forum outside nature (e.g. in the spirit of the *agon*); it is instead a (re)active will directed against life-threatening competitors within "nature." It too must first become (re)active to become active: it directs its resentment-filled energy against all opponents to "truth," i.e. the inhabitants of the alternative ascetic paradigm. Thus, the will behind the ascetic mask of science is, from the very start, driven by a latent animus against ascetic competitors. Whereas this (re)action is articulated in the conventional good-versus-evil duality within priestly metaphysics, it is reformulated in the opposition of "truth" ("moral") and opponents to "truth" ("immoral") in scientific asceticism.

At the same time, scientific asceticism is also directed against expressions of life-affirming, creative energy. By establishing an alternative avenue to the "truth," modern science has denigrated all active realms of existence that do not fall under the purview of scientific rationalism. In the process, it has penetrated all "active" realms as pervasively and thoroughly as Christian metaphysics. Through the force of its metaphysical claims, it has integrated distinct expressions of active will into its interpretative framework. But instead of creating a political hierarchy of wills through the establishment of a single, central institution (a Church, for example),[20] it promotes a decentered and competitive rational–scientific interpretation of existence, in which "nature" as a whole reflects a "disembodied" rationality. But scientific rationality cannot give us an "objective" view of nature, once again, but only an interpretation; and that too emerges from the basis of a weak, ascetic will wishing to realize total mastery by subordinating "disruptive" active will. Self-affirming "immoral" will to power is, after all, both a hindrance to the rationality of scientific organization and, more important, an existential threat to a particular physiological type of (ascetic) will.

The "scientific" type attains power through the force of its ascetic interpretation. Instead of achieving the type of self-mastery and natural

---

[20] The modern corporate university offers the closest institutional structure for scientific rationalism. Historically, of course, the modern university grew out of a religious affiliation, eventually gaining greater independence and developing an uneasy rivalry with established religion.

authority characteristic of the strong type within nature (which remains beyond its physiological grasp), the scientific will gains authority through the force of an ascetic interpretation that denies active will its natural arena. To realize that end, it purports to discover rational, mechanical processes ("natural laws") at work in "nature," which can eliminate, absorb, or marginalize (active, "irrational") disturbances.

Nietzsche's final critique of scientific asceticism explains how Darwinism can "succeed" in determining a position within nature allegedly free from moral judgments, while embedding morality within its system as a whole. Darwin's "science" supposedly works with functional categories such as fitness and survival and evaluates on the basis of survival and the fitness for survival, not on the "moral" outcome of struggle. But if this were true, then *all* forms of human existence, *no matter how morally repugnant*, would have to be accepted and tolerated within the Darwinian paradigm. All interpretations of nature would also have to be recognized independently of their moral justification or legitimacy. In short, a radically understood Darwinism would have to eliminate any and all moral evaluations even within the parameters of civilization and within all forms of competition.

Yet, Darwin's interpretation continues to adhere to ascetic life-principles. It assumes it can present a total description of existence, i.e. evolution by natural selection, from an ascetic position outside life. But the perspective of scientific truth must first assume an unacknowledged basis from which to ground that particular understanding. In Nietzsche's words: "Strictly speaking, there is no 'presuppositionless' knowledge, the thought of such a thing is unthinkable, paralogical: a philosophy, a 'faith' always has to be there first, for knowledge to win from it a direction, a meaning, a limit, a method, a *right* to exist" (*GM* III, 24).

The scientific perspective, then, continues to combat nature from a position outside nature. Scientific asceticism never implicitly challenges, questions, or desires to overthrow morality; it only wishes to establish an *alternative* basis from which to project the *same* denatured (i.e. ascetic) will to power. The "scientist" as type judges life according to a higher "truth," one which he himself embodies and defines. "Morality" as ascetic life-principle is therefore never challenged by the scientific outlook; indeed, it is actually promoted and furthered through a competitive, essentially compatible (ascetic) program: "this 'modern science' is, for the time being, the *best* ally for the ascetic ideal, for the simple reason that it is the most unconscious, involuntary, secret and subterranean!" (*GM* III, 25).

Nietzsche, therefore, concludes that modern science not only fails to oppose the ascetic perspective; it actually extends its principles, practices, and preconditions through other means. Science has not realized its promise to overcome the (priestly) moral perspective. Indeed, modern science has allowed asceticism to conveniently coexist with the priestly perspective by inhabiting an alternative ascetic foundation, which derives its *raison d'être* from combating religious faith.

MODERN SCIENTIFIC ATHEISM: THE CORE OF THE ASCETIC IDEAL

In *GM* II, 27, Nietzsche abruptly shifts to the culmination of his argument. Whereas in previous sections addressing "science," specifically *GM* II, 24–26, Nietzsche turns out to have been addressing the "comedians of the Christian moral ideal" (*GM* III, 26), i.e. contemporary free-thinkers, modern scholars, and other practitioners of "objective" knowledge and "pure" *Wissenschaft*,[21] he suddenly changes tack in *GM* III, 27, and starts to talk more respectfully of the modern scientific imperative. He contrasts the "comedians of the ideal" in the previous sections with a positive new counterforce – those brave scientific souls who approach "truth" *without* ideals: "Everywhere else where spirit is at work in a rigorous, powerful and honest way, it now completely lacks an ideal" (*GM* III, 27).

It is here, in my opinion, where Nietzsche subtly references natural scientists such as Darwin and his followers, his polemical targets, for it is their rigorous "will to truth" which has led them to go so far as to challenge the Christian faith in God and a benign universe. For Nietzsche, they are the modern exponents of "science" in its highest (and most honest) articulation. Nietzsche clearly admires their strength to go down the lonely avenue – without "ideals" – to which their "will to truth" has taken them.[22]

---

[21] *Wissenschaft* applies to all humanistic disciplines (*Geisteswissenschaften*), including e.g. theology, philology, and history. But the term also refers to the *Naturwissenschaften* ("natural sciences"), which extend to Darwinian biological science. In my reading of the final sections of *GM* III, Nietzsche moves from a critique of the more general academic sciences – starting in *GM* III, 24 – to his final challenge to *all* forms of modern science (including Darwinism) in *GM* III, 27, since *both* branches of *Wissenschaft* were grounded for him in the same ascetic fallacy.

[22] Clark attempts to salvage empirical science, such as that of Darwin, from Nietzsche's explicit critique of the "will to truth" (*Nietzsche on Truth*, 188). She criticizes scholars like Kaufmann who assume that "the will to truth and the ascetic ideal would make it impossible to take the value of truth for granted, that if Nietzsche attacked one, he had to attack the other" (*Nietzsche on Truth*, 197), and she argues for a "positive," non-ascetic understanding of the "will to truth."

But, interestingly, Nietzsche does not stop here. In a subtle continuation of his line of thought in this important section, he argues in the following sentences that the only way out of the nihilism of two millennia of asceticism,[23] which has presently culminated in the dead end of modern science, would be to radicalize the scientific imperative itself. This would not be done by opposing asceticism as such, i.e. from a counter-ascetic position (the stand of modern science), but by taking the genealogical strand of asceticism within modern science to its ultimate conclusion:

> Unconditional, honest atheism (– *its* air alone is what we breathe, we more spiritual men of the age!) is, **in that sense,**[24] *not* opposed to the ascetic ideal as it appears to be; instead, it is only one of the ideal's last phases of development, one of its final forms and inherent logical conclusions, – it is the awe-inspiring *catastrophe* of a two-thousand-year discipline in truth-telling, which finally forbids itself the *lie entailed in the belief in God*. (GM III, 27; emphasis in bold mine)

"Honest, unconditional atheism" – here, the very last chapter in Nietzsche's long genealogical account of asceticism – represents asceticism's final gasp. It is the point when scientific asceticism asks itself the question: "*What does all will to truth mean?*" (GM III, 27). Nietzsche's form of "honest atheism" not only denies belief in God; scientific atheism does that as well. Far more significantly, it also rejects any effort to derive metaphysical consolation from *not* believing in God (i.e. modern forms of

---

[23] Certainly, the genealogical strand of asceticism existed long before, as *GM* makes clear; however, it only became "world-historical" through the vehicle of an expansionist Christian metaphysics among weakened, suffering wills.

[24] Kaufmann's translation of this passage gives an inadequate rendering of a seemingly insignificant word: he translates the slightly outdated German word "*demgemäss*" with "therefore." (I have rendered it here as "in that sense.") Kaufmann's choice of "therefore" creates the impression that the "unconditional honest atheism," to which Nietzsche now refers, is the same brand of (popular) "atheism" he mentions in the previous sentence (though, significantly, at first within quotation marks, the second time without). Kaufmann creates a false parallelism to the previously mentioned *popular* "atheism," when Nietzsche here actually introduces a *new* brand of atheism – namely, *his* form. For Nietzsche, this "unconditional honest" atheism is the only form which truly merits being called atheism without quotations marks. Thus, Nietzsche does not establish a definite conclusion (through the use of "therefore"); he creates a *Steigerung*, a heightening of the previously mentioned. Many translators follow Kaufmann's lead and translate it in his sense, and many of Nietzsche's readers in English therefore miss this highly significant nuance. The subtle point is that Nietzsche does *not* align with the perspectives of modern scientific atheism, but instead sees how *that* brand of atheism represents the final historical dead end of millennia of asceticism and must be transcended. (For a more detailed discussion, see Dirk R. Johnson, "Translating Nietzsche's Atheism(s): A World beyond the Ethical Imperative" [paper presented at the Friedrich Nietzsche Society Conference, University of Sussex, September 2004].) The final position that Nietzsche sets out here corresponds to Stage 6 of "How the 'True World' Finally Became a Fable" in *TI*, and I strongly take issue with Clark's reading, which maintains that Stage 6 indicates Nietzsche's *return* to a position consonant with the empirical sciences (Clark, "Development of Nietzsche's Later Position" 74–75).

atheism) – for it understands *both* God *and* "*non*-God" to be founded on the same ascetic fallacy.

Nietzsche's form of "honest unconditional atheism" is, therefore, a decisive step *beyond* Darwin's scientific brand of atheism; that "Darwinian" atheism is encapsulated, rather, in Nietzsche's formulation: "Everywhere else where spirit is at work in a rigorous, powerful and honest way, it now completely lacks an ideal – the popular expression for this abstinence is 'atheism' –: *except for its will to truth*" (*GM* III, 27). For Nietzsche, however, the problem is that *that* "will to truth," which is embodied in modern scientific atheism, is just a further expression of the ascetic ideal; *it is not a final reckoning with it*: "But this will, this *remnant* of an ideal, if you believe me, is that ideal itself in its strictest, more spiritual formulation, completely esoteric, totally stripped of externals, and thus not so much its remnant as its *kernel*" (*GM* III, 27). In other words, the only way that science can effectively overcome the ascetic imperative is if it takes its own ascetic "will to truth" and directs it against its foundation and existential imperative. This process alone would represent the death of asceticism at the hands of its own internal, perverse "logic."

For Nietzsche, only "honest unconditional atheism" – namely, *his* particular *breed* of atheism – represents that final reckoning with the ascetic legacy, because it takes this step and pushes "the will to truth" to this ultimate, radical conclusion.[25] It recognizes that "the will to truth," currently enshrined as the bulwark of modern science, stands exposed as the final core of two thousand years of (Christian) asceticism. And only by pushing that "will to truth" to its final conclusion ("what does all will to truth mean?") can one liberate oneself from the metaphysical demands of the modern scientific imperative and ascend to a "higher" Dionysian awareness – an active, affirmative, non-ascetic stance toward existence.

CONCLUSIONS

Nietzsche breaks through to this position by radicalizing Darwin's perspectives. In the middle period, his "Darwinian meditations" liberated

---

[25] There are two interesting, enigmatic passages directly linked to this notion: "When the Christian Crusaders in the East fell upon that invincible order of Assassins, the order of free spirits *par excellence* ... they received an inkling of that symbol and watchword that was reserved for the highest ranks alone as their *secretum*: 'nothing is true, everything is permitted'" (*GM* III, 24). Nietzsche recognizes the behavior of Pontius Pilate as another example of this principle: "The noble scorn of a Roman, when faced with an unashamed mangling of the word 'truth', gave the New Testament its only statement *of any value* — its critique, even its annihilation: 'What is truth!'" (*A* 46).

him from the last vestiges of Wagnerian metaphysics. Through the impact of Darwin, he subscribed to a naturalist interpretation of human behavior and genealogical modes of explanation. But over time, he began to question the assumptions on which Darwin's faith in naturalism was grounded. He grew skeptical of attempts to offer a metaphysical narrative account of life and nature. This position emerged from exploiting some of Darwin's insights. For example, by intensifying the idea of struggling wills and focusing on the internal hierarchy of the individual biological entity (rather than external outcome, or survival), Nietzsche challenged the metaphysical implications of Darwin's model. Instead, his "will to power" advanced an open-ended understanding of struggle, one where metaphysical interpretations themselves were expressive of a specific *type* of will.

GM serves a dual purpose. On the one hand, it counters the "English psychologists'" hypothesis that man's genealogy can be traced back to more rudimentary forms. On the other, it presents its own alternative genealogy. Nietzsche's genealogical tree has two main branches. The first incorporates all strong, active wills within an open-ended history, one whose lineage has yet to be established and whose traditions have yet to be fixed.[26] The other has its roots in priestly asceticism. That branch represents the "genealogy of morals." By excavating asceticism as the instinctual source for morality, Nietzsche could focus on the types hiding behind ascetic "moral" interpretations. And he could recognize how various strands of asceticism linked similar human types based on a common genealogical bond.

But Nietzsche's attempt to expose the ascetic ideal in its diverse manifestations was not to prove the inherent superiority of one perspective over another. It was not, for example, to contrast the philosopher favorably with the priest; or to prove the philosopher's superiority to the scientist; or to pass judgment on the priest. The problem was the type's fixation on a specific role and identity, thereby limiting its inherent potential as a result of the specific limitations of the type. This represented the legacy of the ascetic mold. In order to get beyond the shell, the individual would first have to understand and pass through *all* identities and to acknowledge

[26] Nietzsche's project in the final period was to discover sympathetic thinkers from the past – i.e. historical exponents of what he came to call "immoralism" (e.g. Thucydides, Tacitus, Sallust, Machiavelli, etc.) – and to establish, from that point on, a new genealogical lineage of "immoralism" (for a more detailed analysis, see Dirk R. Johnson, "'Höherer Réealismus' or Philosophical Réealignment? Nietzsche, Paul Rée and the Search for a 'Tradition'" [paper presented at the Friedrich Nietzsche Society Conference, University of St. Andrews, September 1997]).

them as acceptable existential possibilities, in order finally to recognize the limits – and the conditionality – of various competitive perspectives.

Nietzsche's so-called "philosopher of the future" no longer accepts the role of (ascetic) philosopher. Rather, he suggests a fuller and more complete, non-circumscribed human type, who no longer stays fixed in the predetermined mold of asceticism, but who can sense and overcome the temptations presented by ascetic poses and interpretations. This new "philosopher" no longer conforms to the outer distinctions between artist, philosopher, priest, and scientist, but can subsume *all* those identities – as well as numerous others – within a total, non-ascetic vision of life.

At that point, the type no longer needs the (ascetic) shell, for he has stopped adopting a "disinterested" ascetic stance vis-à-vis nature. He will not be defined by the ascetic role and its constraints; he will have become emboldened to venture past all roles, embarking on a full, non-ascetic immersion into life. Beyond roles and ascetic restraints and siren-calls, he can once again recapture the Dionysian outlook – the "highest of all possible beliefs." Like Goethe, he will then be able fight against "separation of reason, sensibility, feeling, will" and discipline himself to "wholeness" and to "*totality*"; he will "*create* himself":

A spirit like this who has *become free* stands in the middle of the world with a cheerful and trusting fatalism in the *belief* that only the individual is reprehensible, that everything is redeemed and affirmed in the whole – *he does not negate any more* ... But a belief like this is the highest of all possible beliefs: I have christened it with the name *Dionysus*. (*TI* "Skirmishes" 49)

Conclusion

Nietzsche's philosophy in his final years was premised on a fundamental anti-Darwinism. This antagonism did not emerge suddenly; nor was it "wrong" about the fundamentals of Darwinian science. It was the product of years of serious reflection on the philosophical underpinnings of modern science, in particular Darwinism. But how can so many prominent scholars seem to get this issue so wrong? I would like to suggest several possible reasons. The first is that Nietzsche himself did not make his antagonism explicit. Though *GM* was meant as a polemical response to the Darwinists, it was written in such a way that one could fairly believe that he had composed it in their spirit and that it mirrored their convictions. Rather than see how the text undermined them, the "genealogists" could (and without significant stretch) believe that its methods vindicated them. Their assumption is understandable, particularly since his polemic was one of the first at that time to argue on the principles of "naturalism" and to reject the transcendental bases for morality. If one considers that Darwin's genealogical methods were still being developed, challenged, and contested, his approach was truly radical, and it seemed to take the side of scientific naturalism.

Second, commentators do not recognize the important link between Nietzsche's gradually unfolding middle-period critique of the *moralistes*, particularly on the basis of their altruism–egoism distinction, and his late-period challenge to the ascetic ideal. By randomly identifying "scientific" traces and superficial biological markers in his works (such as references to instincts and drives, decadence and degeneration[1]), these readers ignore his more than ten-year *philosophical* investigation into the *moral* suppositions behind the biological discourse of his time. Both the theory

---

[1] Richardson seeks (somewhat anachronistically) to project into Nietzsche's thought a systematic *theory* of "instincts" and "drives," though Nietzsche never comes anywhere near to developing a coherent "theory" on this question (Richardson, *Nietzsche's New Darwinism*, 6).

of evolution and its related terms (i.e. "adaptation, self-preservation, progress, democracy, utility and scarcity"[2]) were products of the same linguistic heritage. Furthermore, Nietzsche's anti-Christian pronouncements seemed to give voice to the Darwinists' own anti-religious reservations – and there could be little doubt that *GM* was in part directed against Christianity and its priesthood. For this reason, commentators such as Mathias Risse foreground his attack against *Christian* morality and not his broader campaign against morality as such.[3] And so, while scholars have little problem in detecting the work's anti-Christian animus, they infer that he shares that same anti-clerical, anti-Church bias with the Darwinists.

The latter position is conditioned by the success of Darwinian naturalism, which has placed the transcendental moral claims of Christianity and the methods of scientific naturalism at loggerheads ever since, presenting the modern era with only two possible explanations for the "moral" phenomenon. Since Nietzsche clearly shared many of the anti-metaphysical assumptions of the "genealogists" and argued using features of their paradigm, he must have sympathized with their objectives. If one has to place him in one of two ideological "camps," then, it would seem logical that he belongs to the scientific naturalists.

But such a perspective fails to take into account Nietzsche's notion of the *agon*. According to this principle, the strong will does not seek to attack and to discredit one platform from the firm grounding of another, but to release its brand of active energy by targeting a will or group of wills that has achieved momentary supremacy. The goal of the practice is not to replace the position with an alternative totalizing truth, but to enter into the "system" of thought and subvert some of its foundational principles. Taking on an "equal" rival, one which forces you to maximize your own active reserves, is a sign of respect and gratitude. Thereby the higher type reveals his active, aggressive instincts and seeks obstacles and goads to its higher will. In short, the agonistic spirit does not demand a straightforward rejection of the polemical rival. As I have indicated, Nietzsche shares many of Darwin's key insights and agrees with some

---

[2] Gregory Moore, "Nietzsche and Evolutionary Theory," in *A Companion to Nietzsche*, ed. Keith Ansell-Pearson (Oxford: Blackwell Publishing, 2006), 530.

[3] Risse, "The Second Treatise," 56. Maudemarie Clark also suggests that what Nietzsche opposes is essentially *Christian* morality, since "what we in the West, including those of us who do not accept or even reject Christianity, call 'morality' is *in fact* Christian morality" (Clark, "Introduction," xx). And Daniel Conway uses the epithet "*Christian* morality" twenty times (!) when referring to his critique of *morality*, as though Nietzsche somehow had intended to spare morality *per se* from his indictment (Conway, "For Whom the Bell Tolls," 88–105).

of his assumptions, including, but not limited to, the "natural" origins of morality; the primacy of (human) will; the notion of some form of struggle.

At the same time, the seeming congruence on these questions does not necessitate overall agreement. From within Darwinism, Nietzsche could locate the weak points, the inconsistencies, the metaphysical remnants of the Christian ideal, and his theory of active will meant that he could win for himself a position from which to attack the ascetic ideal – or, as Nietzsche himself characterizes his approach in the Preface to *GM*, "to replace the improbable with the more probable and in some circumstances to replace one error with another" (*GM* "Preface" 4). The task in the end was not to vanquish "all obstacles in general but instead to conquer the ones where you can apply your whole strength, suppleness, and skill with weapons" (*EH* "Wise" 7).

Another common misconception is that Nietzsche's philosophy also represents a "totality," that is, even if Nietzsche does not agree with Darwin on all questions, his philosophy does have related objectives. From this standpoint, one can argue that both thinkers were respectively "right": Nietzsche does not even care to challenge Darwin but fashions a naturalistic philosophy that acknowledges and incorporates the scientific revolution initiated by Darwin. Seen in that light, his philosophy was then the first truly "naturalized" one, accepting man as a product of nature and attempting to rebuild modern philosophy, as well as modern ethics, on post-Darwinian foundations. In that reading, his insights do not challenge Darwin in any significant way, but rather seek to develop a philosophical system with a newly won anthropological awareness inspired by him. In the fashion of rendering unto Caesar what is Caesar's, these perspectives grant Darwin his primacy in the scientific realm, while they then probe Nietzsche's texts for the deeper implications of Darwin's scientific discoveries for modern philosophy.

Allied to that position is a stubborn skepticism that Nietzsche's philosophy could with any degree of credibility call into question modern science, particularly Darwinism. The implication is that a post-Darwinian philosophy cannot hope to compete with the uncontestable truths of modern science but must to some degree work as the handmaiden of science. The current divide in contemporary philosophy reflects this dilemma: while analytic philosophy disregards any efforts at philosophical speculation that diverge from the principles and methods of scientific induction, Continental philosophers argue for the possibility of philosophical "truth" that can liberate itself from scientific expectations and methodology. However, even the "Continentals" do not question that modern science has *its* claims to certain truths, while philosophy engages in a different form of truth-searching.

But if one were to address the question in the terms which Nietzsche expresses at the finale of *GM* III, modern science has not found the position of an "unconditional, honest atheism," for it has not yet questioned "its will to truth" (*GM* III, 27). The implications of this position, then, would not be to replace modern science with just another philosophical "truth" or to make certain that scientific truth-claims correlate with philosophy, but, instead, to argue for a new philosophical awareness, one where the search for "truth," the ultimate remnant of the millennia-old ascetic ideal as Nietzsche sees it, is no longer a constituent, defining element. Whether that search is concealed behind the mask of philosophy or science, it must be transcended. Indeed, Nietzsche's higher type will distinguish itself by being a skeptic ("Zarathustra is a skeptic"); it will recognize the symptoms of physiological weakness and degeneration that lie behind the siren-call of "truth";[4] and it will set its own values. These values will not correlate with the "truths" of modern science; they will transcend them, for higher types will regard "truth" itself as inimical to their understanding of great health and well-being. In fact, those "truths" will fall victim to the superior, affirmative will of the *Übermensch*.

But to understand this position, one must grasp the full implication of Nietzsche's assault on the metaphysical enterprise and how he had arrived at that final antagonism. The reason scholarship has not fully appreciated his subversion of the Darwinist model, in my opinion, is that it has not recognized how his particular understanding of the will to power pulls the rug from under any form of totalizing system. By arguing that interpretations are premised on the constitution of individual wills, Nietzsche began to focus attention on the "nature" of the will. This approach brooked no exception. For him, the "human, all too human" became primary; and the scientific will, too, was dissected dispassionately, in an effort to reveal the nature of the instincts embodied in the natural scientists' "will to truth." But once he had determined that the *same* instinctual confusion and degeneration and the *same* spirit of nihilism and *décadence* inhabited the "scientific" will as they did other forms of asceticism, then he had effectively reduced the phenomenon of Darwinism, too, to a constellation

---

[4] "Anyone who does not just understand the word 'Dionysian' but understands *himself* in the word 'Dionysian' does not need to refute Plato or Christianity or Schopenhauer – *he smells the decay*" (*EH* "Birth of Tragedy" 2).

of *Darwinist* wills, whose instinctual ambivalence was reflected in their sustained *need* for the absolute truth-claims of science.

Until this point, I have argued how Nietzsche's developing perspectives subverted Darwin's positions, culminating in his "mature" anti-Darwinism. But we now must come to the implications of his position. Of course, there are many, but I will limit myself to a single one: what does my reading imply for the meaning and purpose of *GM*? If that polemical text is meant to implicate Darwinism, as I have argued until now, what does such a position suggest for the numerous readings that do not find a serious antagonism? Nietzsche's late texts, including *GM*, were polemics. According to what Nietzsche himself stated about the works written after *Z*: "After the yea-saying part of my task had been solved it was time for the no-saying, *no-doing* half: the revaluation of values so far, the great war, – summoning a day of decision" (*EH* "Beyond Good and Evil" 1). Nietzsche's targets were the triumphant cultural movements in modernity, more specifically, the wills to power *behind* those movements. His late texts were above all *cultural polemics*.

For Nietzsche, the contemporary "culture" was not just an abstraction, theoretical construct, or insignificant part of philosophizing; it was central, for "culture" represented the majority confluence of wills. Though those wills had a certain prehistory and were ongoing products of previous "historical" precedents (e.g. the phenomenon of enslaved wills; the success of Christian metaphysics via the interpretative will to power of Paul, and so forth), as his analysis in *GM* illustrates, these determining forces had already been ingrained into the will, had left their physiological stamp, so to speak, and had conditioned the instincts in a particular direction – namely, to reflect a "denatured," ascetic hierarchization and interpretation. The triumph of the "moral" interpretation – first as a result of the expansionist will to power of Christian metaphysics, then through the infiltration of learning by the priesthood and the subsequent triumph of an "alternative" basis of ascetic learning in the guise of "objective science" – had led to a deeper ingraining of the ascetic ideal into the physiology of the human will. As a result, the current culture now reflected the widespread triumph of the ascetic ideal expressed through its numerous contemporary manifestations – either in the form of traditional Christian religion, modern "philosophy," secular science, or in other transcendental speculative systems (*GM* III, 23–27).

With this approach, Nietzsche eliminated, as no longer relevant, the question of whether certain perspectives better expressed the "truth"; instead, he became interested in the nature of will that sought power through the "will to truth." In the end, he reduced the issue to the following simple equation: is it a weak will, one that reflects instinctual decline, world-weariness and resentment, the spirit of nihilism and ascetic rejection of "the world"; or a "Dionysian" will that constantly overcomes the spirit of pessimism and can say "yes" to life, even wishing for its eternal return? Nietzsche diagnosed his age as one where the preponderant naysaying forces of nihilism had finally triumphed over the "rarer" forms of higher spirits, whose institutional basis for a higher agonistic culture had been undermined by nihilist wills.

At the close of *GM* III, the finale of the text as a whole, Nietzsche comes to his ultimate, devastating conclusion: modern science has not at all overcome Christian asceticism; on the contrary, science is the last, and perhaps most stubborn interpretational outpost of the ascetic ideal.[5] Through the various forms of "science," ascetic wills have found an alternative guise under which to articulate their resentment against life. Indeed, modern science expresses one of the last stages of the ongoing "slave revolt" in morality, whose trajectory Nietzsche follows throughout *GM* to its current flourishing in the various nihilist manifestations of the modern era.

In that sense, *GM* and *A*, written one year apart, represent two branches of a single overarching polemical attack against two powerful trends – at times independent, at times intersecting. Whereas *A* focuses on the will to power behind a resurgent, politicized Christianity, newly tinged by shades of *racial* anti-Semitism, *GM* directs its attention to the nihilist forces behind a "scientific" perspective that equally threatened to undermine the promise of a Dionysian higher culture. In fact, the "naturalist" theories of the "genealogists" had begun to inform the ideological arsenal of *both* (on the surface) contradictory camps, so that each faction could instrumentalize Darwinist "truths" in its own interpretative "spirit" with the single goal of realizing its specific will to power.

Understood in this way, it becomes perhaps clearer now how *GM* was able to appeal to such a broad, eclectic ideological constituency and how it could be appropriated as a seminal "theoretical" text by both major parties. Whereas the work in its earliest reception attracted anti-Christian anti-Semites, who found theoretical arguments to fuel their vision of a "naturalized" master-narrative of anti-Judaic hatred – one which now had

---

[5] "The opposite, as I said, is the case … science today is a *hiding place* for all kinds of ill-humour, unbelief, gnawing worms, *despectio sui*, bad conscience – it is the *disquiet* of the lack of ideals itself, the suffering from a *lack* of great love, the discontent over *enforced* contentedness" (*GM* III, 23).

the "advantage" of being grounded in the latest findings of Darwinian biological science – it also spoke to a generation of scientifically minded anti-Christian "genealogists," who demanded an alternative "scientific" master-narrative of man's "moral" development. Thus, *GM* specifically targets the emergence and spread of *ressentiment* forces in the contemporary culture at large – whether in the "disembodied" guise of a "disinterested" naturalist science or in the form of a revitalized Christianity, which – far from being marginalized or rendered historically superfluous by scientific "progress" – could adapt and articulate its message in the new voice of scientific biologism. Rather than prove that their Christian beliefs were mere superstition, the newly discovered biological "truths" could lend legitimacy, credibility, and urgency to long-nourished hatreds and suppressed eliminationist fantasies.

Of course, the irony of Nietzsche's final polemical position was that the nuances of his insights were not appreciated in his cultural climate and were then appropriated by the very same forces of *ressentiment* whose subterranean "will to power" he attempted to expose and against whom his texts were directed. To some extent, his fear of ideological misappropriation, which had already begun in his lifetime, can explain the stridency and frustration characteristic of his final writings. But the stridency and prophetic tenor of his final works arose from an even deeper, more pessimistic reservoir. For his theories did not only expose the will to power behind various incarnations of the ascetic ideal. More important, his insights made him understand the *procedural mechanism* through which *ressentiment*-driven will would be "enacted" in contemporary culture through the spirit of interpretation. The means of such articulation would no longer be the direct and immediate release of (re)active energy, but the subtler means of theory.

Instead of eliminating man's "animal" nature or representing a "higher" stage of his "moral" development, the new scientific paradigm would lead to his increased *brutalization* as a result of the suppression and interiorization of his once active, instinctual (i.e. "animal") reserve. Forever denied an outlet for his outer-directed energy, modern man would permanently dam up his assertive will to power and look for other means to vent that force, namely, through a theoretical and "logical" "justification" of once proscribed behavior.[6] That shunted will would derive compensatory

---

[6] In *GM* II, 21, Nietzsche argues that the "death of God" has not reduced feelings of guilt, inadequacy, and the bad conscience, as one might expect, but has only pushed them ever deeper into the psychology of the human will, so that the "bad conscience now so firmly establishes itself,

master-narratives of revenge, domination, and elimination, which could both explain its tortured soul to itself and allow for the release of dangerously bottled-up (re)active energy.[7]

Thus, Nietzsche saw himself standing at a fateful juncture in man's historical "development" – one that in many ways represented a clear break with the past and that extended indefinitely into the "future." Having eliminated all the possibilities for the expression of active (and now) "immoral" energy (and therefore the preparatory basis for a higher culture), the "last man" had finalized the "slave revolt" in morality, propelling the ascetic ideal in its various incarnations to its "world-historical" triumph. It was the victory of the "last man," and it required the *Übermensch* as its only possible redemption.

But now, triumphant modern man was left with himself and his own tortured soul. Unable to find release for his *ressentiment*-laden (re)active energy, he had to locate new targets, new outlets. His (re)active resentment had to go even further "underground," so to speak, leading to a plethora of "theories" that could justify and assuage his thirst for compensatory revenge and annihilation. A host of new permissible "enemies" needed to be fashioned – e.g. "inferiors," the "weak," the "backward," the "feeble-minded," the "class enemy," the "race enemy," the "system"[8] – which could allow annihilationist and eliminationist energy, *anarchic*

---

eating into him, broadening out and growing, like a polyp, so wide and deep that in the end, with the impossibility of paying back the debt [guilt], is conceived the impossibility of discharging the penance, the idea that it cannot be paid off ('*eternal* punishment')." Thus, while the Christian God had at least allowed for a (temporary) paying-off of "debt/guilt," modern forms of secularism and atheism have left modern man with the after-effects of the Christian inheritance but with *no ability to pay off the demands of his bad conscience*: "now the prospect for a once-and-for-all-payment *is to be* foreclosed, out of pessimism, now our glance *is to* bounce and recoil disconsolately off an iron impossibility, now those concepts 'debt' and 'duty' *are to be* reversed" (*GM* II, 21). This process has now turned the internalized pain and suffering of the will into a *permanent* predicament.

[7] "Alas for this crazy, pathetic beast man! What ideas he has, what perversity, what hysterical nonsense, what *bestiality of thought* immediately erupts, the moment he is prevented, if only gently, from being a *beast in deed!*" (*GM* II, 22).

[8] Nietzsche argues that "modern man," the "tame man," regards himself as being at the pinnacle of civilization because he can feel himself to be *relatively* superior to the mass of "less-desirables" that permeate the lower ranks of society. This relative superiority also allows him to control their destiny: "the 'tame man', who is incurably mediocre and unedifying, has already learnt to view himself as the aim and pinnacle, the meaning of history, the 'higher man'; – yes, the fact that he has a certain right to feel like that in so far as he feels distanced from the superabundance of failed, sickly, tired and exhausted people of whom today's Europe is beginning to reek, and in so far as he is at least *relatively successful*, at least still capable of living, at least saying 'yes' to life" (italics mine) (*GM* I, 11). The theory of evolution offers such "higher men" a "scientific" explanation for their alleged "success," i.e. their *relative* superiority over the broad mass of the less fortunate.

energy, to be both theoretically justified and vented.[9] For, according to Nietzsche, all will to power must be released in some form – be it in (re)active, resentment-driven versions or (in rarer cases) in the spirit of self-affirmation.

But because the immediate, outer-directed expression of energy was prohibited and had to be rechanneled inwards, there would be an exponential growth of theoretical systems that could nourish the embers of unventilated (re)active energy. The dawning new age on the horizon would no longer see open conflict between individual strong types according to the affirmative spirit of the *agon*, but the phenomenon of confrontational, suppressed forces of resentment continuously seething and fulminating under the surface of "civilization," waiting for their moment to achieve numerical superiority.[10] At that point, nothing could prevent them from "acting" out their long-suppressed resentment in the fulfillment of their *ressentiment*-driven master-narratives of existence. For the only force capable of stemming the destructive tide of (re)active energy was the "higher types," those who could intervene and prevent resentment forces from achieving dominance and annihilating one another. However, this was precisely the foundation of "higher culture" that the modern age had eliminated, leaving "civilization" in the hands of the anarchic forces of nihilism.

---

[9] Stone shows how the notion of a "lethal chamber," where racially and physiologically "undesirables" could be eliminated, was prevalent in the climate of Edwardian England, particularly among eugenicists, possibly serving as the inspiration for the gas chambers of the Third Reich. "Here I want only to ask, since the field of eugenics was established in Britain, and was eagerly taken on board by German scientists, might it not also be the case that the notion of the 'lethal chamber', which had existed in British literature on eugenics since the turn of the century, also fed into the fantasies which eventually led to the gas chambers?" (Stone, *Breeding Superman*, 132).

[10] In an ironic twist on Plato's allegory of the cave, Nietzsche plumbs the psychological depths of "modern man" to reveal the furnace of *ressentiment* in which modern "ideals" are fabricated:

– No! Wait a moment! You haven't heard anything yet about the masterpieces of those black magicians who can turn anything black into whiteness, milk and innocence: – haven't you noticed their perfect *raffinement*, their boldest, subtlest, most ingenious and mendacious stunt? Pay attention! These cellar rats of revenge and hatred – what do they turn revenge and hatred into? Have you ever heard these words? Would you suspect, if you just went by what they said, that the men around you were nothing but men of *ressentiment*? ...

– "I understand, I'll open my ears once more (oh! oh! oh! and *hold* my nose). Now, at last, I can hear what they have been saying so often: 'We good people – *we are the just*' – what they are demanding is not called retribution, but 'the triumph of *justice*'; what they hate is not their enemy, oh no!, they hate '*injustice*', 'godlessness'; what they believe and hope for is not the prospect of revenge, the delirium of sweet revenge (– Homer early on dubbed it 'sweeter than honey'), but the victory of God, the *just* God, over the Godless; all that remains for them to love on earth are not their brothers in hate but their 'brothers in love', as they say, all good and just people on earth."(*GM* I, 14)

In conclusion, three underlying concerns inform the polemical intentions of *GM*. All three are consequences of Nietzsche's final anti-Darwinism. First, Nietzsche feared that the emergence and spread of the "genealogical" perspective through scientific Darwinism had made it more difficult to realize a Dionysian culture. The success of the Darwinist paradigm pointed to the victory of "moral" forces; the decline of a "master morality"; and the difficulty of forming a pocket of resistance within the "culture." *GM* was to offer that pocket. Second, Nietzsche feared that the theories of Darwin had already begun to stabilize into scientific "truths." *GM* was meant to rip away that pretence. Instead of the drive to "truth" or pure "knowledge," Nietzsche revealed how the spirit of *ressentiment* stood behind modern science's "will to truth." At the end of the "scientific" quest, he recognized nihilist wills, who would suffocate the possibility for a resurgent Dionysian culture:[11] "Here there is snow, here life is silenced; the last crows heard here are called 'what for?', 'in vain', '*nada*' – here nothing flourishes or grows any more" (*GM* III, 26).

Finally, Nietzsche intuited that the complete triumph of nihilist wills bore in it the seeds of a greater barbarism than in all previous stages of humanity. For while in earlier epochs, the forces of "morality" had always been held in check by a "natural" and clearly visible opponent – namely, the actual political expressions and institutions of a "master morality" (e.g. the vestiges of the ancient state within early Christianity;[12] the noble classes within the Medieval period; the promise of a renewal of the "higher type" in the Renaissance;[13] even, most recently, the temporary triumph of Napoleonic elites over the senseless nationalism and political particularization of early modern Europe[14]), which had secured a certain "balance of power" between forces – the complete disappearance of those

---

[11] Another feature of this form of criticism was the ever-present danger of disgust (*Ekel*) and pity (*Mitleid*) with the realities of the modern era, which could tire, depress, and sap the energy, self-confidence, and morale of all fledgling "higher types," the only possible harbingers of a resurgent Dionysian culture (see *GM* I, 12, *GM* II, 24, and *GM* III, 13).

[12] "[T]he *imperium Romanum*, the most magnificent form of organization ever to be achieved under difficult conditions, compared to which everything before or after has just been patched together, botched and dilettantish, – those holy anarchists made a 'piety' out of destroying 'the world', *which is to say* the *imperium Romanum*, until every stone was overturned" (*A* 58).

[13] "[T]he last *great* age, the age of the Renaissance ... a moment when a higher order of values, the noble, life-affirming values, the values that guarantee the future, had triumphed" (*EH* "Wagner" 2).

[14] "Finally, when a *force majeure* of genius and will became visible on the bridge between two centuries of decadence, one strong enough to make Europe into a unity, a political *and economic* unity for the purpose of world governance, the Germans with their 'Wars of Liberation' cheated Europe out of the meaning, the miracle of meaning, in the existence of Napoleon" (*EH* "Wagner" 2).

residual "immoral" institutions in the modern era meant that a social and political corrective to the force of "moral" wills no longer existed.[15] Those earlier residual institutions had once served a beneficial purpose, even for their "moral" rivals: they had trained the latter to become more "clever," to hone their "minds," and to hatch plans of overthrow during millennia of clandestine warfare. But now, without a more powerful rival to serve as a counterbalance, everyone could become the "immoral" target of particular wills to power if such wills achieved supremacy, and no political entity could step in to prevent eliminationist fantasies from becoming nihilist reality.[16]

At the same time, the millennia of pain and cruelty that had been inflicted on the instinctual self, pushing man's outer-directed impulses ever deeper into the physiological storehouse of the will,[17] combined with the disappearance of the "immoral" rivals of the "master morality," had led to an increased "spiritualization" of *ressentiment*. These (re)active wills now no longer had any *direct* opposition to their objectives, and they could pursue the "logic" of their systems with single-minded, relentless abandon. They could seek out and temporarily unite with other like-spirited types, who could help them realize their collective will to power and eliminate obstacles to the fulfillment of their (re)active wills – all to seek out emotional redress for, and freedom from, the pain of internalized suffering, a suffering which could only be (at least momentarily) assuaged through the compensatory rush of "justified" pain, cruelty, and violence. But in the end, debilitated, they would wake from their "intoxication" and would have to confront the consequences of their unleashed *barbarism*:

[T]he ascetic priest has insouciantly taken into service the *whole* pack of wild hounds in man, releasing now one, then another, always with the same purpose of waking man out of his long-drawn-out melancholy, of putting to flight,

---

[15] Belief in the Christian God and the fear of His retribution were for centuries the main *internal* deterrents to the release of *ressentiment*-driven energy; but the decline of faith in the modern era means that there is no longer even an internal bulwark against eliminationist fantasies.

[16] The existence of the "immoral" power structures of the "masters" had been the only *institutional* guarantee for the realization of earthly "justice" and the only bulwark against the forces of seething *ressentiment*: "Everywhere that justice is practised and maintained, the stronger power can be seen looking for means of putting an end to the senseless ravages of *ressentiment* amongst those inferior to it (whether groups or individuals), partly by lifting the object of *ressentiment* out of the hands of revenge, partly by substituting, for revenge, a struggle against the enemies of peace and order, partly by working out compensation, suggesting, sometimes enforcing it, and partly by promoting certain equivalences for wrongs into a norm which *ressentiment*, from now on, has to take into account" (*GM* II, 11).

[17] See *GM* II, 21.

at least temporarily, his dull pain, his lingering misery, always with a religious interpretation and "justification" as well. Every such excess of emotion has to be *paid* for afterwards, it goes with saying – it makes the sick person even sicker. (*GM* III, 20)

For more than a century, *GM*'s purported proximity to Darwinist doctrines has led a whole host of modern readers to detect congruence between Nietzsche's philosophy and Darwin's science. The ideological spectrum has ranged widely – from standard early Social Darwinist readings and eugenicist interpretations, anti-Semitic and Wagnerian appropriations, and National Socialist amalgamations, to the current revival of interest in Nietzsche's supposedly "naturalist" rhetoric or in the "ethical" implications of *GM*.[18] Despite distinct differences in approach, none of these perspectives takes the polemical, culturally contingent, anti-Darwinian nature of the text at face value. Rather, they treat *GM* as a straightforward articulation of the biologist–naturalist preoccupations of the age. That is, they see Nietzsche operating in the shadow of Darwin, not as his spiritual antagonist. In the case of some of the earliest appropriations in particular, this misunderstanding has led his spiritual opponents to go so far as to co-opt and distort his message to reflect the *exact opposite* of his *clearly articulated* intentions – with disastrous consequences.

But the type of anti-Darwinian reading I have proposed here suggests not only that one cannot logically appropriate Nietzsche for such purposes, but, what is more, that Nietzsche prophetically exposes the will to power behind those very forces as well as the dangerous mechanism by which they will realize their (re)active, nihilist will to power through interpretation in the coming age of anarchy and barbarism. Understood in this way, Nietzsche remains to this day an uncomfortable reminder – in our age of social leveling and scientific nihilism – of the ever-lurking dangers of the spirit of *ressentiment*.

---

[18] Richard Brown argues that Nietzsche "appears to be a precursor" of Edward O. Wilson and his "biology of ethics" (Brown, "Nihilism: 'Thus Speaks Physiology'," in *Nietzsche and the Rhetoric of Nihilism: Essays on Interpretation, Language, and Politics*, ed. Tom Darby, Béla Egyed, and Ben Jones [Ottowa: Carleton University Press, 1973], 136). Daniel Dennett calls *GM* "one of the first and still subtlest of the Darwinian investigations of the evolution of ethics" (Dennett, *Darwin's Dangerous Idea*, 182)!

Bibliography

Abbey, Ruth. *Nietzsche's Middle Period*. New York: Oxford University Press, 2000.

Abel, Günter. "Nietzsche contra 'Selbsterhaltung': Steigerung der Macht und Ewige Wiederkehr." *Nietzsche Studien* 10/11 (1981/82): 367–84.

Acampora, Christa Davis. "On Sovereignty and Overhumanity: Why It Matters How We Read Nietzsche's *Genealogy* II:2." In Acampora, ed., *Nietzsche's On the Genealogy of Morals*, 147–62.

Acampora, Christa Davis, ed. *Nietzsche's On the Genealogy of Morals*. Lanham, MD: Rowman & Littlefield, 2006.

Acampora, Christa Davis, and Ralph R. Acampora, eds. *A Nietzschean Bestiary*. Lanham, MD: Rowman & Littlefield, 2004.

Allison, David B. *Reading the New Nietzsche: The Birth of Tragedy, The Gay Science, Thus Spoke Zarathustra, and On the Genealogy of Morals*. Lanham, MD: Rowman & Littlefield, 2001.

Allison, David B., ed. *The New Nietzsche: Contemporary Styles of Interpretation*. New York: Dell, 1977.

Amigoni, David, and Jeff Wallace, eds. *Charles Darwin, the Origin of Species: New Interdisciplinary Essays*. New York: St. Martin's Press, 1995.

Ansell-Pearson, Keith. *Viroid Life: Perspectives on Nietzsche and the Transhuman Condition*. London: Routledge, 1997.

Ansell-Pearson, Keith, ed. *A Companion to Nietzsche*. Oxford: Blackwell Publishing, 2006.

Aschheim, Steven E. *The Nietzsche Legacy in Germany, 1890–1990*. Berkeley: University of California Press, 1992.

Babich, Babette. "The Genealogy of Morals and Right Reading: On the Nietzschean Aphorism and the Art of the Polemic." In Acampora, ed., *Nietzsche's On the Genealogy of Morals*, 177–90.

Nietzsche's Philosophy of Science: Reflecting Science on the Ground of Art and Life. Albany: State University of New York Press, 1994.

Bannister, Robert C. "The Survival of the Fittest is Our Doctrine: History or Histrionics?" *Journal of the History of Ideas* 31 (1970): 377–81.

Barzun, Jacques. *Darwin, Marx, Wagner: Critique of a Heritage*. Garden City, NY: Doubleday, 1958.

Beatty, John. "Speaking of Species: Darwin's Strategy." In Kohn, ed., *Darwinian Heritage*, 265–81.
  "What's in a Word? Coming to Terms in the Darwinian Revolution." *Journal of the History of Biology* 15 (1982): 215–39.
Beddall, Barbara G. "Wallace, Darwin and the Theory of Natural Selection: A Study in the Development of Ideas and Attitudes." *Journal of the History of Biology* 1 (1968): 261–323.
Beer, C.G. "Darwin, Instinct and Ethnology." *Journal of the History of the Behavioral Sciences* 19 (1983): 68–79.
Beer, Gillian. *Darwin's Plots: Evolutionary Narrative in Darwin, George Eliot, and Nineteenth-Century Fiction.* London: Routledge & Kegan Paul, 1983.
  "Darwin's Reading and the Fictions of Development." In Kohn, ed., *Darwinian Heritage*, 543–87.
Behler, Ernst. *Confrontations: Derrida, Heidegger, Nietzsche.* Stanford: Stanford University Press, 1991.
Benton, Ted. "Social Darwinism and Socialist Darwinism in Germany: 1860–1900." *Rivista di Filosofia* 73 (1982): 79–121.
Bernasconi, Robert, and Sybol Cook, eds. *Race and Racism in Continental Philosophy.* Bloomington: Indiana University Press, 2003.
Blondel, Eric. *Nietzsche, the Body and Culture.* Stanford: Stanford University Press, 1991.
Bock, Kenneth E. "Darwin and Social Theory." *Philosophy of Science* 22 (1955): 123–34.
Bowler, Peter J. *Charles Darwin: The Man and His Influence.* Oxford: Blackwell, 1990.
  "Darwinism and the Argument from Design: Suggestions for a Revaluation." *Journal of the History of Biology* 10 (1977): 29–43.
  "Malthus, Darwin, and the Concept of Struggle." *Journal of the History of Ideas* (1976): 631–50.
  "Scientific Attitudes to Darwinism in Britain and America." In Kohn, ed., *Darwinian Heritage*, 641–81.
Bradie, Michael. *The Secret Chain: Evolution and Ethics.* Albany: State University of New York Press, 1994.
Brennecke, Detlef. "Die blonde Bestie. Vom Missverständnis eines Schlagwortes." *Nietzsche Studien* 5 (1976): 113–45.
Brobjer, Thomas H. *Nietzsche and the "English": The Influence of British and American Thinking on His Philosophy.* Amherst, NY: Humanity Books, 2008.
  "Nietzsche's magnum opus." *History of European Ideas* 32 (2006): 278–94.
Brose, Karl. *Geschichtsphilosophische Strukturen im Werk Nietzsches.* Bern: Peter Lang, 1973.
Brown, Frank. "The Evolution of Darwin's Theism." *Journal of the History of Biology* 19 (1986): 1–45.
Brown, Richard. "Nihilism: 'Thus Speaks Physiology'." In *Nietzsche and the Rhetoric of Nihilism: Essays on Interpretation, Language, and Politics,* ed.

Tom Darby, Béla Egyed, and Ben Jones. Ottowa: Carleton University Press, 1973, 133–44.

Browne, Janet. "Darwin and the Expression of the Emotions." In Kohn, ed., *Darwinian Heritage*, 307–26.

"Essay Review: New Developments in Darwin Studies?" *Journal of the History of Biology* 15 (1982): 275–80.

Burckhardt, Jacob. *Griechische Kulturgeschichte*, 4 vols. Stuttgart: Kröner, 1948.

Weltgeschichtliche Betrachtungen. Leipzig: Kröner, 1934.

Burckhardt, Richard W. Jr. "Darwin on Animal Behavior and Evolution." In Kohn, ed., *Darwinian Heritage*, 327–65.

Campioni, Giuliano. *Der französische Nietzsche*. Berlin: de Gruyter, 2009.

Cannon, Walter. "The Bases of Darwin's Achievement: A Revaluation." *Victorian Studies* 5 (1961): 109–34.

"Darwin's Vision in 'On the Origin of Species'." In *The Art of Victorian Prose*, ed. George Levine and William Madden. New York: Oxford University Press, 1968, 154–76.

"The Problem of Miracles in the 1830s." *Victorian Studies* 4 (1960): 5–32.

Cassirer, Ernst. *The Problem of Knowledge: Philosophy, Science, and History since Hegel*. New Haven: Yale University Press, 1950.

Chamberlain, Houston Stewart, and John Lees. *Foundations of the Nineteenth Century*. New York: John Lane, 1914.

Clagett, Marshall. *Critical Problems in the History of Science*. Madison: University of Wisconsin Press, 1959.

Clark, Maudemarie. "The Development of Nietzsche's Later Position on Truth." In Richardson and Leiter, *Nietzsche*, 59–84.

"Introduction." In Friedrich Nietzsche, *On the Genealogy of Morality*. Indianapolis: Hackett Publishing Co., 1998, vii–xxxiv.

Nietzsche on Truth and Philosophy. New York: Cambridge University Press, 1990.

Colp, Ralph, Jr. "Charles Darwin's Reprobation of Nature: 'Clumsy, Wasteful, Blundering Low & Cruel'." *New York State Journal of Medicine* 81 (1981): 1116–19.

"The Contacts between Karl Marx and Charles Darwin." *Journal of the History of Ideas* 35 (1974): 329–38.

Conway, Daniel. "For Whom the Bell Tolls." *Journal of Nietzsche Studies* 35/36 (2008): 88–105.

"How We Became What We Are: Tracking the 'Beasts of Prey'." In Acampora, ed., *Nietzsche's On the Genealogy of Morals*, 305–20.

Nietzsche's On the Genealogy of Morals. London: Continuum, 2008.

Cornell, J.F. "Analogy and Technology in Darwin's Vision of Nature." *Journal of the History of Biology* 17 (1984): 303–44.

"God's Magnificent Law: The Bad Influence of Theistic Metaphysics on Darwin's Estimation of Natural Selection." *Journal of the History of Biology* 20 (1987): 381–412.

Cowan, Michael. *Cult of the Will*. University Park, PA: Penn State University Press, 2008.

"*Nichts ist so sehr zeitgemäß als Willensschwäche*: Friedrich Nietzsche and the Psychology of the Will." *Nietzsche Studien* 34 (2005): 48–74.

Corsi, Pietro, and Paul J. Weindling. "Darwinism in Germany, France, and Italy." In Kohn, ed., *Darwinian Heritage*, 683–729.

Cox, Christoph. *Nietzsche: Naturalism and Interpretation*. Berkeley: University of California Press, 1999.

Crook, D.P. "Darwinism – The Political Implications." *History of European Ideas* 2 (1981): 19–34.

Danto, Arthur. *Nietzsche as Philosopher*. New York: Macmillan, 1965.

Darwin, Charles. *The Descent of Man, and Selection in Relation to Sex*. Princeton: Princeton University Press, 1981.

The Origin of Species, ed. Gillian Beer. New York: Oxford University Press, 1996.

The Autobiography of Charles Darwin, ed. Nora Barlow. New York: W.W. Norton & Co., 1993.

De Beer, Gavin. "How Darwin Came by His Theory of Natural Selection." *New Scientist* 21 (1964): 216–18.

"Other Men's Shoulders." *Annals of Science* 20 (1964): 303–22.

Deleuze, Gilles. *Nietzsche and Philosophy*. New York: Columbia University Press, 1983.

Dennett, Daniel. *Darwin's Dangerous Idea: Evolution and the Meanings of Life*. New York: Simon & Schuster, 1995.

Desmond, Adrian, and James R. Moore. *Darwin*. New York: W.W. Norton & Co., 1991.

Dewey, John. *The Influence of Darwin on Philosophy, and Other Essays in Contemporary Thought*. New York: P. Smith, 1951.

Diemer, Alwin. *Konzeption und Begriff der Forschung in den Wissenschaften des 19. Jahrhunderts*. Meisenheim am Glan: Hain, 1978.

Djuric, Mihailo. *Nietzsche und die Metaphysik*. New York: de Gruyter, 1985.

Donnellan, Brendan. "Friedrich Nietzsche and Paul Rée: Cooperation and Conflict." *Journal of the History of Ideas* 43 (1982): 595–612.

Nietzsche and the French Moralists. Bonn: Bouvier, 1982.

Düsing, Edith. *Nietzsches Denkweg: Theologie, Darwinismus, Nihilismus*. Munich: W. Fink, 2006.

Durant, John. "The Ascent of Nature in Darwin's *Descent of Man*." In Kohn, ed., *Darwinian Heritage*, 283–303.

Darwinism and Divinity: Essays on Evolution and Religious Belief. Oxford: B. Blackwell, 1985.

Eiseley, Loren C. *Darwin's Century: Evolution and the Men Who Discovered It*. Garden City, NY: Doubleday, 1958.

Ellegård, Alvar. *Darwin and the General Reader: The Reception of Darwin's Theory of Evolution in the British Periodical Press, 1859–1872*. Göteborg: Elanders, 1958.

Eng, Erling. "The Confrontation between Reason and Imagination: The Example of Darwin." *Diogenes* 95 (1976): 58–67.

Ewald, Oskar. "Darwin and Nietzsche." *Zeitschrift für Philosophie und philosophische Kritik* 136 (1909): 159–79.

Fay, Margaret. "Did Marx Offer to Dedicate *Capital* to Darwin?" *Journal of the History of Ideas* 39 (1978): 233–46.

Foot, Philippa. "Nietzsche: The Revaluation of Values." In *Nietzsche: A Collection of Critical Essays*, ed. Robert Solomon. Garden City, NY: Anchor Books, 1973, 156–68.

Foucault, Michel, and Paul Rabinow. *The Foucault Reader*. New York: Pantheon Books, 1984.

Freeman, Derek. "The Evolutionary Theories of Charles Darwin and Herbert Spencer." *Current Anthropology* 15 (1974): 211–37.

Gale, Barry G. "Darwin and the Concept of a Struggle for Existence: A Study in the Extrascientific Origins of Scientific Ideas." *Isis* 63 (1972): 321–44.

Geuss, Raymond. *Morality, Culture, and History: Essays on German Philosophy*. Cambridge: Cambridge University Press, 1999.

Ghiselin, Michael T. "The Individual in the Darwinian Revolution." *New Literary History* 3 (1971): 113–34.

Gilman, Sander L. *Conversations with Nietzsche: A Life in the Words of His Contemporaries*. New York: Oxford University Press, 1987.

Glick, Thomas F. *The Comparative Reception of Darwinism*. Austin: University of Texas Press, 1974.

Goldhagen, Daniel Jonah. *Hitler's Willing Executioners: Ordinary Germans and the Holocaust*. New York: Knopf, 1996.

Golomb, Jacob. *Nietzsche and Jewish Culture*. New York: Routledge, 1997.

Gossman, Lionel. *Basel in the Age of Burckhardt: A Study in Unseasonable Ideas*. Chicago: University of Chicago Press, 2000.

Grau, Gerd Günther. *Christlicher Glaube und intellektuelle Redlichkeit: Eine religionsphilosophische Studie über Nietzsche*. Frankfurt am Main: G. Schulte-Bulmke, 1958.

Ideologie und Wille zur Macht: Zeitgemässe Betrachtungen über Nietzsche. Berlin: de Gruyter, 1984.

Greene, John C. "Darwin as a Social Evolutionist." *Journal of the History of Biology* 10 (1977): 1–27.

"Reflections on the Progress of Darwin Studies." *Journal of the History of Biology* 8 (1975): 243–73.

Gregory, Frederick. *Nature Lost? Natural Science and the German Theological Traditions of the Nineteenth Century*. Cambridge, MA: Harvard University Press, 1992.

Scientific Materialism in Nineteenth Century Germany. Dordrecht, Holland: D. Reidel Publishing Co., 1977.

Grinnell, George. "The Rise and Fall of Darwin's First Theory of Transmutation." *Journal of the History of Biology* 7 (1974): 259–73.

Gruber, Howard E. *Darwin on Man: A Psychological Study of Scientific Creativity.* New York: E.P. Dutton, 1974.

Gruber, Howard E., and Robert T. Keegan. "Love, Death, and Continuity in Darwin's Thinking." *Journal of the History of the Behavioral Sciences* 19 (1983): 15–29.

Günzel, Stephan. "Review of Friedrich Nietzsche, *Werke. Kritische Gesamtausgabe, Neunte Abteilung, Der handschriftliche Nachlass ab Frühjahr 1885 in differenzierter Transkription,* Vol. 1–3, ed. Marie-Luise Haase und Michael Kohlenbach." *Nietzscheforschung* 10 (2003): 348–53.

Haas, Ludwig. "*Der Darwinismus bei Nietzsche.*" Ph.D. dissertation, Giessen, 1932.

Haase, Marie-Luise. "Friedrich Nietzsche liest Francis Galton." *Nietzsche Studien* 18 (1989): 633–58.

"Nietzsche und ..." *Nietzscheforschung* 10 (2003): 17–36.

Habermas, Jürgen, and Frederick Lawrence. *The Philosophical Discourse of Modernity: Twelve Lectures.* Cambridge, MA: MIT Press, 1987.

Halliday, R.J. "Social Darwinism: A Definition." *Victorian Studies* 14 (1971): 389–405.

Hasler, Ueli. *Beherrschte Natur: Die Anpassung der Theologie an die bürgerliche Naturauffassung im 19. Jahrhundert (Schleiermacher, Ritschl, Herrmann).* Berne: Peter Lang, 1982.

Hatab, Lawrence J. "How Does the Ascetic Ideal Function in Nietzsche's *Genealogy?*" *Journal of Nietzsche Studies* 35/36 (2008): 106–23.

Nietzsche's "On the Genealogy of Morality": An Introduction. Cambridge: Cambridge University Press, 2008.

Havas, Randall. *Nietzsche's Genealogy: Nihilism and the Will to Knowledge.* Ithaca, NY: Cornell University Press, 1995.

Hawkins, Mike. *Social Darwinism in European and American Thought, 1860–1945: Nature as Model and Nature as Threat.* Cambridge: Cambridge University Press, 1997.

Heidegger, Martin. *Nietzsche,* 2 vols. Pfullingen: Neske, 1961.

Helfland, Michael S. "T.H. Huxley's 'Evolution and Ethics': The Politics of Evolution and the Evolution of Politics." *Victorian Studies* 20 (1977): 154–77.

Helmstadter, Richard J., and Bernard V. Lightman. *Victorian Faith in Crisis: Essays on Continuity and Change in Nineteenth-Century Religious Belief.* Stanford: Stanford University Press, 1990.

Henke, D. "Nietzsches Darwinismuskritik aus der Sicht der gegenwärtigen Evolutionsforschung." *Nietzsche Studien* 13 (1984): 189–210.

Hensel, Eva. *Der Positivismus Nietzsches, sein Ursprung und seine Überwindung.* Königsberg: Hartung, 1914.

Herbert, Sandra. "Darwin, Malthus, and Selection." *Journal of the History of Biology* 4 (1971): 209–17.

"The Place of Man in the Development of Darwin's Theory of Transmutation (1)." *Journal of the History of Biology* 7 (1974): 217–58.

"The Place of Man in the Development of Darwin's Theory of Transmutation (ii)." *Journal of the History of Biology* 10 (1977): 155–227.

Hodge, M.J.S., and David Kohn. "The Immediate Origins of Natural Selection." In Kohn, ed., *Darwinian Heritage*, 185–205.

Higgins, Kathleen Marie. *Nietzsche's Zarathustra*. Philadelphia: Temple University Press, 1987.

Himmelfarb, Gertrude. *Darwin and the Darwinian Revolution*. Chicago: Ivan R. Dee, Inc., 1996.

Hobbes, Thomas. *Leviathan*. New York: Penguin Books, 1985.

Höffe, Otfried, ed. *Friedrich Nietzsche: Zur Genealogie der Moral*. Berlin: Akademie Verlag, 2004.

Hollingdale, R. J. *Nietzsche: The Man and His Philosophy*. Cambridge: Cambridge University Press, 1999.

Hollinrake, Roger. *Nietzsche, Wagner, and the Philosophy of Pessimism*. London: George Allen and Unwin, 1982.

Holub, Robert C. *Friedrich Nietzsche*. New York: Twayne Publishers, 1995.

Hull, David L. "Darwinism as a Historical Entity: A Historiographic Proposal." In Kohn, ed., *Darwinian Heritage*, 773–812.

Huntley, William B. "David Hume and Charles Darwin." *Journal of the History of Ideas* 33 (1972): 457–70.

Horn, Anette. "'Eine Philosophie, welche im Grunde der Instinct für eine persönliche Diät ist?': Krankheit und Gesundheit im Denken Nietzsches." *Acta Germanica* 22 (1994): 39–55.

Hume, David. *Hume on Human Nature and the Understanding*, ed. A.G.N. Flew. New York: Collier Books, 1962.

Huszar, George de. "Nietzsche's Theory of Decadence." *Journal of the History of Ideas* 6 (1945): 259–72.

Hyman, Stanley Edgar. *The Tangled Bank: Darwin, Marx, Frazer and Freud as Imaginative Writers*. New York: Atheneum, 1962.

Janaway, Christopher. *Beyond Selflessness: Reading Nietzsche's Genealogy*. Oxford: Oxford University Press, 2007.

"Beyond Selflessness in Ethics and Inquiry." *Journal of Nietzsche Studies* 35/36 (2008): 124–40.

Janz, Curt Paul. *Friedrich Nietzsche: Biogr. in 3 Bd.*, vol. 1. Munich: Hanser, 1978.

Jaspers, Karl. *Nietzsche und das Christentum*. Hameln: F. Seifert, 1946.

Johnson, Dirk. "Il Sodalizio di Friedrich Nietzsche con Paul Rée: 'Réealismo superiore' o réeallineamento filosofico?" *Rivista di filosofia* (2005): 233–62.

"Nietzsche's Early Darwinism: The 'David Strauss' Essay of 1873." *Nietzsche Studien* 30 (2001): 62–79.

"On the Way to the 'Anti-Darwin': Nietzsche's Darwinian Meditations in the Middle Period." *Tijdschrift voor filosofie* 65 (2003): 657–78.

"Review of Gregory Moore, *Nietzsche, Biology, and Metaphor*." *Journal of Nietzsche Studies* 35/36 (2008).

Jones, Greta. "The Social History of Darwin's Descent of Man." *Economy and Society* 7 (1978): 1–23.

Jordanova, L. J. *Languages of Nature: Critical Essays on Science and Literature.* London: Free Association Books, 1986.

Kaufmann, Walter. *Nietzsche: Philosopher, Psychologist, Antichrist.* Princeton: Princeton University Press, 1967.

Kelly, Alfred. *The Descent of Darwin: The Popularization of Darwinism in Germany, 1860–1914.* Chapel Hill: University of North Carolina Press, 1981.

Klossowski, Pierre. *Nietzsche and the Vicious Circle.* London: Athlone Press, 1997.

Kofman, Sarah. *Nietzsche and Metaphor.* London: Athlone Press, 1993.

Kohn, David. "Darwin's Ambiguity: The Secularization of Biological Meaning." *British Journal for the History of Science* 22 (1989): 215–39.

——— "Darwin's Principle of Divergence as Internal Dialogue." In Kohn, ed., *Darwinian Heritage,* 245–57.

Kohn, David, ed. *The Darwinian Heritage.* Princeton: Princeton University Press, 1985.

Kołakowski, Leszek. *The Alienation of Reason: A History of Positivist Thought.* Garden City, NY: Doubleday, 1968.

Krell, David Farrell. *Exceedingly Nietzsche: Aspects of Contemporary Nietzsche-Interpretation.* London: Routledge, 1988.

Kuhn, Elisabeth. *Friedrich Nietzsches Philosophie des europäischen Nihilismus.* Berlin: de Gruyter, 1992.

Kuhn, Thomas S. "The History of Science." In *International Encyclopedia of the Social Sciences* 14, ed. David Sills. New York, 1968.

——— *The Structure of Scientific Revolutions.* Chicago: University of Chicago Press, 1996.

Lampert, Laurence. *Nietzsche and Modern Times: A Study of Bacon, Descartes, and Nietzsche.* New Haven: Yale University Press, 1993.

Lampl, Hans Erich. "Ex Oblivione: Das Féré Palimpsest." *Nietzsche Studien* 15 (1986): 225–49.

——— "Flaire du Livre: Friedrich Nietzsche und Théodule Ribot." *Nietzsche Studien* 18 (1989): 573–86.

Lange, Friedrich Albert. *The History of Materialism and Criticism of Its Present Importance.* New York: Harcourt, Brace & Company, 1925.

La Vergata, Antonello. "Images of Darwin: A Historiographic Overview." In Kohn, ed., *Darwinian Heritage,* 901–72.

Leiter, Brian. *Nietzsche on Morality.* London: Routledge, 2002.

Leiter, Brian, and Neil Sinhababu, eds. *Nietzsche and Morality.* Oxford: Oxford University Press, 2007.

Lenoir, Timothy. *The Strategy of Life: Teleology and Mechanics in Nineteenth-Century German Biology.* Dordrecht, Holland: D. Reidel Publishing Company, 1982

Levine, George. "By Knowledge Possessed: Darwin, Nature, and Victorian Narrative." *New Literary History* 24 (1993): 363–91.

Lindberg, David C., and Ronald L. Numbers, eds. *God and Nature: Historical Essays on the Encounter between Christianity and Science*. Berkeley: University of California Press, 1986.

Loewenberg, Bert James. "The Mosaic of Darwinian Thought." *Victorian Studies* 3 (1959): 3–18.

Long, Thomas A. "Nietzsche's Philosophy of Medicine." *Nietzsche Studien* 19 (1990): 112–28.

Longo, Silvano. *"Die Aufdeckung der leiblichen Vernunft bei Friedrich Nietzsche."* Ph.D. dissertation, Würzburg, 1987.

Lonsbach, Richard Maximilian. *Friedrich Nietzsche und die Juden: Ein Versuch*. Stockholm: Bermann-Fischer, 1939.

Lovejoy, Arthur. *The Great Chain of Being*. Cambridge, MA: Harvard University Press, 1936.

Löwith, Karl. *Nietzsches Philosophie der Ewigen Wiederkehr des Gleichen*. Berlin: Verlag die Runde, 1935.

Magnus, Bernd. *Nietzsche's Existential Imperative*. Bloomington: Indiana University Press, 1978.

Mandelbaum, Maurice. "Darwin's Religious Views." *Journal of the History of Ideas* 19 (1958): 363–78.

Malthus, T.R. *An Essay on the Principle of Population*, ed. Geoffrey Gilbert. Oxford: Oxford University Press, 1993.

Manier, Edward. "History, Philosophy and Sociology of Biology: A Family Romance." *Studies in History and Philosophy of Science* 11 (1980): 1–24.

The Young Darwin and His Cultural Circle: A Study of Influences Which Helped Shape the Language and Logic of the First Drafts of the Theory of Natural Selection. Dordrecht, Holland: D. Reidel Publishing Co., 1978.

Mann, Gunter. "Biologie und Geschichte: Ansätze und Versuche zur biologistischen Theorie der Geschichte im 19. und beginnenden 20. Jahrhundert." *Medizinhistorisches Journal* 10 (1975): 281–306.

"Dekadenz – Degeneration – Untergangsangst im Lichte der Biologie des 19. Jahrhunderts." *Medizinhistorisches Journal* 20 (1985): 6–35.

"Medizinisch-Biologische Ideen und Modelle in der Gesellschaftslehre des 19. Jahrhunderts." *Medizinhistorisches Journal* 4 (1969): 1–23.

May, Simon. *Nietzsche's Ethics and His War on "Morality"*. Oxford: Oxford University Press, 1999.

Mayr, Ernst. "Darwin's Five Theories of Evolution." In Kohn, ed., *Darwinian Heritage*, 755–72.

Migotti, Mark. "Slave Morality, Socrates, and the Bushmen: A Reading of the First Essay of *On the Genealogy of Morals*." *Philosophy and Phenomenological Research* 58, no. 4 (1998): 745–79.

Mittasch, Alwin. *Friedrich Nietzsche als Naturphilosoph*. Stuttgart: A. Kröner, 1952.

Monro, D.H. *A Guide to the British Moralists*. London: Fontana, 1972.

Montinari, Mazzino. *Nietzsche lesen*. Berlin: de Gruyter, 1982.

Moore, Gregory. "Nietzsche and Evolutionary Theory." In Ansell-Pearson, ed., *A Companion to Nietzsche*, 517–31.

Nietzsche, Biology, and Metaphor. Cambridge: Cambridge University Press, 2002.

Moore, James R. "Darwin of Down: The Evolutionist as Squarson-Naturalist." In Kohn, ed., *Darwinian Heritage*, 435–81.

Moore, James R., ed. *History, Humanity, and Evolution: Essays for John C. Greene*. New York: Cambridge University Press, 1989.

Mostert, Pieter. "Nietzsche's Reception of Darwinism." *Bijdragen tot de Dierkunde* 49 (1979): 235–46.

Müller-Lauter, Wolfgang. "Der Organismus als innerer Kampf. Der Einfluss von Wilhelm Roux auf Friedrich Nietzsche." *Nietzsche Studien* 7 (1978): 189–223.

Nietzsche: His Philosophy of Contradictions and the Contradictions of His Philosophy. Urbana: University of Illinois Press, 1999.

Nehamas, Alexander. *Nietzsche: Life as Literature*. Cambridge, MA: Harvard University Press, 1985.

Oldroyd, David R. "How did Darwin Arrive at his Theory? The Secondary Literature to 1982." *History of Science* 22 (1984): 325–74.

Ospovat, Dov. "Darwin after Malthus." *Journal of the History of Biology* 12 (1979): 211–30.

"God and Natural Selection: The Darwinian Idea of Design." *Journal of the History of Biology* 13 (1980): 169–94.

Owen, David. *Nietzsche's Genealogy of Morality*. Montreal: McGill-Queen's University Press, 2007.

"Nietzsche's *Genealogy* Revisited." *Journal of Nietzsche Studies* 35/36 (2008): 141–54.

Pancaldi, Giuliano. "Darwin's Intellectual Development (Commentary)." In Kohn, ed., *Darwinian Heritage*, 259–63.

Paradis, James G., and Thomas Postlewait, eds. *Victorian Science and Victorian Values: Literary Perspectives*. New York: New York Academy of Sciences, 1981.

Pasley, Malcolm, ed. *Nietzsche: Imagery and Thought*. Berkeley: University of California Press, 1978.

Pieper, Annemarie. *Ein Seil geknüpft zwischen Tier und Übermensch: philosophische Erläuterungen zu Nietzsches erstem Zarathustra*. Stuttgart: Klett-Cotta, 1990.

Plutarch. *The Lives of the Noble Grecians and Romans*, vol. II. New York: Random House, 1992.

Popper, Karl. *The Myth of the Framework: In Defense of Science and Rationality*. London: Routledge, 1994.

"Natural Selection and the Emergence of Mind." *Dialectica* 32 (1978): 339–55.

Provine, William B. "Adaptation and Mechanisms of Evolution after Darwin: A Study in Persistent Controversies." In Kohn, ed., *Darwinian Heritage*, 825–66.

Randall, John H. "The Changing Impact of Darwin on Philosophy." *Journal of the History of Ideas* 22 (1961): 435–62.

Rée, Paul. *Basic Writings*, ed. Robin Small. Urbana: University of Illinois Press, 2003.

Der Ursprung der moralischen Empfindungen. Chemnitz: E. Schmeitzner, 1877.

Die Entstehung des Gewissens. Berlin: C. Duncker, 1885.

Reschke, Renate. "Review of Friedrich Nietzsche, *Werke. Kritische Gesamtausgabe*, Neunte Abteilung, *Der handschriftliche Nachlass ab Frühjahr 1885 in differenzierter Transkription*, Vol. 4–5, ed. Marie-Luise Haase und Martin Stingelin in Verbindung mit der Berlin-Brandenburgischen Akademie der Wissenschaften." *Nietzscheforschung* 13 (2006): 287–95.

Roger, Jacques. "Darwinism Today (Commentary)." In Kohn, ed., *Darwinian Heritage*, 813–23.

Rogers, James A. "Darwinism and Social Darwinism." *Journal of the History of Ideas* 33 (1972): 265–80.

Richards, Robert J. *Darwin and the Emergence of Evolutionary Theories of Mind and Behavior*. Chicago: University of Chicago Press, 1987.

Richardson, John. *Nietzsche's New Darwinism*. New York: Oxford University Press, 2004.

Nietzsche's System. New York: Oxford University Press, 1996.

Richardson, John, and Brian Leiter, eds. *Nietzsche*. Oxford: Oxford University Press, 2001.

Richter, Claire. *Nietzsche et les Théories biologiques contemporaines*. Paris: Mercure de France, 1911.

Richter, Raoul. *Essays*. Leipzig: Felix Meiner, 1913.

Ridley, Aaron. *Nietzsche's Conscience: Six Character Studies from the Genealogy*. Ithaca, NY: Cornell University Press, 1998.

Risse, Mathias. "The Second Treatise in *On the Genealogy of Morality*: Nietzsche on the Origin of the Bad Conscience." *European Journal of Philosophy* 9 (2001): 55–81.

Runkle, Gerald. "Marxism and Charles Darwin." *Journal of Politics* 23 (1961): 108–26.

Ruse, Michael. *Can a Darwinian be a Christian? The Relationship between Science and Religion*. Cambridge: Cambridge University Press, 2001.

"Charles Darwin's Theory of Evolution: An Analysis." *Journal of the History of Biology* 8 (1975): 219–41.

The Darwinian Paradigm: Essays on Its History, Philosophy and Religious Implications. London: Routledge, 1989.

The Darwinian Revolution: Science Red in Tooth and Claw. Chicago: University of Chicago Press, 1979.

"Darwin's Debt to Philosophy: An Examination of the Influence of the Philosophical Ideas of John F.W. Herschel and William Whewell on the Development of Charles Darwin's Theory of Natural Selection." *Studies in History and Philosophy of Science* 6 (1975): 159–81.

Safranski, Rüdiger. *Nietzsche: A Political Biography.* New York: W.W. Norton, 2002.

Salaquarda, Jörg. "Gesundheit und Krankheit bei Friedrich Nietzsche." *Studi Tedeschi* 17 (1974): 73–108.

"Nietzsche und Lange." *Nietzsche Studien* 7 (1978): 235–53.

Salin, Edgar. *Jakob Burckhardt und Nietzsche.* Heidelberg: L. Schneider, 1948.

Santaniello, Weaver. *Nietzsche, God, and the Jews.* Albany: State University of New York Press, 1994.

"Nietzsche's *Antichrist*: 19th-Century Christian Jews and the Real 'Big Lie'." *Modern Judaism* 17 (1997): 163–77.

"A Post-Holocaust Re-Examination of Nietzsche and the Jews: *Vis-à-vis* Christendom and Nazism." In Golomb, ed., *Nietzsche and Jewish Culture,* 21–54.

Schaberg, William H., and Alexander Nehamas. *The Nietzsche Canon: A Publication History and Bibliography.* Chicago: University of Chicago Press, 1995.

Schacht, Richard. *Making Sense of Nietzsche: Reflections Timely and Untimely.* Urbana: University of Illinois Press, 1995.

Nietzsche, Genealogy, Morality: Essays on Nietzsche's Genealogy of Morals. Berkeley: University of California Press, 1994.

Schalk, Fritz. *Die französischen Moralisten: La Rochefoucauld, Vauvenargues, Montesquieu, Chamfort, Rivarol.* Leipzig: In der Dieterich'schen Verlagsbuchhandlung, 1938.

Schank, Gerd. *"Rasse" und "Züchtung" bei Nietzsche.* Berlin: de Gruyter, 2000.

Schwartz, Joel S. "Charles Darwin's Debt to Malthus and Edward Blyth." *Journal of the History of Biology* 7 (1974): 301–18.

Schipperges, Heinrich. *Am Leitfaden des Leibes: Zur Anthropologik und Therapeutik Friedrich Nietzsches.* Stuttgart: Klett, 1975.

Schweber, Silvan. "Darwin and the Political Economists: Divergence of Character." *Journal of the History of Biology* 13 (1980): 195–289.

"The Origin of the Origin Revisited." *Journal of the History of Biology* 19 (1977): 229–316.

"The Wider British Context in Darwin's Theorizing." In Kohn, ed., *Darwinian Heritage,* 35–69.

Schlechta, Karl, and Anni Anders. *Der Fall Nietzsche.* Munich: C. Hanser, 1959.

Friedrich Nietzsche: Von den Verborgenen Anfängen seines Philosophierens. Stuttgart: F. Fromann, 1962.

Scott, Jacqueline. "On the Use and Abuse of Race in Philosophy: Nietzsche, Jews, and Race." In Bernasconi, ed., *Race and Racism in Continental Philosophy,* 53–73.

Skowron, Michael. "Nietzsches 'Anti-Darwinismus'." *Nietzsche Studien* 37 (2008): 160–94.

Small, Robin. *Nietzsche and Rée: A Star Friendship.* Oxford: Oxford University Press, 2005.

   Nietzsche in Context. Burlington, VT: Ashgate, 2001.

Smith, C.U.M. "'Clever Beasts Who Invented Knowing': Nietzsche's Evolutionary Biology of Knowledge." *Biology and Philosophy* 2 (1987): 65–91.

Smith, Douglas. *Transvaluations: Nietzsche in France, 1872–1972.* Oxford: Oxford University Press, 1996.

Sober, Elliott. "Darwin on Natural Selection: A Philosophical Perspective." In Kohn, ed., *Darwinian Heritage*, 867–99.

Stack, George J. *Lange and Nietzsche.* Berlin: de Gruyter, 1983.

Staten, Henry. *Nietzsche's Voice.* Ithaca, NY: Cornell University Press, 1990.

Stegmaier, Werner. "Darwin, Darwinismus, Nietzsche." *Nietzsche Studien* 16 (1987): 246–87.

   Nietzsches "Genealogie der Moral". Darmstadt: Wissenschaftliche Buchgesellschaft, 1994.

Stevens, Jacqueline. "On the Morals of Genealogy." *Political Theory* 31 (2003): 558–88.

Stone, Dan. *Breeding Superman: Nietzsche, Race and Eugenics in Edwardian and Interwar Britain.* Liverpool: Liverpool University Press, 2002.

Tanner, Michael. *Nietzsche.* Oxford: Oxford University Press, 1994.

Thatcher, David S. "Nietzsche, Bagehot and the Morality of Custom." *Victorian Newsletter* 62 (1982): 7–13.

   "Nietzsche's Debt to Lubbock." *Journal of the History of Ideas* 44 (1983): 293–309.

Thomas, R. Hinton. *Nietzsche in German Politics and Society, 1890–1918.* Dover, NH: Manchester University Press, 1983.

Thompson, Janna. "The New Social Darwinism: The Politics of Sociobiology." *Politics* 17 (1982): 121–28.

Tille, Alexander. *Von Darwin bis Nietzsche: Ein Buch Entwicklungsethik.* Leipzig: Naumann, 1893.

Turner, Frank M. *Between Science and Religion: The Reaction to Scientific Naturalism in Late Victorian England.* New Haven: Yale University Press, 1974.

Venturelli, Aldo. *Kunst, Wissenschaft und Geschichte bei Nietzsche.* Berlin: de Gruyter, 2003.

Vorzimmer, Peter. "Darwin, Malthus, and the Theory of Natural Selection." *Journal of the History of Ideas* 30 (1969): 527–42.

   "Darwin's Question about the Breeding of Animals (1839)." *Journal of the History of Biology* 2 (1969): 269–81.

Wahrig-Schmidt, Bettina. "'Irgendwie, jedenfalls physiologisch': Friedrich Nietzsche, Alexandre Herzen (Fils) und Charles Féré 1888." *Nietzsche Studien* 17 (1988): 434–64.

Weikart, Richard. *From Darwin to Hitler: Evolutionary Ethics, Eugenics, and Racism in Germany*. New York: Palgrave Macmillan, 2004.

"The Origins of Social Darwinism in Germany, 1859–1895." *Journal of the History of Ideas* 54 (1993): 468–88.

Weiner, Marc. *Richard Wagner and the Anti-Semitic Imagination*. Lincoln: University of Nebraska Press, 1995.

Williams, W.D. *Nietzsche and the French*. Oxford: Blackwell, 1952.

Wilson, A.N. *God's Funeral*. New York: W.W. Norton, 1999.

Wokler, Robert. "From *l'homme physique* to *l'homme moral* and Back: Towards a History of Enlightenment Anthropology." *History of the Human Sciences* 6 (1993): 121–38.

Young, Robert. "Darwinism and the Division of Labor." *Listener* (17 August 1972): 202–05.

"Darwinism *Is* Social." In Kohn, ed., *Darwinian Heritage*, 609–38.

"Darwin's Metaphor: Does Nature Select?" *Monist* 55 (1971): 442–503.

Darwin's Metaphor: Nature's Place in Victorian Culture. Cambridge: Cambridge University Press, 1985.

"Evolutionary Biology and Ideology: Then and Now." *Social Studies* 1 (1971): 177–206.

"Malthus and the Evolutionists: The Common Context of Biological and Social Theory." *Past and Present* 43 (1969): 109–41.

Yovel, Yirmiyahu. *Nietzsche as Affirmative Thinker*. Boston: M. Nijhoff Publishers, 1986.

Zeitlin, Irving M. *Nietzsche: A Re-Examination*. Cambridge: Polity Press, 1994.

Index

CPSIA information can be obtained at www.ICGtesting.com
Printed in the USA
LVOW07s2139190813

348699LV00013B/337/P